A Practical Guide to Forecasting Financial Market Volatility

For other titles in the Wiley Finance series
please see www.wiley.com/finance

A Practical Guide to Forecasting Financial Market Volatility

Ser-Huang Poon

John Wiley & Sons, Ltd

Other Wiley Editorial Offices

John Wiley & Sons Inc., 111 River Street, Hoboken, NJ 07030, USA

Jossey-Bass, 989 Market Street, San Francisco, CA 94103-1741, USA

Wiley-VCH Verlag GmbH, Boschstr. 12, D-69469 Weinheim, Germany

John Wiley & Sons Australia Ltd, 33 Park Road, Milton, Queensland 4064, Australia

John Wiley & Sons (Asia) Pte Ltd, 2 Clementi Loop #02-01, Jin Xing Distripark, Singapore 129809

John Wiley & Sons Canada Ltd, 22 Worcester Road, Etobicoke, Ontario, Canada M9W 1L1

Wiley also publishes its books in a variety of electronic formats. Some content that appears
in print may not be available in electronic books.

Library of Congress Cataloging-in-Publication Data

Poon, Ser-Huang.
   A practical guide for forecasting financial market volatility / Ser Huang
Poon.
      p. cm. — (The Wiley finance series)
   Includes bibliographical references and index.
   ISBN-13 978-0-470-85613-0 (cloth : alk. paper)
   ISBN-10 0-470-85613-0 (cloth : alk. paper)
   1. Options (Finance)—Mathematical models.   2. Securities—Prices—
   Mathematical models.   3. Stock price forecasting—Mathematical models.   I. Title.
II. Series.
      HG6024.A3P66   2005
      332.64′01′5195—dc22   2005005768

British Library Cataloguing in Publication Data

A catalogue record for this book is available from the British Library

ISBN-13   978-0-470-85613-0 (HB)
ISBN-10   0-470-85613-0 (HB)

I dedicate this book to my mother

Contents

Foreword

If one invests in a financial asset today the return received at some pre-specified point in the future should be considered as a random variable. Such a variable can only be fully characterized by a distribution function or, more easily, by a density function. The main, single and most important feature of the density is the expected or mean value, representing the location of the density. Around the mean is the uncertainty or the volatility. If the realized returns are plotted against time, the jagged oscillating appearance illustrates the volatility. This movement contains both welcome elements, when surprisingly large returns occur, and also certainly unwelcome ones, the returns far below the mean. The well-known fact that a poor return can arise from an investment illustrates the fact that investing can be risky and is why volatility is sometimes equated with risk.

Volatility is itself a stock variable, having to be measured over a period of time, rather than a flow variable, measurable at any instant of time. Similarly, a stock price is a flow variable but a return is a stock variable. Observed volatility has to be observed over stated periods of time, such as hourly, daily, or weekly, say.

Having observed a time series of volatilities it is obviously interesting to ask about the properties of the series: is it forecastable from its own past, do other series improve these forecasts, can the series be modeled conveniently and are there useful multivariate generalizations of the results? Financial econometricians have been very inventive and industrious considering such questions and there is now a substantial and often sophisticated literature in this area.

The present book by Professor Ser-Huang Poon surveys this literature carefully and provides a very useful summary of the results available.

By so doing, she allows any interested worker to quickly catch up with the field and also to discover the areas that are still available for further exploration.

Clive W.J. Granger
December 2004

Preface

Volatility forecasting is crucial for option pricing, risk management and portfolio management. Nowadays, volatility has become the subject of trading. There are now exchange-traded contracts written on volatility. Financial market volatility also has a wider impact on financial regulation, monetary policy and macroeconomy. This book is about financial market volatility forecasting. The aim is to put in one place models, tools and findings from a large volume of published and working papers from many experts. The material presented in this book is extended from two review papers ('Forecasting Financial Market Volatility: A Review' in the *Journal of Economic Literature*, 2003, 41, 2, pp. 478–539, and 'Practical Issues in Forecasting Volatility' in the *Financial Analysts Journal*, 2005, 61, 1, pp. 45–56) jointly published with Clive Granger.

Since the main focus of this book is on volatility forecasting performance, only volatility models that have been tested for their forecasting performance are selected for further analysis and discussion. Hence, this book is oriented towards practical implementations. Volatility models are not pure theoretical constructs. The practical importance of volatility modelling and forecasting in many finance applications means that the success or failure of volatility models will depend on the characteristics of empirical data that they try to capture and predict. Given the prominent role of option price as a source of volatility forecast, I have also devoted much effort and the space of two chapters to cover Black–Scholes and stochastic volatility option pricing models.

This book is intended for first- and second-year finance PhD students and practitioners who want to implement volatility forecasting models but struggle to comprehend the huge volume of volatility research. Readers who are interested in more technical aspects of volatility modelling could refer to, for example, Gourieroux (1997) on ARCH models, Shephard (2003) on stochastic volatility and Fouque, Papanicolaou and Sircar (2000) on stochastic volatility option pricing. Books that cover specific aspects or variants of volatility models include Franses and van Dijk (2000) on nonlinear models, and Beran (1994) and Robinson (2003) on long memory models. Specialist books that cover financial time series modelling in a more general context include Alexander (2001), Tsay (2002) and Taylor (2005). There are also a number of edited series that contain articles on volatility modelling and forecasting, e.g. Rossi (1996), Knight and Satchell (2002) and Jarrow (1998).

I am very grateful to Clive for his teaching and guidance in the last few years. Without his encouragement and support, our volatility survey works and this book would not have got started. I would like to thank all my co-authors on volatility research, in particular Bevan Blair, Namwon Hyung, Eric Jondeau, Martin Martens, Michael Rockinger, Jon Tawn, Stephen Taylor and Konstantinos Vonatsos. Much of the writing here reflects experience gained from joint work with them.

1
Volatility Definition and Estimation

1.1 WHAT IS VOLATILITY?

It is useful to start with an explanation of what volatility is, at least for the purpose of clarifying the scope of this book. Volatility refers to the spread of all likely outcomes of an uncertain variable. Typically, in financial markets, we are often concerned with the spread of asset returns. Statistically, volatility is often measured as the sample standard deviation

$$\widehat{\sigma} = \sqrt{\frac{1}{T-1} \sum_{t=1}^{T} (r_t - \mu)^2},$$ (1.1)

where r_t is the return on day t, and μ is the average return over the T-day period.

Sometimes, variance, σ^2, is used also as a volatility measure. Since variance is simply the square of standard deviation, it makes no difference whichever measure we use when we compare the volatility of two assets. However, variance is much less stable and less desirable than standard deviation as an object for computer estimation and volatility forecast evaluation. Moreover standard deviation has the same unit of measure as the mean, i.e. if the mean is in dollar, then standard deviation is also expressed in dollar whereas variance will be expressed in dollar square. For this reason, standard deviation is more convenient and intuitive when we think about volatility.

Volatility is related to, but not exactly the same as, risk. Risk is associated with undesirable outcome, whereas volatility as a measure strictly for uncertainty could be due to a positive outcome. This important difference is often overlooked. Take the Sharpe ratio for example. The Sharpe ratio is used for measuring the performance of an investment by comparing the mean return in relation to its 'risk' proxy by its volatility.

The Sharpe ratio is defined as

$$\text{Sharpe ratio} = \frac{\begin{pmatrix}\text{Average} \\ \text{return, } \mu\end{pmatrix} - \begin{pmatrix}\text{Risk-free interest} \\ \text{rate, e.g. T-bill rate}\end{pmatrix}}{\text{Standard deviation of returns, } \sigma}.$$

The notion is that a larger Sharpe ratio is preferred to a smaller one. An unusually large positive return, which is a desirable outcome, could lead to a reduction in the Sharpe ratio because it will have a greater impact on the standard deviation, σ, in the denominator than the average return, μ, in the numerator.

More importantly, the reason that volatility is not a good or perfect measure for risk is because volatility (or standard deviation) is only a measure for the spread of a distribution and has no information on its shape. The only exception is the case of a normal distribution or a lognormal distribution where the mean, μ, and the standard deviation, σ, are sufficient statistics for the entire distribution, i.e. with μ and σ alone, one is able to reproduce the empirical distribution.

This book is about volatility only. Although volatility is not the sole determinant of asset return distribution, it is a key input to many important finance applications such as investment, portfolio construction, option pricing, hedging, and risk management. When Clive Granger and I completed our survey paper on volatility forecasting research, there were 93 studies on our list plus several hundred non-forecasting papers written on volatility modelling. At the time of writing this book, the number of volatility studies is still rising and there are now about 120 volatility forecasting papers on the list. Financial market volatility is a 'live' subject and has many facets driven by political events, macroeconomy and investors' behaviour. This book will elaborate some of these complexities that kept the whole industry of volatility modelling and forecasting going in the last three decades. A new trend now emerging is on the trading and hedging of volatility. The Chicago Board of Exchange (CBOE) for example has started futures trading on a volatility index. Options on such futures contracts are likely to follow. Volatility swap contracts have been traded on the over-the-counter market well before the CBOE's developments. Previously volatility was an input to a model for pricing an asset or option written on the asset. It is now the principal subject of the model and valuation. One can only predict that volatility research will intensify for at least the next decade.

1.2   FINANCIAL MARKET STYLIZED FACTS

To give a brief appreciation of the amount of variation across different
financial assets, Figure 1.1 plots the returns distributions of a normally

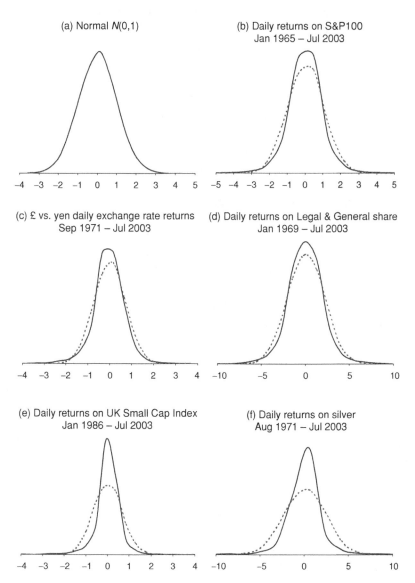

Figure 1.1   Distribution of daily financial market returns. (*Note*: the dotted line is
the distribution of a normal random variable simulated using the mean and standard
deviation of the financial asset returns)

distributed random variable, and the respective daily returns on the US Standard and Poor market index (S&P100),[1] the yen–sterling exchange rate, the share of Legal & General (a major insurance company in the UK), the UK Index for Small Capitalisation Stocks (i.e. small companies), and silver traded at the commodity exchange. The normal distribution simulated using the mean and standard deviation of the financial asset returns is drawn on the same graph to facilitate comparison.

From the small selection of financial asset returns presented in Figure 1.1, we notice several well-known features. Although the asset returns have different degrees of variation, most of them have long 'tails' as compared with the normally distributed random variable. Typically, the asset distribution and the normal distribution cross at least three times, leaving the financial asset returns with a longer left tail and a higher peak in the middle. The implications are that, for a large part of the time, financial asset returns fluctuate in a range smaller than a normal distribution. But there are some occasions where financial asset returns swing in a much wider scale than that permitted by a normal distribution. This phenomenon is most acute in the case of UK Small Cap and silver. Table 1.1 provides some summary statistics for these financial time series.

The normally distributed variable has a skewness equal to zero and a kurtosis of 3. The annualized standard deviation is simply $\sqrt{252}\sigma$, assuming that there are 252 trading days in a year. The financial asset returns are not adjusted for dividend. This omission is not likely to have any impact on the summary statistics because the amount of dividends distributed over the year is very small compared to the daily fluctuations of asset prices. From Table 1.1, the Small Cap Index is the most negatively skewed, meaning that it has a longer left tail (extreme losses) than right tail (extreme gains). Kurtosis is a measure for tail thickness and it is astronomical for S&P100, Small Cap Index and silver. However, these skewness and kurtosis statistics are very sensitive to outliers. The skewness statistic is much closer to zero, and the amount of kurtosis dropped by 60% to 80%, when the October 1987 crash and a small number of outliers are excluded.

Another characteristic of financial market volatility is the time-varying nature of returns fluctuations, the discovery of which led to Rob Engle's Nobel Prize for his achievement in modelling it. Figure 1.2 plots the time series history of returns of the same set of assets presented

---

[1] The data for S&P100 prior to 1986 comes from S&P500. Adjustments were made when the two series were grafted together.

Table 1.1 Summary statistics for a selection of financial series

	N(0, 1)	S&P100	Yen/£ rate	Legal & General	UK Small Cap	Silver
Start date		Jan 65	Sep 71	Jan 69	Jan 86	Aug 71
Number of observations	8000	9675	7338	7684	4432	7771
Daily average[a]	0	0.024	−0.021	0.043	0.022	0.014
Daily Standard Deviation	1	0.985	0.715	2.061	0.648	2.347
Annualized average	0	6.067	−5.188	10.727	5.461	3.543
Annualized Standard Deviation	15.875	15.632	11.356	32.715	10.286	37.255
Skewness	0	−1.337	−0.523	0.026	−3.099	0.387
Kurtosis	3	37.140	7.664	6.386	42.561	45.503
Number of outliers removed		1			5	9
Skewness[b]		−0.055			−0.917	−0.088
Kurtosis[b]		7.989			13.972	15.369

[a] Returns not adjusted for dividends.
[b] These two statistical measures are computed after the removal of outliers.
All series have an end date of 22 July, 2003.

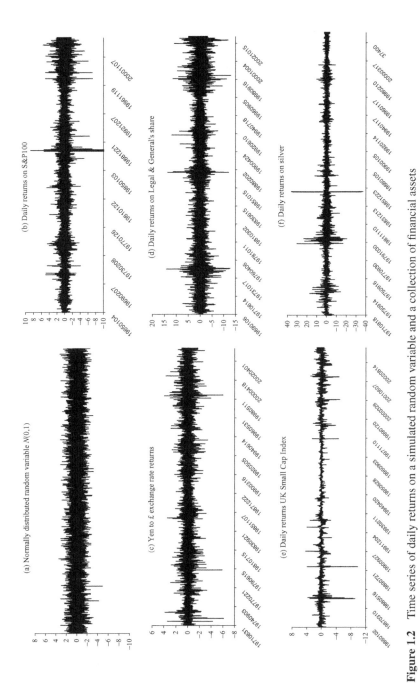

Figure 1.2 Time series of daily returns on a simulated random variable and a collection of financial assets

in Figure 1.1. The amplitude of the returns fluctuations represents the amount of variation with respect to a short instance in time. It is clear from Figures 1.2(b) to (f) that fluctuations of financial asset returns are 'lumpier' in contrast to the even variations of the normally distributed variable in Figure 1.2(a). In the finance literature, this 'lumpiness' is called volatility clustering. With volatility clustering, a turbulent trading day tends to be followed by another turbulent day, while a tranquil period tends to be followed by another tranquil period. Rob Engle (1982) is the first to use the ARCH (autoregressive conditional heteroscedasticity) model to capture this type of volatility persistence; 'autoregressive' because high/low volatility tends to persist, 'conditional' means time-varying or with respect to a point in time, and 'heteroscedasticity' is a technical jargon for non-constant volatility.[2]

There are several salient features about financial market returns and volatility that are now well documented. These include fat tails and volatility clustering that we mentioned above. Other characteristics documented in the literature include:

(i) Asset returns, r_t, are not autocorrelated except possibly at lag one due to nonsynchronous or thin trading. The lack of autocorrelation pattern in returns corresponds to the notion of *weak form market efficiency* in the sense that returns are not predictable.

(ii) The autocorrelation function of $|r_t|$ and r_t^2 decays slowly and $corr\,(|r_t|\,,|r_{t-1}|) > corr\left(r_t^2, r_{t-1}^2\right)$. The decay rate of the autocorrelation function is much slower than the exponential rate of a stationary AR or ARMA model. The autocorrelations remain positive for very long lags. This is known as the long memory effect of volatility which will be discussed in greater detail in Chapter 5. In the table below, we give a brief taste of the finding:

	$\sum \rho(|r|)$	$\sum \rho(r^2)$	$\sum \rho(ln|r|)$	$\sum \rho(|Tr|)$
S&P100	35.687	3.912	27.466	41.930
Yen/£	4.111	1.108	0.966	5.718
L&G	25.898	14.767	29.907	28.711
Small Cap	25.381	3.712	35.152	38.631
Silver	45.504	8.275	88.706	60.545

---

[2] It is worth noting that the ARCH effect appears in many time series other than financial time series. In fact Engle's (1982) seminal work is illustrated with the UK inflation rate.

(iii) The numbers reported above are the sum of autocorrelations for the first 1000 lags. The last column, $\rho(|Tr|)$, is the autocorrelation of absolute returns after the most extreme 1% tail observations were truncated. Let $r_{0.01}$ and $r_{0.99}$ be the 98% confidence interval of the empirical distribution,

$$Tr = Min\,[r, r_{0.99}]\,, \text{ or } Max\,[r, r_{0.01}]\,. \qquad (1.2)$$

The effect of such an outlier truncation is discussed in Huber (1981). The results reported in the table show that suppressing the large numbers markedly increases the long memory effect.

(iv) Autocorrelation of powers of an absolute return are highest at power one: $corr\,(|r_t|, |r_{t-1}|) > corr\,\left(r_t^d, r_{t-1}^d\right), d \neq 1$. Granger and Ding (1995) call this property the Taylor effect, following Taylor (1986). We showed above that other means of suppressing large numbers could make the memory last longer. The absolute returns $|r_t|$ and squared returns r_t^2 are proxies of daily volatility. By analysing the more accurate volatility estimator, we note that the strongest autocorrelation pattern is observed among realized volatility. Figure 1.3 demonstrates this convincingly.

(v) Volatility asymmetry: it has been observed that volatility increases if the previous day returns are negative. This is known as the leverage effect (Black, 1976; Christie, 1982) because the fall in stock price causes leverage and financial risk of the firm to increase. The phenomenon of volatility asymmetry is most marked during large falls. The leverage effect has not been tested between contemporaneous returns and volatility possibly due to the fact that it is the previous day residuals returns (and its sign dummy) that are included in the conditional volatility specification in many models. With the availability of realized volatility, we find a similar, albeit slightly weaker, relationship in volatility and the sign of contemporaneous returns.

(vi) The returns and volatility of different assets (e.g. different company shares) and different markets (e.g. stock vs. bond markets in one or more regions) tend to move together. More recent research finds correlation among volatility is stronger than that among returns and both tend to increase during bear markets and financial crises.

The art of volatility modelling is to exploit the time series properties and stylized facts of financial market volatility. Some financial time series have their unique characteristics. The Korean stock market, for

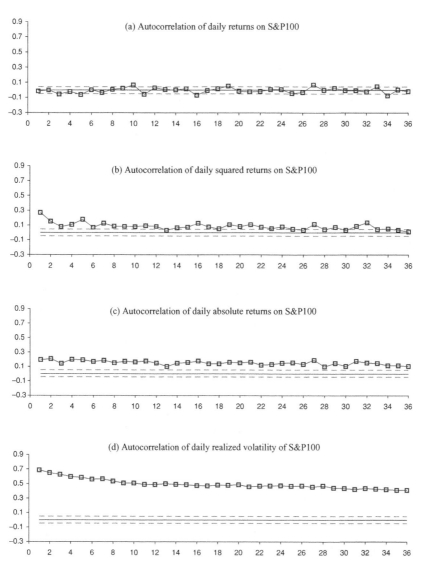

Figure 1.3 Aurocorrelation of daily returns and proxies of daily volatility of S&P100. (*Note*: dotted lines represent two standard errors)

example, clearly went through a regime shift with a much higher volatility level after 1998. Many of the Asian markets have behaved differently since the Asian crisis in 1997. The difficulty and sophistication of volatility modelling lie in the controlling of these special and unique features of each individual financial time series.

1.3 VOLATILITY ESTIMATION

Consider a time series of returns r_t, $t = 1, \cdots, T$, the standard deviation, σ, in (1.1) is the *unconditional volatility* over the T period. Since volatility does not remain constant through time, the *conditional volatility*, $\sigma_{t,\tau}$ is a more relevant information for asset pricing and risk management at time t. Volatility estimation procedure varies a great deal depending on how much information we have at each sub-interval t, and the length of τ, the volatility reference period. Many financial time series are available at the daily interval, while τ could vary from 1 to 10 days (for risk management), months (for option pricing) and years (for investment analysis). Recently, intraday transaction data has become more widely available providing a channel for more accurate volatility estimation and forecast. This is the area where much research effort has been concentrated in the last two years.

When monthly volatility is required and daily data is available, volatility can simply be calculated using Equation (1.1). Many macroeconomic series are available only at the monthly interval, so the current practice is to use absolute monthly value to proxy for macro volatility. The same applies to financial time series when a daily volatility estimate is required and only daily data is available. The use of absolute value to proxy for volatility is the equivalent of forcing $T = 1$ and $\mu = 0$ in Equation (1.1). Figlewski (1997) noted that the statistical properties of the sample mean make it a very inaccurate estimate of the true mean especially for small samples. Taking deviations around zero instead of the sample mean as in Equation (1.1) typically increases volatility forecast accuracy.

The use of daily return to proxy daily volatility will produce a very noisy volatility estimator. Section 1.3.1 explains this in a greater detail. Engle (1982) was the first to propose the use of an ARCH (autoregressive conditional heteroscedasticity) model below to produce conditional volatility for inflation rate r_t;

$$r_t = \mu + \varepsilon_t, \quad \varepsilon_t \sim N\left(0, \sqrt{h_t}\right).$$
$$\varepsilon_t = z_t \sqrt{h_t},$$
$$h_t = \omega + \alpha_1 \varepsilon_{t-1}^2 + \alpha_2 \varepsilon_{t-2}^2 + \cdots. \tag{1.3}$$

The ARCH model is estimated by maximizing the likelihood of $\{\varepsilon_t\}$. This approach of estimating conditional volatility is less noisy than the absolute return approach but it relies on the assumption that (1.3) is the true return-generating process, ε_t is Gaussian and the time series is long enough for such an estimation.

While Equation (1.1) is an unbiased estimator for σ^2, the square root of $\widehat{\sigma}^2$ is a biased estimator for σ due to Jensen inequality.[3] Ding, Granger and Engle (1993) suggest measuring volatility directly from absolute returns. Davidian and Carroll (1987) show absolute returns volatility specification is more robust against asymmetry and nonnormality. There is some empirical evidence that deviations or absolute returns based models produce better volatility forecasts than models that are based on squared returns (Taylor, 1986; Ederington and Guan, 2000a; McKenzie, 1999). However, the majority of time series volatility models, especially the ARCH class models, are squared returns models. There are methods for estimating volatility that are designed to exploit or reduce the influence of extremes.[4] Again these methods would require the assumption of a Gaussian variable or a particular distribution function for returns.

1.3.1 Using squared return as a proxy for daily volatility

Volatility is a latent variable. Before high-frequency data became widely available, many researchers have resorted to using daily squared returns, calculated from market daily closing prices, to proxy daily volatility. Lopez (2001) shows that ε_t^2 is an unbiased but extremely imprecise estimator of σ_t^2 due to its asymmetric distribution. Let

$$Y_t = \mu + \varepsilon_t, \quad \varepsilon_t = \sigma_t z_t, \tag{1.4}$$

and $z_t \sim N(0, 1)$. Then

$$E\left[\varepsilon_t^2 \middle| \Phi_{t-1}\right] = \sigma_t^2 E\left[z_t^2 \middle| \Phi_{t-1}\right] = \sigma_t^2$$

since $z_t^2 \sim \chi_{(1)}^2$. However, since the median of a $\chi_{(1)}^2$ distribution is 0.455, ε_t^2 is less than $\frac{1}{2}\sigma_t^2$ more than 50% of the time. In fact

$$\Pr\left(\varepsilon_t^2 \in \left[\frac{1}{2}\sigma_t^2, \frac{3}{2}\sigma_t^2\right]\right) = \Pr\left(z_t^2 \in \left[\frac{1}{2}, \frac{3}{2}\right]\right) = 0.2588,$$

which means that ε_t^2 is 50% greater or smaller than σ_t^2 nearly 75% of the time!

---

[3] If $r_t \sim N\left(0, \sigma_t^2\right)$, then $E\left(|r_t|\right) = \sigma_t \sqrt{2/\pi}$. Hence, $\widehat{\sigma}_t = |r_t|/\sqrt{2/\pi}$ if r_t has a conditional normal distribution.

[4] For example, the maximum likelihood method proposed by Ball and Torous (1984), the high–low method proposed by Parkinson (1980) and Garman and Klass (1980).

Under the null hypothesis that returns in (1.4) are generated by a GARCH(1,1) process, Andersen and Bollerslev (1998) show that the population R^2 for the regression

$$\varepsilon_t^2 = \alpha + \beta \widehat{\sigma}_t^2 + \upsilon_t$$

is equal to κ^{-1} where κ is the kurtosis of the standardized residuals and κ is finite. For conditional Gaussian error, the R^2 from a correctly specified GARCH(1,1) model cannot be greater than 1/3. For thick tail distribution, the upper bound for R^2 is lower than 1/3. Christodoulakis and Satchell (1998) extend the results to include compound normals and the Gram–Charlier class of distributions confirming that the mis-estimation of forecast performance is likely to be worsened by nonnormality known to be widespread in financial data.

Hence, the use of ε_t^2 as a volatility proxy will lead to low R^2 and undermine the inference on forecast accuracy. Blair, Poon and Taylor (2001) report an increase of R^2 by three to four folds for the 1-day-ahead forecast when intraday 5-minutes squared returns instead of daily squared returns are used to proxy the actual volatility. The R^2 of the regression of $|\varepsilon_t|$ on σ_t^{intra} is 28.5%. Extra caution is needed when interpreting empirical findings in studies that adopt such a noisy volatility estimator. Figure 1.4 shows the time series of these two volatility estimates over the 7-year period from January 1993 to December 1999. Although the overall trends look similar, the two volatility estimates differ in many details.

1.3.2   Using the high–low measure to proxy volatility

The high–low, also known as the range-based or extreme-value, method of estimating volatility is very convenient because daily high, low, opening and closing prices are reported by major newspapers, and the calculation is easy to program using a hand-held calculator. The high–low volatility estimator was studied by Parkinson (1980), Garman and Klass (1980), Beckers (1993), Rogers and Satchell (1991), Wiggins (1992), Rogers, Satchell and Yoon (1994) and Alizadeh, Brandt and Diebold (2002). It is based on the assumption that return is normally distributed with conditional volatility σ_t. Let H_t and L_t denote, respectively, the highest and the lowest prices on day t. Applying the Parkinson (1980) H-L measure to a price process that follows a geometric Brownian

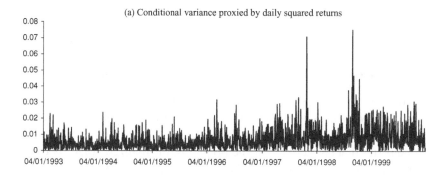

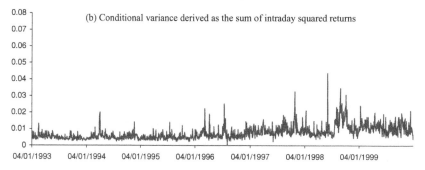

Figure 1.4   S&P100 daily volatility for the period from January 1993 to December 1999

motion results in the following volatility estimator (Bollen and Inder, 2002):

$$\widehat{\sigma}_t^2 = \frac{(\ln H_t - \ln L_t)^2}{4 \ln 2}$$

The Garman and Klass (1980) estimator is an extension of Parkinson (1980) where information about opening, p_{t-1}, and closing, p_t, prices are incorporated as follows:

$$\widehat{\sigma}_t^2 = 0.5 \left(\ln \frac{H_t}{L_t} \right)^2 - 0.39 \left(\ln \frac{p_t}{p_{t-1}} \right)^2.$$

We have already shown that financial market returns are not likely to be normally distributed and have a long tail distribution. As the $H\text{-}L$ volatility estimator is very sensitive to outliers, it will be useful to apply the trimming procedures in Section 1.4. Provided that there are no destabilizing large values, the $H\text{-}L$ volatility estimator is very efficient and, unlike the realized volatility estimator introduced in the next section, it is least affected by market microstructure effect.

1.3.3   Realized volatility, quadratic variation and jumps

More recently and with the increased availability of tick data, the term *realized volatility* is now used to refer to volatility estimates calculated using intraday squared returns at short intervals such as 5 or 15 minutes.[5] For a series that has zero mean and no jumps, the realized volatility converges to the continuous time volatility. To understand this, we assume for the ease of exposition that the instantaneous returns are generated by the continuous time martingale,

$$dp_t = \sigma_t dW_t, \tag{1.5}$$

where dW_t denotes a standard Wiener process. From (1.5) the conditional variance for the one-period returns, $r_{t+1} \equiv p_{t+1} - p_t$, is $\int_t^{t+1} \sigma_s^2 ds$ which is known as the *integrated volatility* over the period t to $t + 1$. Note that while asset price p_t can be observed at time t, the volatility σ_t is an unobservable latent variable that scales the stochastic process dW_t continuously through time.

Let m be the sampling frequency such that there are m continuously compounded returns in one unit of time and

$$r_{m,t} \equiv p_t - p_{t-1/m} \tag{1.6}$$

and realized volatility

$$RV_{t+1} = \sum_{j=1,\cdots,m} r_{m,t+j/m}^2.$$

If the discretely sampled returns are serially uncorrelated and the sample path for σ_t is continuous, it follows from the theory of quadratic variation (Karatzas and Shreve, 1988) that

$$p \lim_{m \to \infty} \left(\int_t^{t+1} \sigma_s^2 ds - \sum_{j=1,\cdots,m} r_{m,t+j/m}^2 \right) = 0.$$

Hence time t volatility is theoretically observable from the sample path of the return process so long as the sampling process is frequent enough.

---

[5] See Fung and Hsieh (1991) and Andersen and Bollerslev (1998). In the foreign exchange markets, quotes for major exchange rates are available round the clock. In the case of stock markets, close-to-open squared return is used in the volatility aggregation process during market close.

When there are jumps in price process, (1.5) becomes

$$dp_t = \sigma_t dW_t + \kappa_t dq_t,$$

where dq_t is a Poisson process with $dq_t = 1$ corresponding to a jump at time t, and zero otherwise, and κ_t is the jump size at time t when there is a jump. In this case, the quadratic variation for the cumulative return process is then given by

$$\int_t^{t+1} \sigma_s^2 ds + \sum_{t < s \leq t+1} \kappa^2(s), \qquad (1.7)$$

which is the sum of the integrated volatility and jumps.

In the absence of jumps, the second term on the right-hand side of (1.7) disappears, and the quadratic variation is simply equal to the integrated volatility. In the presence of jumps, the realized volatility continues to converge to the quadratic variation in (1.7)

$$p \lim_{m \to \infty} \left(\int_t^{t+1} \sigma_s^2 ds + \sum_{t < s \leq t+1} \kappa^2(s) - \sum_{j=1}^m r_{m,t+j/m}^2 \right) = 0. \qquad (1.8)$$

Barndorff-Nielsen and Shephard (2003) studied the property of the standardized *realized bipower variation* measure

$$BV_{m,t+1}^{[a,b]} = m^{[(a+b)/2-1]} \sum_{j=1}^{m-1} \left| r_{m,t+j/m} \right|^a \left| r_{m,t+(j+1)/m} \right|^b, \quad a, b \geq 0.$$

They showed that when jumps are large but rare, the simplest case where $a = b = 1$,

$$\mu_1^{-2} BV_{m,t+1}^{[1,1]} = \mu_1^{-2} \sum_{j=1}^{m-1} \left| r_{m,t+j/m} \right| \left| r_{m,t+(j+1)/m} \right| \to \int_t^{t+1} \sigma_s^2 ds$$

where $\mu_1 = \sqrt{2/\pi}$. Hence, the realized volatility and the realized bipower variation can be substituted into (1.8) to estimate the jump component, κ_t. Barndorff-Nielsen and Shephard (2003) suggested imposing a nonnegative constraint on κ_t. This is perhaps too restrictive. For nonnegative volatility, $\kappa_t + \mu_1^{-2} BV_t > 0$ will be sufficient.

Characteristics of financial market data suggest that returns measured at an interval shorter than 5 minutes are plagued by spurious serial correlation caused by various market microstructure effects including nonsynchronous trading, discrete price observations, intraday periodic volatility patterns and bid–ask bounce.[6] Bollen and Inder (2002), Ait-Sahalia, Mykland and Zhang (2003) and Bandi and Russell (2004) have given suggestions on how to isolate microstructure noise from realized volatility estimator.

1.3.4   Scaling and actual volatility

The forecast of multi-period volatility $\sigma_{T,T+j}$ (i.e. for j period) is taken to be the sum of individual multi-step point forecasts $\Sigma_{j=1}^{s} h_{T+j|T}$. These multi-step point forecasts are produced by recursive substitution and using the fact that $\varepsilon_{T+i|T}^2 = h_{T+i|T}$ for $i > 0$ and $\varepsilon_{T+i|T}^2 = \varepsilon_{T+i}^2$ for $T + i \leq 0$. Since volatility of financial time series has complex structure, Diebold, Hickman, Inoue and Schuermann (1998) warn that forecast estimates will differ depending on the current level of volatility, volatility structure (e.g. the degree of persistence and mean reversion etc.) and the forecast horizon.

If returns are *iid* (independent and identically distributed, or strict white noise), then variance of returns over a long horizon can be derived as a simple multiple of single-period variance. But, this is clearly not the case for many financial time series because of the stylized facts listed in Section 1.2. While a point forecast of $\widehat{\sigma}_{T-1,T|t-1}$ becomes very noisy as $T \to \infty$, a cumulative forecast, $\widehat{\sigma}_{t,T|t-1}$, becomes more accurate because of errors cancellation and volatility mean reversion except when there is a fundamental change in the volatility level or structure.[7]

Complication in relation to the choice of forecast horizon is partly due to volatility mean reversion. In general, volatility forecast accuracy improves as data sampling frequency increases relative to forecast horizon (Andersen, Bollerslev and Lange, 1999). However, for forecasting volatility over a long horizon, Figlewski (1997) finds forecast error doubled in size when daily data, instead of monthly data, is used to forecast volatility over 24 months. In some cases, where application is of very long horizon e.g. over 10 years, volatility estimate calculated using

---

[6] The bid–ask bounce for example induces negative autocorrelation in tick data and causes the realized volatility estimator to be upwardly biased. Theoretical modelling of this issue so far assumes the price process and the microstructure effect are not correlated, which is open to debate since market microstructure theory suggests that trading has an impact on the efficient price. I am grateful to Frank de Jong for explaining this to me at a conference.

[7] $\widehat{\sigma}_{t,T|t-1}$ denotes a volatility forecast formulated at time $t-1$ for volatility over the period from t to T. In pricing options, the required volatility parameter is the expected volatility over the life of the option. The pricing model relies on a riskless hedge to be followed through until the option reaches maturity. Therefore the required volatility input, or the implied volatility derived, is a cumulative volatility forecast over the option maturity and not a point forecast of volatility at option maturity. The interest in forecasting $\sigma_{t,T|t-1}$ goes beyond the riskless hedge argument, however.

weekly or monthly data is better because volatility mean reversion is difficult to adjust using high frequency data. In general, model-based forecasts lose supremacy when the forecast horizon increases with respect to the data frequency. For forecast horizons that are longer than 6 months, a simple historical method using low-frequency data over a period at least as long as the forecast horizon works best (Alford and Boatsman, 1995; and Figlewski, 1997).

As far as sampling frequency is concerned, Drost and Nijman (1993) prove, theoretically and for a special case (i.e. the GARCH(1,1) process, which will be introduced in Chapter 4), that volatility structure should be preserved through intertemporal aggregation. This means that whether one models volatility at hourly, daily or monthly intervals, the volatility structure should be the same. But, it is well known that this is not the case in practice; volatility persistence, which is highly significant in daily data, weakens as the frequency of data decreases. [8] This further complicates any attempt to generalize volatility patterns and forecasting results.

1.4   THE TREATMENT OF LARGE NUMBERS

In this section, I use large numbers to refer generally to extreme values, outliers and rare jumps, a group of data that have similar characteristics but do not necessarily belong to the same set. To a statistician, there are always two 'extremes' in each sample, namely the minimum and the maximum. The H-L method for estimating volatility described in the previous section, for example, is also called the extreme value method. We have also noted that these H-L estimators assume conditional distribution is normal. In extreme value statistics, normal distribution is but one of the distributions for the tail. There are many other extreme value distributions that have tails thinner or thicker than the normal distribution's. We have known for a long time now that financial asset returns are not normally distributed. We also know the standardized residuals from ARCH models still display large kurtosis (see McCurdy and Morgan, 1987; Milhoj, 1987; Hsieh, 1989; Baillie and Bollerslev, 1989). Conditional heteroscedasticity alone could not account for all the tail thickness. This is true even when the Student-t distribution is used to construct

---

[8] See Diebold (1988), Baillie and Bollerslev (1989) and Poon and Taylor (1992) for examples. Note that Nelson (1992) points out separately that as the sampling frequency becomes shorter, volatility modelled using discrete time model approaches its diffusion limit and persistence is to be expected provided that the underlying returns is a diffusion or a near-diffusion process with no jumps.

the likelihood function (see Bollerslev, 1987; Hsieh, 1989). Hence, in the literature, the extreme values and the tail observations often refer to those data that lie outside the (conditional) Gaussian region. Given that jumps are large and are modelled as a separate component to the Brownian motion, jumps could potentially be seen as a set similar to those tail observations provided that they are truly rare.

Outliers are by definition unusually large in scale. They are so large that some have argued that they are generated from a completely different process or distribution. The frequency of occurrence should be much smaller for outliers than for jumps or extreme values. Outliers are so huge and rare that it is very unlikely that any modelling effort will be able to capture and predict them. They have, however, undue influence on modelling and estimation (Huber, 1981). Unless extreme value techniques are used where scale and marginal distribution are often removed, it is advisable that outliers are removed or trimmed before modelling volatility. One such outlier in stock market returns is the October 1987 crash that produced a 1-day loss of over 20% in stock markets worldwide.

The ways that outliers have been tackled in the literature largely depend on their sizes, the frequency of their occurrence and whether these outliers have an additive or a multiplicative impact. For the rare and additive outliers, the most common treatment is simply to remove them from the sample or omit them in the likelihood calculation (Kearns and Pagan, 1993). Franses and Ghijsels (1999) find forecasting performance of the GARCH model is substantially improved in four out of five stock markets studied when the additive outliers are removed. For the rare multiplicative outliers that produced a residual impact on volatility, a dummy variable could be included in the conditional volatility equation after the outlier returns has been dummied out in the mean equation (Blair, Poon and Taylor, 2001).

$$r_t = \mu + \psi_1 D_t + \varepsilon_t, \qquad \varepsilon_t = \sqrt{h_t} z_t$$
$$h_t = \omega + \beta h_{t-1} + \alpha \varepsilon_{t-1}^2 + \psi_2 D_{t-1}$$

where D_t is 1 when t refers to 19 October 1987 and 0 otherwise. Personally, I find a simple method such as the trimming rule in (1.2) very quick to implement and effective.

The removal of outliers does not remove volatility persistence. In fact, the evidence in the previous section shows that trimming the data using (1.2) actually increases the 'long memory' in volatility making it appear to be extremely persistent. Since autocorrelation is defined as

$$\rho\left(r_t, r_{t-\tau}\right) = \frac{Cov\left(r_t, r_{t-\tau}\right)}{Var\left(r_t\right)},$$

the removal of outliers has a great impact on the denominator, reduces $Var\left(r_t\right)$ and increases the individual and the cumulative autocorrelation coefficients.

Once the impact of outliers is removed, there are different views about how the extremes and jumps should be handled vis-à-vis the rest of the data. There are two schools of thought, each proposing a seemingly different model, and both can explain the long memory in volatility. The first believes structural breaks in volatility cause mean level of volatility to shift up and down. There is no restriction on the frequency or the size of the breaks. The second advocates the regime-switching model where volatility switches between high and low volatility states. The means of the two states are fixed, but there is no restriction on the timing of the switch, the duration of each regime and the probability of switching. Sometimes a three-regime switching is adopted but, as the number of regimes increases, the estimation and modelling become more complex. Technically speaking, if there are infinite numbers of regimes then there is no difference between the two models. The regime-switching model and the structural break model will be described in Chapter 5.

2

Volatility Forecast Evaluation

Comparing forecasting performance of competing models is one of the most important aspects of any forecasting exercise. In contrast to the efforts made in the construction of volatility models and forecasts, little attention has been paid to forecast evaluation in the volatility forecasting literature. Let $\widehat{X}_t$ be the predicted variable, X_t be the actual outcome and $\varepsilon_t = \widehat{X}_t - X_t$ be the forecast error. In the context of volatility forecast, $\widehat{X}_t$ and X_t are the predicted and actual conditional volatility. There are many issues to consider:

(i) The form of X_t: should it be σ_t^2 or σ_t?
(ii) Given that volatility is a latent variable, the impact of the noise introduced in the estimation of X_t, the actual volatility.
(iii) Which form of ε_t is more relevant for volatility model selection; $\Sigma \varepsilon_t^2$, $\Sigma |\varepsilon_t|$ or $\Sigma |\varepsilon_t|/X_t$? Do we penalize underforecast, $\widehat{X}_t < X_t$, more than overforecast, $\widehat{X}_t > X_t$?
(iv) Given that all error statistics are subject to noise, how do we know if one model is truly better than another?
(v) How do we take into account when X_t and X_{t+1} (and similarly for ε_t and $\widehat{X}_t$) cover a large amount of overlapping data and are serially correlated?

All these issues will be considered in the following sections.

2.1 THE FORM OF X_t

Here we argue that X_t should be σ_t, and that if σ_t cannot be estimated with some accuracy it is best not to perform comparison across predictive models at all. The practice of using daily squared returns to proxy daily conditional variance has been shown time and again to produce wrong signals in model selection.

Given that all time series volatility models formulate forecasts based on past information, they are not designed to predict shocks that are new to the system. Financial market volatility has many stylized facts. Once a shock has entered the system, the merit of the volatility model depends on how well it captures these stylized facts in predicting the volatility of the following days. Hence we argue that X_t should be σ_t. Conditional variance σ_t^2 formulation gives too much weight to the errors caused by 'new' shocks and especially the large ones, distorting the less extreme forecasts where the models are to be assessed.

Note also that the square of a variance error is the fourth power of the same error measured from standard deviation. This can complicate the task of forecast evaluation given the difficulty in estimating fourth moments with common distributions let alone the thick-tailed ones in finance. The confidence interval of the mean error statistic can be very wide when forecast errors are measured from variances and worse if they are squared. This leads to difficulty in finding significant differences between forecasting models.

Davidian and Carroll (1987) make similar observations in their study of variance function estimation for heteroscedastic regression. Using high-order theory, they show that the use of square returns for modelling variance is appropriate only for approximately normally distributed data, and becomes nonrobust when there is a small departure from normality. Estimation of the variance function that is based on logarithmic transformation or absolute returns is more robust against asymmetry and nonnormality.

Some have argued that perhaps X_t should be $ln\sigma_t$ to rescale the size of the forecast errors (Pagan and Schwert, 1990). This is perhaps one step too far. After all, the magnitude of the error directly impacts on option pricing, risk management and investment decision. Taking the logarithm of the volatility error is likely to distort the loss function which is directly proportional to the magnitude of forecast error. A decision maker might be more risk-averse towards the larger errors.

We have explained in Section 1.3.1 the impact of using squared returns to proxy daily volatility. Hansen and Lunde (2004b) used a series of simulations to show that '... the substitution of a squared return for the conditional variance in the evaluation of ARCH-type models can result in an inferior model being chosen as [the] best with a probability converges to one as the sample size increases ... '. Hansen and Lunde (2004a) advocate the use of realized volatility in forecast evaluation but caution the noise introduced by market macrostructure when the intraday returns are too short.

2.2   ERROR STATISTICS AND THE FORM OF ε_t

Ideally an evaluation exercise should reflect the relative or absolute usefulness of a volatility forecast to investors. However, to do that one
needs to know the decision process that require these forecasts and the
costs and benefits that result from using better forecasts. Utility-based
criteria, such as that used in West, Edison and Cho (1993), require some
assumptions about the shape and property of the utility function. In practice these costs, benefits and utility function are not known and one often
resorts to simply use measures suggested by statisticians.

Popular evaluation measures used in the literature include
Mean Error (ME)

$$\frac{1}{N} \sum_{t=1}^{N} \varepsilon_t = \frac{1}{N} \sum_{t=1}^{N} (\widehat{\sigma}_t - \sigma_t),$$

Mean Square Error (MSE)

$$\frac{1}{N} \sum_{t=1}^{N} \varepsilon_t^2 = \frac{1}{N} \sum_{t=1}^{N} (\widehat{\sigma}_t - \sigma_t)^2,$$

Root Mean Square Error (RMSE)

$$\sqrt{\frac{1}{N} \sum_{t=1}^{N} \varepsilon_t^2} = \sqrt{\frac{1}{N} \sum_{t=1}^{N} (\widehat{\sigma}_t - \sigma_t)^2},$$

Mean Absolute Error (MAE)

$$\frac{1}{N} \sum_{t=1}^{N} |\varepsilon_t| = \frac{1}{N} \sum_{t=1}^{N} |\widehat{\sigma}_t - \sigma_t|,$$

Mean Absolute Percent Error (MAPE)

$$\frac{1}{N} \sum_{t=1}^{N} \frac{|\varepsilon_t|}{\sigma_t} = \frac{1}{N} \sum_{t=1}^{N} \frac{|\widehat{\sigma}_t - \sigma_t|}{\sigma_t}.$$

Bollerslev and Ghysels (1996) suggested a heteroscedasticity-
adjusted version of MSE called HMSE where

$$\text{HMSE} = \frac{1}{N} \sum_{t=1}^{N} \left[\frac{\sigma_t}{\widehat{\sigma}_t} - 1 \right]^2$$

This is similar to squared percentage error but with the forecast error scaled by predicted volatility. This type of performance measure is not appropriate if the absolute magnitude of the forecast error is a major concern. It is not clear why it is the predicted and not the actual volatility that is used in the denominator. The squaring of the error again will give greater weight to large errors.

Other less commonly used measures include *mean logarithm of absolute errors* (MLAE) (as in Pagan and Schwert, 1990), the Theil-U statistic and one based on asymmetric loss function, namely LINEX:

Mean Logarithm of Absolute Errors (MLAE)

$$\frac{1}{N}\sum_{t=1}^{N}\ln|\varepsilon_t| = \frac{1}{N}\sum_{t=1}^{N}\ln|\widehat{\sigma}_t - \sigma_t|$$

Theil-U measure

$$\text{Theil-}U = \frac{\sum_{t=1}^{N}(\widehat{\sigma}_t - \sigma_t)^2}{\sum_{t=1}^{N}\left(\widehat{\sigma}_t^{BM} - \sigma_t\right)^2}, \tag{2.1}$$

where $\widehat{\sigma}_t^{BM}$ is the benchmark forecast, used here to remove the effect of any scalar transformation applied to σ_t.

LINEX has asymmetric loss function whereby the positive errors are weighted differently from the negative errors:

$$\text{LINEX} = \frac{1}{N}\sum_{t=1}^{N}[\exp\{-a(\widehat{\sigma}_t - \sigma_t)\} + a(\widehat{\sigma}_t - \sigma_t) - 1]. \tag{2.2}$$

The choice of the parameter a is subjective. If $a > 0$, the function is approximately linear for overprediction and exponential for underprediction. Granger (1999) describes a variety of other asymmetric loss functions of which the LINEX is an example. Given that most investors would treat gains and losses differently, the use of asymmetric loss functions may be advisable, but their use is not common in the literature.

2.3 COMPARING FORECAST ERRORS OF DIFFERENT MODELS

In the special case where the error distribution of one forecasting model dominates that of another forecasting model, the comparison is straightforward (Granger, 1999). In practice, this is rarely the case, and most comparisons of forecasting results are made based on the error statistics described in Section 2.2. It is important to note that these error statistics are themselves subject to error and noise. So if an error statistic of model A is higher than that of model B, one cannot conclude that model B is better than A without performing tests of significance. For statistical inference, West (1996), West and Cho (1995) and West and McCracken (1998) show how standard errors for ME, MSE, MAE and RMSE may be derived taking into account serial correlation in the forecast errors and uncertainty inherent in volatility model parameter estimates.

If there are T number of observations in the sample and T is large, there are two ways in which out-of-sample forecasts may be made. Assume that we use n number of observations for estimation and make $T - n$ number of forecasts. The *recursive scheme* starts with the sample $\{1, \cdots, n\}$ and makes first forecast at $n + 1$. The second forecast for $n + 2$ will include the last observation and form the information set $\{1, \cdots, n + 1\}$. It follows that the last forecast for T will include all but the last observation, i.e. the information set is $\{1, \cdots, T - 1\}$. In practice, the *rolling scheme* is more popular, where a fixed number of observations is used in the estimation. So the forecast for $n + 2$ will be based on information set $\{2, \cdots, n + 1\}$, and the last forecast at T will be based on $\{T - n, \cdots, T - 1\}$. The rolling scheme omits information in the distant past. It is also more manageable in terms of computation when T is very large. The standard errors developed by West and co-authors are based on asymptotic theory and work for recursive scheme only. For smaller sample and rolling scheme forecasts, Diebold and Mariano's (1995) small sample methods are more appropriate.

Diebold and Mariano (1995) propose three tests for 'equal accuracy' between two forecasting models. The tests relate prediction error to some very general loss function and analyse loss differential derived from errors produced by two competing models. The three tests include an asymptotic test that corrects for series correlation and two exact finite sample tests based on sign test and the Wilcoxon sign-rank test. Simulation results show that the three tests are robust against non-Gaussian, nonzero mean, serially and contemporaneously correlated forecast errors. The two sign-based tests in particular continue to work well among small samples. The Diebold and Mariano tests have been used in a number of volatility forecasting contests. We provide the test details here.

Let $\{\widehat{X}_{it}\}_{t=1}^{T}$ and $\{\widehat{X}_{jt}\}_{t=1}^{T}$ be two sets of forecasts for $\{X_{t}\}_{t=1}^{T}$ from models i and j respectively. Let the associated forecast errors be $\{e_{it}\}_{t=1}^{T}$ and $\{e_{jt}\}_{t=1}^{T}$. Let $g(\cdot)$ be the loss function (e.g. the error statistics in Section 2.2) such that

$$g(X_t, \widehat{X}_{it}) = g(e_{it}).$$

Next define loss differential

$$d_t \equiv g(e_{it}) - g(e_{jt}).$$

The null hypothesis is equal forecast accuracy and zero loss differential $E(d_t) = 0$.

2.3.1   Diebold and Mariano's asymptotic test

The first test targets on the mean

$$\overline{d} = \frac{1}{T} \sum_{t=1}^{T} |g(e_{it}) - g(e_{jt})|$$

with test statistic

$$S_1 = \frac{\overline{d}}{\sqrt{\frac{1}{T} 2\pi \widehat{f}_d(0)}} \qquad S_1 \sim N(0,1)$$

$$2\pi \widehat{f}_d(0) = \sum_{\tau=-(T-1)}^{T-1} 1\left(\frac{\tau}{S(T)}\right) \widehat{\gamma}_d(\tau)$$

$$\widehat{\gamma}_d(\tau) = \frac{1}{T} \sum_{t=|\tau|+1}^{T} (d_t - \overline{d})(d_{t-|\tau|} - \overline{d}).$$

The operator $1(\tau/S(T))$ is the lag window, and $S(T)$ is the truncation lag with

$$1\left(\frac{\tau}{S(T)}\right) = \begin{cases} 1 & \text{for } \left|\frac{\tau}{S(T)}\right| \le 1 \\ 0 & \text{otherwise} \end{cases}.$$

Assuming that k-step ahead forecast errors are at most $(k-1)$-dependent, it is therefore recommended that $S(T) = (k-1)$. It is not likely that $\widehat{f}_d(0)$ will be negative, but in the rare event that $\widehat{f}_d(0) < 0$, it should be treated as zero and the null hypothesis of equal forecast accuracy be rejected automatically.

2.3.2 Diebold and Mariano's sign test

The sign test targets on the median with the null hypothesis that

$$Med (d) = Med \left(g(e_{it}) - g\left(e_{jt}\right)\right)$$
$$= 0.$$

Assuming that $d_t \sim iid$, then the test statistic is

$$S_2 = \sum_{t=1}^{T} I_+ (d_t)$$

where

$$I_+ (d_t) = \begin{cases} 1 & \text{if } d_t > 0 \\ 0 & \text{otherwise} \end{cases}.$$

For small sample, S_2 should be assessed using a table for cumulative binomial distribution. In large sample, the Studentized verson of S_2 is asymptotically normal

$$S_{2a} = \frac{S_2 - 0.5T}{\sqrt{0.25T}} \overset{a}{\sim} N(0, 1).$$

2.3.3 Diebold and Mariano's Wilcoxon sign-rank test

As the name indicates, this test is based on both the sign and the rank of loss differential with test statistic

$$S_3 = \sum_{t=1}^{T} I_+ (d_t) \operatorname{rank} (|d_t|)$$

represents the sum of the ranks of the absolute values of the positive observations. The critical values for S_3 have been tabulated for small sample. For large sample, the Studentized verson of S_3 is again asymptotically normal

$$S_{2a} = \frac{S_3 - \dfrac{T(T+1)}{4}}{\sqrt{\dfrac{T(T+1)(2T+1)}{24}}} \overset{a}{\sim} N(0, 1).$$

2.3.4   Serially correlated loss differentials

Serial correlation is explicitly taken care of in S_1. For S_2 and S_3 (and their asymptotic counter parts S_{2a} and S_{3a}), the following k-set of loss differentials have to be tested jointly

$$\{d_{ij,1}, d_{ij,1+k}, d_{ij,1+2k}, \cdots\},$$
$$\{d_{ij,2}, d_{ij,2+k}, d_{ij,2+2k}, \cdots\},$$
$$\vdots$$
$$\{d_{ij,k}, d_{ij,2k}, d_{ij,3k}, \cdots\}.$$

A test with size bounded by α is then tested k times, each of size α/k, on each of the above k loss-differentials sequences. The null hypothesis of equal forecast accuracy is rejected if the null is rejected for *any* of the k samples.

2.4   REGRESSION-BASED FORECAST EFFICIENCY AND ORTHOGONALITY TEST

The regression-based method for examining the informational content of forecasts is by far the most popular method in volatility forecasting. It involves regressing the actual volatility, X_t, on the forecasts literature, $\widehat{X}_t$, as shown below:

$$X_t = \alpha + \beta \widehat{X}_t + \upsilon_t . \qquad (2.3)$$

Conditioning upon the forecast, the prediction is unbiased only if $\alpha = 0$ and $\beta = 1$.

Since the error term, υ_t, is heteroscedastic and serially correlated when overlapping forecasts are evaluated, the standard errors of the parameter estimates are often computed on the basis of Hansen and Hodrick (1980). Let Y be the row matrix of regressors including the constant term. In (2.3), $Y_t = \begin{pmatrix} 1 & \widehat{X}_t \end{pmatrix}$ is a 1×2 matrix. Then

$$\widehat{\Psi} = T^{-1} \sum_{t=1}^{T} \upsilon_t^2 Y_t' Y_t$$

$$+ T^{-1} \sum_{k=1}^{T} \sum_{t=k+1}^{T} Q(k,t) \upsilon_k \upsilon_t \left(Y_t' Y_k + Y_k' Y_t \right),$$

where υ_k and υ_t are the residuals for observation k and t from the regression. The operator $Q(k, t)$ is an indicator function taking the value 1 if there is information overlap between Y_k and Y_t. The adjusted covariance matrix for the regression coefficients is then calculated as

$$\widehat{\Omega} = \left(Y'Y \right)^{-1} \widehat{\Psi} \left(Y'Y \right)^{-1}. \tag{2.4}$$

Canina and Figlewski (1993) conducted some simulatation studies and found the corrected standard errors in (2.4) are close to the true values, and the use of overlapping data reduced the standard error between one-quarter and one-eighth of what would be obtained with only nonoverlapping data.

In cases where there are more than one forecasting model, additional forecasts are added to the right-hand side of (2.3) to check for incremental explanatory power. Such a forecast encompassing test dates back to Theil (1966). Chong and Hendry (1986) and Fair and Shiller (1989, 1990) provide further theoretical exposition of such methods for testing forecast efficiency. The first forecast is said to subsume information contained in other forecasts if these additional forecasts do not significantly increase the adjusted regression R^2. Alternatively, an orthogonality test may be conducted by regressing the residuals from (2.3) on other forecasts. If these forecasts are orthogonal, i.e. do not contain additional information, then the regression coefficients will not be different from zero.

While it is useful to have an unbiased forecast, it is important to distinguish between bias and predictive power. A biased forecast can have predictive power if the bias can be corrected. An unbiased forecast is useless if all forecast errors are big. For $\widehat{X}_i$ to be considered as a good forecast, $Var(\upsilon_t)$ should be small and R^2 for the regression should tend to 100%. Blair, Poon and Taylor (2001) use the proportion of explained variability, P, to measure explanatory power

$$P = 1 - \frac{\sum \left(X_i - \widehat{X}_i \right)^2}{\sum (X_i - \mu_X)^2}. \tag{2.5}$$

The ratio in the right-hand side of (2.5) compares the sum of squared prediction errors (assuming $\alpha = 0$ and $\beta = 1$ in (2.3)) with the sum of squared variation of X_i. P compares the amount of variation in the forecast errors with that in actual volatility. If prediction errors are small,

P is closer to 1. Given that a regression model that produces (2.5) is more restrictive than (2.3), P is likely to be smaller than conventional R^2. P can even be negative since the ratio on the right-hand side of (2.5) can be greater than 1. A negative P means that the forecast errors have a greater amount of variation than the actual volatility, which is not a desirable characteristic for a well-behaved forecasting model.

2.5   OTHER ISSUES IN FORECAST EVALUATION

In all forecast evaluations, it is important to distinguish in-sample and out-of-sample forecasts. In-sample forecast, which is based on parameters estimated using all data in the sample, implicitly assumes parameter estimates are stable across time. In practice, time variation of parameter estimates is a critical issue in forecasting. A good forecasting model should be one that can withstand the robustness of out-of-sample test – a test design that is closer to reality.

Instead of striving to make some statistical inference, model performance could be judged on some measures of economic significance. Examples of such an approach include portfolio improvement derived from better volatility forecasts (Fleming, Kirby and Ostdiek, 2000, 2002). Some papers test forecast accuracy by measuring the impact on option pricing errors (Karolyi, 1993). In the latter case, pricing error in the option model will be cancelled out when the option implied volatility is reintroduced into the pricing formula. So it is not surprising that evaluation which involves comparing option pricing errors often prefers the implied volatility method to all other time series methods.

Research in financial market volatility has been concentrating on modelling and less on forecasting. Work on combined forecast is rare, probably because the groups of researchers in time series models and option pricing do not seem to mix. What has not yet been done in the literature is to separate the forecasting period into 'normal' and 'exceptional' periods. It is conceivable that different forecasting methods are better suited to different trading environment and economic conditions.

3
Historical Volatility Models

Compared with the other types of volatility models, the historical volatility models (HIS) are the easiest to manipulate and construct. The well-known Riskmetrics EWMA (equally weighted moving average) model from JP Morgan is a form of historical volatility model; so are models that build directly on realized volatility that have became very popular in the last few years. Historical volatility models have been shown to have good forecasting performance compared with other time series volatility models. Unlike the other two time series models (viz. ARCH and stochastic volatility (SV)) conditional volatility is modelled separately from returns in the historical volatility models, and hence they are less restrictive and are more ready to respond to changes in volatility dynamic. Studies that find historical volatility models forecast better than ARCH and/or SV models include Taylor (1986, 1987), Figlewski (1997), Figlewski and Green (1999), Andersen, Bollerslev, Diebold and Labys (2001) and Taylor, J. (2004). With the increased availability of intraday data, we can expect to see research on the realized volatility variant of the historical model to intensify in the next few years.

3.1 MODELLING ISSUES

Unlike ARCH SV models where returns are the main input, HIS models do not normally use returns information so long as the volatility estimates are ready at hand. Take the simplest form of ARCH(1) for example,

$$r_t = \mu + \varepsilon_t, \qquad \varepsilon_t \sim N(0, \sigma_t) \qquad (3.1)$$
$$\varepsilon_t = z_t \sigma_t, \qquad z_t \sim N(0, 1)$$
$$\sigma_t^2 = \omega + \alpha_1 \varepsilon_{t-1}^2. \qquad (3.2)$$

The conditional volatility σ_t^2 in (3.2) is modelled as a 'byproduct' of the return equation (3.1). The estimation is done by maximizing the likelihood of observing $\{\varepsilon_t\}$ using the normal, or other chosen, density. The construction and estimation of SV models are similar to those of ARCH, except that there is now an additional innovation term in (3.2).

In contrast, the HIS model is built directly on conditional volatility, e.g. an AR(1) model:

$$\sigma_t = \gamma + \beta_1 \sigma_{t-1} + \upsilon_t. \tag{3.3}$$

The parameters γ and β_1 are estimated by minimizing in-sample forecast errors, υ_t, where

$$\upsilon_t = \sigma_t - \widehat{\gamma} - \widehat{\beta}_1 \widehat{\sigma}_{t-1},$$

and the forecaster has the choice of reducing mean square errors, mean absolute errors etc., as in the case of choosing an appropriate forecast error statistic in Section 2.2.

The historical volatility estimates σ_t in (3.3) can be calculated as sample standard deviations if there are sufficient data for each t interval. If there is not sufficient information, then the H-L method of Section 1.3.2 may be used, and in the most extreme case, where only one observation is available for each t interval, one often resorts to using absolute return to proxy for volatility at t. In Section 1.3.1 we have highlighted the danger of using daily absolute or squared returns to proxy 'actual' daily volatility for the purpose of forecast evaluation, as this could lead to very misleading model ranking. The problem with the use of daily absolute return in volatility modelling is less severe provided that long distributed lags are included (Nelson, 1992; Nelson and Foster, 1995). With the increased availability of intraday data, historical volatility estimates can be calculated quite accurately as realized volatility following Section 1.3.3.

3.2   TYPES OF HISTORICAL VOLATILITY MODELS

There are now two major types of HIS models: the single-state and the regime-switching models. All the HIS models differ by the number of lag volatility terms included in the model and the weights assigned to them, reflecting the choice on the tradeoff between increasing the amount of information and more updated information.

3.2.1   Single-state historical volatility models

The simplest historical price model is the *random walk* model, where the difference between consecutive period volatility is modelled as a random noise;

$$\sigma_t = \sigma_{t-1} + \upsilon_t,$$

So the best forecast for tomorrow's volatility is today's volatility:

$$\widehat{\sigma}_{t+1} = \sigma_t,$$

where σ_t alone is used as a forecast for σ_{t+1}.

In contrast, the *historical average* method makes a forecast based on the entire history

$$\widehat{\sigma}_{t+1} = \frac{1}{t}(\sigma_t + \sigma_{t-1} + \cdots + \sigma_1).$$

The simple *moving average* method below,

$$\widehat{\sigma}_{t+1} = \frac{1}{\tau}(\sigma_t + \sigma_{t-1} + \cdots + \sigma_{t-\tau-1}),$$

is similar to the historical average method, except that older information is discarded. The value of τ (i.e. the lag length to past information used) could be subjectively chosen or based on minimizing in-sample forecast error, $\varsigma_{t+1} = \sigma_{t+1} - \widehat{\sigma}_{t+1}$. The multi-period forecasts $\widehat{\sigma}_{t+\tau}$ for $\tau > 1$ will be the same as the one-step-ahead forecast $\widehat{\sigma}_{t+1}$ for all three methods above.

The *exponential smoothing* method below,

$$\sigma_t = (1 - \beta)\sigma_{t-1} + \beta\widehat{\sigma}_{t-1} + \xi_t \quad \text{and} \quad 0 \le \beta \le 1,$$
$$\widehat{\sigma}_{t+1} = (1 - \beta)\sigma_t + \beta\widehat{\sigma}_t,$$

is similar to the historical method, but more weight is given to the recent past and less weight to the distant past. The smoothing parameter β is estimated by minimizing the in-sample forecast errors ξ_t.

The *exponentially weighted moving average* method (EWMA) below is the moving average method with exponential weights:

$$\widehat{\sigma}_{t+1} = \sum_{i=1}^{\tau} \beta^i \sigma_{t-i-1} \bigg/ \sum_{i=1}^{\tau} \beta^i.$$

Again the smoothing parameter β is estimated by minimizing the in-sample forecast errors ξ_t. The JP Morgan *Riskmetrics*^{TM} model is a procedure that uses the EWMA method.

All the historical volatility models above have a fixed weighting scheme or a weighting scheme that follows some declining pattern. Other types of historical model have weighting schemes that are not prespecified. The simplest of such models is the *simple regression* method,

$$\sigma_t = \gamma + \beta_1 \sigma_{t-1} + \beta_2 \sigma_{t-2} + \cdots + \beta_n \sigma_{t-n} + \upsilon_t,$$
$$\widehat{\sigma}_{t+1} = \gamma + \beta_1 \sigma_t + \beta_2 \sigma_{t-1} + \cdots + \beta_n \sigma_{t-n+1},$$

which expresses volatility as a function of its past values and an error term.

The *simple regression* method is principally autoregressive. If past volatility errors are also included, one gets the *ARMA* model

$$\widehat{\sigma}_{t+1} = \beta_1 \sigma_t + \beta_2 \sigma_{t-1} + \cdots + \gamma_1 v_t + \gamma_2 v_{t-1} + \cdots.$$

Introducing a differencing order I(d), we get ARIMA when $d = 1$ and ARFIMA when $d < 1$.

3.2.2 Regime switching and transition exponential smoothing

In this section, we have the *threshold autoregressive* model from Cao and Tsay (1992):

$$\sigma_t = \phi_0^{(i)} + \phi_1^{(i)}\sigma_{t-1} + \cdots + \phi_p^{(i)}\sigma_{t-p} + v_t, \quad i = 1, 2, \ldots, k$$

$$\widehat{\sigma}_{t+1} = \phi_0^{(i)} + \phi_1^{(i)}\sigma_t + \cdots + \phi_p^{(i)}\sigma_{t+1-p},$$

where the thresholds separate volatility into states with independent *simple regression* models and noise processes in each state. The prediction $\widehat{\sigma}_{t+1}$ could be based solely on current state information i assuming the future will remain on current state. Alternatively it could be based on information of all states weighted by the transition probability for each state. Cao and Tsay (1992) found the threshold autoregressive model outperformed EGARCH and GARCH in forecasting of the 1- to 30-month volatility of the S&P value-weighted index. EGARCH provided better forecasts for the S&P equally weighted index, possibly because the equally weighted index gives more weights to small stocks where the leverage effect could be more important.

The *smooth transition exponential smoothing* model is from Taylor, J. (2004):

$$\widehat{\sigma}_t = \alpha_{t-1}\varepsilon_{t-1}^2 + (1 - \alpha_{t-1})\widehat{\sigma}_{t-1}^2 + v_t, \tag{3.4}$$

where

$$\alpha_{t-1} = \frac{1}{1 + \exp(\beta + \gamma V_{t-1})},$$

and $V_{t-1} = a\varepsilon_{t-1} + b|\varepsilon_{t-1}|$ is the transition variable. The smoothing parameter α_{t-1} varies between 0 and 1, and its value depends on the size and the sign of ε_{t-1}. The dependence on ε_{t-1} means that multi-step-ahead forecasts cannot be made except through simulation. (The same would apply to many nonlinear ARCH and SV models as we will show in the next few chapters.)

One-day-ahead forecasting results show that the smooth transition exponential smoothing model performs very well against several ARCH counterparts and even outperformed, on a few occasions, the realized volatility forecast. But these rankings were not tested for statistical significance, so it is difficult to come to a conclusion given the closeness of many error statistics reported.

3.3 FORECASTING PERFORMANCE

Taylor (1987) was one of the earliest to test time-series volatility forecasting models before ARCH/GARCH permeated the volatility literature. Taylor (1987) used extreme value estimates based on high, low and closing prices to forecast 1 to 20 days DM/$ futures volatility and found a weighted average composite forecast performed best. Wiggins (1992) also gave support to extreme-value volatility estimators.

In the pre-ARCH era, there were many studies that covered a wide range of issues. Sometimes forecasters would introduce 'learning' by allowing parameters and weights of combined forecasts to be dynamically updated. These frequent updates did not always lead to better results, however. Dimson and Marsh (1990) found *ex ante* time-varying optimized weighting schemes do not always work well in out-of-sample forecasts. Sill (1993) found S&P500 volatility was higher during recession and that commercial T-Bill spread helped to predict stock-market volatility.

The randow walk and historical average method seems naive at first, but they seem to work very well for medium and long horizon forecasts. For forecast horizons that are longer than 6 months, low-frequency data over a period at least as long as the forecast horizon works best. To provide equity volatility for investment over a 5-year period for example, Alford and Boatsman (1995) recommended, after studying a sample of 6879 stocks, that volatility should be estimated from weekly or monthly returns from the previous 5 years and that adjustment made based on industry and company size. Figlewski (1997) analysed the volatility of the S&P500, the long- and short-term US interest rate and the Deutschemark–dollar exchange rate and the use of monthly data over a long period provides the best long-horizon forecast. Alford and Boatsman (1995), Figlewski (1997) and Figlewski and Green (1999) all stressed the importance of having a long enough estimation period to make good volatility forecasts over long horizon.

4

ARCH

Financial market volatility is known to cluster. A volatile period tends to persist for some time before the market returns to normality. The ARCH (AutoRegressive Conditional Heteroscedasticity) model proposed by Engle (1982) was designed to capture volatility persistence in inflation. The ARCH model was later found to fit many financial time series and its widespread impact on finance has led to the Nobel Committee's recognition of Rob Engle's work in 2003. The ARCH effect has been shown to lead to high kurtosis which fits in well with the empirically observed tail thickness of many asset return distributions. The leverage effect, a phenomenon related to high volatility brought on by negative return, is often modelled with a sign-based return variable in the conditional volatility equation.

4.1 ENGLE (1982)

The ARCH model, first introduced by Engle (1982), has been extended by many researchers and extensively surveyed in Bera and Higgins (1993), Bollerslev, Chou and Kroner (1992), Bollerslev, Engle and Nelson (1994) and Diebold and Lopez (1995). In contrast to the historical volatility models described in the previous chapter, ARCH models do not make use of the past standard deviations, but formulate conditional variance, h_t, of asset returns via maximum likelihood procedures. (We follow the ARCH literature here by writing $\sigma_t^2 = h_t$.) To illustrate this, first write returns, r_t, as

$$r_t = \mu + \varepsilon_t,$$
$$\varepsilon_t = \sqrt{h_t} z_t, \tag{4.1}$$

where $z_t \sim D(0, 1)$ is a white noise. The distribution D is often taken as normal. The process z_t is scaled by h_t, the conditional variance, which in turn is a function of past squared residual returns. In the ARCH(q) process proposed by Engle (1982),

$$h_t = \omega + \sum_{j=1}^{q} \alpha_j \varepsilon_{t-j}^2 \tag{4.2}$$

with $\omega > 0$ and $\alpha_j \geq 0$ to ensure h_t is strictly positive variance. Typically, q is of high order because of the phenomenon of volatility persistence in financial markets. From the way in which volatility is constructed in (4.2), h_t is known at time $t - 1$. So the one-step-ahead forecast is readily available. The multi-step-ahead forecasts can be formulated by assuming $E\left[\varepsilon_{t+\tau}^2\right] = h_{t+\tau}$.

The unconditional variance of r_t is

$$\sigma^2 = \frac{\omega}{1 - \displaystyle\sum_{j=1}^{q} \alpha_j}.$$

The process is covariance stationary if and only if the sum of the autoregressive parameters is less than one $\sum_{j=1}^{q} \alpha_j < 1$.

4.2 GENERALIZED ARCH

For high-order ARCH(q) process, it is more parsimonious to model volatility as a GARCH(p, q) (generalized ARCH due to Bollerslev (1986) and Taylor (1986)), where additional dependencies are permitted on p lags of past h_t as shown below:

$$h_t = \omega + \sum_{i=1}^{p} \beta_i h_{t-i} + \sum_{j=1}^{q} \alpha_j \varepsilon_{t-j}^2$$

and $\omega > 0$. For GARCH(1, 1), the constraints $\alpha_1 \geq 0$ and $\beta_1 \geq 0$ are needed to ensure h_t is strictly positive. For higher orders of GARCH, the constraints on β_i and α_j are more complex (see Nelson and Cao (1992) for details). The unconditional variance equals

$$\sigma^2 = \frac{\omega}{1 - \displaystyle\sum_{i=1}^{p} \beta_i - \sum_{j=1}^{q} \alpha_j}$$

The GARCH(p, q) model is covariance stationary if and only if $\sum_{i=1}^{p} \beta_i + \sum_{j=1}^{q} \alpha_j < 1$.

Volatility forecasts from GARCH(1, 1) can be made by repeated substitutions. First, we make use of the relationship (4.1) to provide an estimate for the expected squared residuals

$$E\left[\varepsilon_t^2\right] = h_t E\left[z_t^2\right] = h_t.$$

The conditional variance h_{t+1} and the one-step-ahead forecast is known at time t,

$$\widehat{h}_{t+1} = \omega + \alpha_1 \varepsilon_t^2 + \beta_1 h_t. \tag{4.3}$$

The forecast of h_{t+2} makes use of the fact that $E\left[\varepsilon_{t+1}^2\right] = h_{t+1}$ and we get

$$\begin{aligned}
\widehat{h}_{t+2} &= \omega + \alpha_1 \varepsilon_{t+1}^2 + \beta_1 h_{t+1} \\
&= \omega + (\alpha_1 + \beta_1) h_{t+1}.
\end{aligned}$$

Similarly,

$$\begin{aligned}
\widehat{h}_{t+3} &= \omega + (\alpha_1 + \beta_1) h_{t+2} \\
&= \omega + \omega(\alpha_1 + \beta_1) + (\alpha_1 + \beta_1)^2 h_{t+1} \\
&= \omega + \omega(\alpha_1 + \beta_1) + \omega(\alpha_1 + \beta_1)^2 + (\alpha_1 + \beta_1)^2 \left[\alpha_1 \varepsilon_t^2 + \beta_1 h_t\right].
\end{aligned}$$

As the forecast horizon τ lengthens,

$$\widehat{h}_{t+\tau} = \frac{\omega}{1 - (\alpha_1 + \beta_1)} + (\alpha_1 + \beta_1)^\tau \left[\alpha_1 \varepsilon_t^2 + \beta_1 h_t\right]. \tag{4.4}$$

If $\alpha_1 + \beta_1 < 1$, the second term on the RHS of (4.4) dies out eventually and $\widehat{h}_{t+\tau}$ converges to $\omega/[1 - (\alpha_1 + \beta_1)]$, the unconditional variance.

If we write $\upsilon_t = \varepsilon_t^2 - h_t$ and substitute $h_t = \varepsilon_t^2 - \upsilon_t$ into (4.3), we get

$$\begin{aligned}
\varepsilon_t^2 - \upsilon_t &= \omega + \alpha_1 \varepsilon_{t-1}^2 + \beta_1 \varepsilon_{t-1}^2 - \beta_1 \upsilon_{t-1} \\
\varepsilon_t^2 &= \omega + (\alpha_1 + \beta_1) \varepsilon_{t-1}^2 + \upsilon_t - \beta_1 \upsilon_{t-1}. \tag{4.5}
\end{aligned}$$

Hence, ε_t^2, the squared residual returns follow an ARMA process with autoregressive parameter $(\alpha_1 + \beta_1)$. If $\alpha_1 + \beta_1$ is close to 1, the autoregressive process in (4.5) dies out slowly.

4.3 INTEGRATED GARCH

For a GARCH(p, q) process, when $\sum_{i=1}^p \alpha_i + \sum_{j=1}^q \beta_j = 1$, the unconditional variance $\sigma^2 \to \infty$ is no longer definite. The series r_t is not covariance stationary, although it remains strictly stationary and ergodic. The conditional variance is then described as an integrated GARCH (denoted as IGARCH) and there is no finite fourth moment.[1]

---

[1] This is not the same as, and should not be confused with, the 'integrated volatility' described in Section 1.3.3.

An infinite volatility is a concept rather counterintuitive to real phenomena in economics and finance. Empirical findings suggest that GARCH(1, 1) is the most popular structure for many financial time series. It turns out that *Riskmetrics*™ EWMA (exponentially weighted moving average) is a nonstationary version of GARCH(1, 1) where the persistence parameters, α_1 and β_1, sum to 1. To see the parallel, we first make repeated substitution of (4.3) and obtain

$$h_{t+2} = \omega + \alpha\varepsilon_{t+1}^2 + \beta h_{t+1}$$
$$= \omega + \omega\beta + \alpha\varepsilon_{t+1}^2 + \alpha\beta\varepsilon_t^2 + \beta^2 h_t,$$
$$h_{t+\tau} = \omega \sum_{i=1}^{\tau} \beta^{i-1} + \alpha \sum_{i=1}^{\tau} \beta^{i-1}\varepsilon_{t+\tau-1}^2 + \beta^{\tau} h_t.$$

When $\tau \to \infty$, and provided that $\beta < 1$ we can infer that

$$h_t = \frac{\omega}{1-\beta} + \alpha \sum_{i=1}^{\infty} \beta^{i-1}\varepsilon_{t-i}^2. \tag{4.6}$$

Next, we have the EWMA model for the sample standard deviations, where

$$\widehat{\sigma}_t^2 = \left(\frac{1}{1+\lambda+\lambda^2+\cdots+\lambda^n}\right)\left(\sigma_{t-1}^2 + \lambda\sigma_{t-1}^2 + \cdots + \lambda^n\sigma_{t-n}^2\right).$$

As $n \to \infty$, and provided that $\lambda < 1$

$$\widehat{\sigma}_t^2 = (1-\lambda) \sum_{i=1}^{\infty} \lambda^{i-1}\sigma_{t-i}^2. \tag{4.7}$$

If we view ε_t^2 as a proxy for σ_t^2, (4.6) and (4.7) are both autoregressive series with long distributed lags, except that (4.6) has a constant term and (4.7) has not.[2]

While intuitively unconvincing as a volatility process because of the infinite variance, the EWMA model has nevertheless been shown to be powerful in volatility forecasting as it is not constrained by a mean level of volatility (unlike e.g. the GARCH(1, 1) model), and hence it adjusts readily to changes in unconditional volatility.

---

[2] EWMA, a sample standard deviation model, is usually estimated based on minimizing in-sample forecast errors. There is no volatility error in GARCH conditional variance. This is why $\widehat{\sigma}_t^2$ in (4.7) has a hat and h_t in (4.6) has not.

4.4 EXPONENTIAL GARCH

The exponential GARCH (denoted as EGARCH) model is due to Nelson (1991). The EGARCH(p, q) model specifies conditional variance in logarithmic form, which means that there is no need to impose an estimation constraint in order to avoid negative variance;

$$\ln h_t = \alpha_0 + \sum_{j=1}^{q} \beta_j \ln h_{t-j}$$
$$+ \sum_{k=1}^{p} \left[\theta_k \epsilon_{t-k} + \gamma_k \left(|\epsilon_{t-k}| - \sqrt{2/\pi} \right) \right]$$
$$\epsilon_t = \varepsilon_t / \sqrt{h_t}.$$

Here, h_t depends on both the size and the sign of ε_t. With appropriate conditioning of the parameters, this specification captures the stylized fact that a negative shock leads to a higher conditional variance in the subsequent period than a positive shock. The process is covariance stationary if and only if $\sum_{j=1}^{q} \beta_j < 1$.

Forecasting with EGARCH is a bit involved because of the logarithmic transformation. Tsay (2002) showed how forecasts can be formulated with EGARCH(1, 0) and gave the one-step-ahead forecast as

$$\widehat{h}_{t+1} = h_t^{2\alpha_1} \exp\left[(1 - \alpha_1)\alpha_0\right] \exp\left[g\left(\epsilon\right)\right]$$
$$g\left(\epsilon\right) = \theta \epsilon_{t-1} + \gamma \left(|\epsilon_{t-1}| - \sqrt{2/\pi} \right).$$

For the multi-step forecast

$$\widehat{h}_{t+\tau} = h_t^{2\alpha_1} (\tau - 1) \exp\left(\omega\right) \left\{ \exp\left[0.5\left(\theta + \gamma\right)^2\right] \Phi\left(\theta + \gamma\right) \right.$$
$$\left. + \exp\left[0.5\left(\theta - \gamma\right)^2\right] \Phi\left(\theta - \gamma\right) \right\},$$

where

$$\omega = (1 - \alpha_1)\alpha_0 - \gamma\sqrt{2/\pi}$$

and $\Phi\left(\cdot\right)$ is the cumulative density function of the standard normal distribution.

4.5 OTHER FORMS OF NONLINEARITY

Models that also allow for nonsymmetrical dependencies include the GJR-GARCH (Glosten, Jagannathan and Runkle, 1993) as shown below:

$$h_t = \omega + \sum_{i=1}^{p} \beta_i h_{t-i} + \sum_{j=1}^{q} \left(\alpha_j \varepsilon_{t-j}^2 + \delta_j D_{j,t-1} \varepsilon_{t-j}^2 \right)$$

$$D_{t-1} = \begin{cases} 1 & \text{if } \varepsilon_{t-1} < 0 \\ 0 & \text{if } \varepsilon_{t-1} \geq 0 \end{cases},$$

The conditional volatility is positive when parameters satisfy $\alpha_0 > 0$, $\alpha_i \geq 0$, $\alpha_i + \gamma_i \geq 0$ and $\beta_j \geq 0$, for $i = 1, \cdots, p$ and $j = 1, \cdots, q$. The process is covariance stationary if and only if

$$\sum_{i=1}^{p} \beta_i + \sum_{j=1}^{q} \left(\alpha_j + \frac{1}{2}\gamma_j \right) < 1.$$

Take the GJR-GARCH(1, 1) case as an example. The one-step-ahead forecast is

$$\widehat{h}_{t+1} = \omega + \beta_1 h_t + \alpha_1 \varepsilon_t^2 + \delta_1 \varepsilon_t^2 D_t,$$

and the multi-step forecast is

$$\widehat{h}_{t+\tau} = \omega + \left(\frac{1}{2} (\alpha_1 + \gamma_1) + \beta_1 \right) h_{t+\tau-1}$$

and use repeated substitution for $h_{t+\tau-1}$.

The TGARCH (threshold GARCH) model from Zakoïan (1994) is similar to GJR-GARCH but is formulated with absolute return instead:

$$\sigma_t = \alpha_0 + \sum_{i=1}^{p} \left[\alpha_i \left| \varepsilon_{t-i} \right| + \gamma_i D_{i,t-i} \left| \varepsilon_{t-i} \right| \right] + \sum_{j=1}^{q} \beta_j \sigma_{t-j}. \qquad (4.8)$$

The conditional volatility is positive when $\alpha_0 > 0$, $\alpha_i \geq 0$, $\alpha_i + \gamma_i \geq 0$ and $\beta_j \geq 0$, for $i = 1, \cdots, p$ and $j = 1, \cdots, q$. The process is covariance stationary, in the case $p = q = 1$, if and only if

$$\beta_1^2 + \frac{1}{2} \left[\alpha_1^2 + (\alpha_1 + \gamma_1)^2 \right] + \frac{2}{\sqrt{2\pi}} \beta_1 (\alpha_1 + \gamma_1) < 1.$$

QGARCH (quadratic GARCH) and various other nonlinear GARCH models are reviewed in Franses and van Dijk (2000). A QGARCH(1, 1) has the following structure

$$h_t = \omega + \alpha \left(\varepsilon_{t-1} - \gamma \right)^2 + \beta h_{t-1}.$$

4.6   FORECASTING PERFORMANCE

Although Taylor (1986) was one of the earliest studies to test the predictive power of GARCH Akigray (1989) is more commonly cited in many subsequent GARCH studies, although an earlier investigation had appeared in Taylor (1986). In the following decade, there were no fewer than 20 papers that test GARCH predictive power against other time series methods and against option implied volatility forecasts. The majority of these forecast volatility of major stock indices and exchange rates.

The ARCH class models, and their variants, have many supporters. Akigray finds GARCH consistently outperforms EWMA and RW in all subperiods and under all evaluation measures. Pagan and Schwert (1990) find EGARCH is best, especially in contrast to some nonparametric methods. Despite a low R^2, Cumby, Figlewski and Hasbrouck (1993) conclude that EGARCH is better than RW. Figlewski (1997) finds GARCH superiority confined to the stock market and for forecasting volatility over a short horizon only.

In general, models that allow for volatility asymmetry come out well in the forecasting contest because of the strong negative relationship between volatility and shock. Cao and Tsay (1992), Heynen and Kat (1994), Lee (1991) and Pagan and Schwert (1990) favour the EGARCH model for volatility of stock indices and exchange rates, whereas Brailsford and Faff (1996) and Taylor, J. (2004) find GJR-GARCH outperforms GARCH in stock indices. Bali (2000) finds a range of nonlinear models work well for forecasting one-week-ahead volatility of US T-Bill yields. Cao and Tsay (1992) find the threshold autoregressive model (TAR in the previous chapter) provides the best forecast for large stocks and EGARCH gives the best forecast for small stocks, and they suspect that the latter might be due to a leverage effect.

Other studies find no clear-cut result. These include Lee (1991), West and Cho (1995), Brailsford and Faff (1996), Brooks (1998), and McMillan, Speight and Gwilym (2000). All these studies (and many other volatility forecasting studies) share one or more of the following characteristics: (i) they test a large number of very similar models all designed to capture volatility persistence, (ii) they use a large number of forecast error statistics, each of which has a very different loss function, (iii) they forecast and calculate error statistics for variance and not standard deviation, which makes the difference between forecasts of different models even smaller, (iv) they use squared daily, weekly or monthly returns to proxy daily, weekly or monthly 'actual' volatility, which results in extremely noisy 'actual' volatility estimates. The noise in the 'actual' volatility estimates makes the small differences between forecasts of similar models indistinguishable.

Unlike the ARCH class model, the 'simpler' methods, including the EWMA method, do not separate volatility persistence from volatility shocks and most of them do not incorporate volatility mean reversion. The 'simpler' methods tend to provide larger volatility forecasts most of the time because there is no constraint on stationarity or convergence to the unconditional variance, and may result in larger forecast errors and less frequent VaR violations. The GJR model allows the volatility persistence to change relatively quickly when return switches sign from positive to negative and vice versa. If unconditional volatility of all parametric volatility models is the same, then GJR will have the largest probability of an underforecast.[3] This possibly explains why GJR was the worst-performing model in Franses and Van Dijk (1996) because they use MedSE (median standard error) as their sole evaluation criterion. In Brailsford and Faff (1996), the GJR(1, 1) model outperforms the other models when MAE, RMSE and MAPE are used.

There is some merit in using 'simpler' methods, and especially models that include long distributed lags. As ARCH class models assume variance stationarity, the forecasting performance suffers when there are changes in volatility level. Parameter estimation becomes unstable when the data period is short or when there is a change in volatility level. This has led to a GARCH convergence problem in several studies (e.g. Tse and Tung (1992) and Walsh and Tsou (1998)). Taylor (1986), Tse (1991), Tse and Tung (1992), Boudoukh, Richardson and Whitelaw (1997), Walsh and Tsou (1998), Ederington and Guan (1999), Ferreira (1999), and Taylor, J, (2004) all favour some form of exponential smoothing method to GARCH for forecasting volatility of a wide range of assets ranging from equities, exchange rates to interest rates.

---

[3] This characteristic is clearly evidenced in Table 2 of Brailsford and Faff (1996). The GJR(1, 1) model underforecasts 76 (out of 90) times. The RW model has an equal chance of underforecasts and overforecasts, whereas all the other methods overforecast more than 50 (out of 90) times.

5
Linear and Nonlinear Long Memory Models

As mentioned before, volatility persistence is a feature that many time series models are designed to capture. A GARCH model features an exponential decay in the autocorrelation of conditional variances. However, it has been noted that squared and absolute returns of financial assets typically have serial correlations that are slow to decay, similar to those of an I(d) process. A shock in the volatility series seems to have very 'long memory' and to impact on future volatility over a long horizon. The integrated GARCH (IGARCH) model of Engle and Bollerslev (1986) captures this effect, but a shock in this model impacts upon future volatility over an infinite horizon and the unconditional variance does not exist for this model.

5.1 WHAT IS LONG MEMORY IN VOLATILITY?

Let ρ_τ denote the correlation between x_t and $x_{t-\tau}$. The time series x_t is said to have a short memory if $\sum_{\tau=1}^{n} \rho_\tau$ converges to a constant as n becomes large. A long memory series has autocorrelation coefficients that decline slowly at a hyperbolic rate. Long memory in volatility occurs when the effects of volatility shocks decay slowly which is often detected by the autocorrelation of measures of volatility, such as absolute or squared returns. A long memory process is covariance stationary if $\sum_{\tau=1}^{n} \rho_\tau / \tau^{2d-1}$, for some positive $d < \frac{1}{2}$, converges to a constant as $n \to \infty$. When $d \geq \frac{1}{2}$, the volatility series is not covariance stationary although it is still strictly stationary. Taylor (1986) was the first to note that autocorrelation of absolute returns, $|r_t|$, is slow to decay compared with that of r_t^2. The highly popular GARCH model is a short memory model based on squared returns r_t^2. Following the work of Granger and Joyeux (1980) and Hosking (1981), where fractionally integrated series was shown to exhibit long memory property described above, Ding, Granger and Engle (1993) propose a fractionally integrated model based on $|r_t|^d$ where d is a fraction. The whole issue of *Journal of Econometrics*, 1996, vol. 73, no. 1, edited by Richard Baillie and Maxwell King was devoted to long memory and, in particular, fractional integrated series.

There has been a lot of research investigating whether long memory of volatility can help to make better volatility forecasts and explain anomalies in option prices. Hitherto much of this research has used the fractional integrated models described in Section 5.3. More recently, several studies have showed that a number of nonlinear short memory volatility models are capable of producing spurious long memory characteristics in volatility as well. Examples of such nonlinear models include the break model (Granger and Hyung, 2004), the volatility component model (Engle and Lee, 1999), and the regime-switching model (Hamilton and Susmel, 1994; Diebold and Inoue, 2001). In these three models, volatility has short memory between breaks, for each volatility component and within each regime. Without controlling for the breaks, the different components and the changing regimes, volatility will produce spurious long memory characteristics. Each of these short memory nonlinear models provides a rich interpretation of the financial market volatility structure compared with the apparently myopic fractional integrated model which simply requires financial market participants to remember and react to shocks for a long time. Discussion of these competing models is provided in Section 5.4.

5.2   EVIDENCE AND IMPACT OF VOLATILITY LONG MEMORY

The long memory characteristic of financial market volatility is well known and has important implications for volatility forecasting and option pricing. Some evidence of long memory has already been presented in Section 1.3. In Table 5.1, we present some statistics from a wider range of assets and through simulation that we published in the *Financial Analysts Journal* recently. In the table, we report the sum of the first 1000 autocorrelation coefficients for a number of volatility proxies for a selection of stock indices, stocks, exchange rates, interest rates and commodities. We have also presented the statistics for GARCH(1, 1) and GJR-GARCH(1, 1) series, both simulated using high volatility persistence parameters. The statistics for the simulated series are in the range of 0.478 to 2.308 while the empirical statistics are much higher. As noted by Taylor (1986), the absolute return has a longer memory than the square returns. This has been known as the 'Taylor effect'. But, taking logs or trimming the data by capping the values in the 0.1%

tails often lengthens the memory. This phenomenon continues to puzzle volatility researchers.

The impact of volatility long memory on option pricing has been studied in Bollerslev and Mikkelsen (1996, 1999), Taylor (2000) and Ohanissian, Russel and Tsay (2003). The effect is best understood analytically from the stochastic volatility option pricing model which is based on stock having the stochastic process below:

$$dS_t = \mu S dt + \sqrt{v_t} S dz_{s,t},$$

$$dv_t = \kappa \left[\theta - v_t \right] dt + \sigma_v \sqrt{v_t} dz_{v,t},$$

which, in a risk-neutral option pricing framework, becomes

$$dv_t = \kappa \left[\theta - v_t \right] dt - \lambda v_t dt + \sigma_v \sqrt{v_t} dz_{v,t}^*$$

$$= \kappa^* \left[\theta^* - v_t \right] dt + \sigma_v \sqrt{v_t} dz_{v,t}^*, \qquad (5.1)$$

where v_t is the instantaneous variance, κ is the speed of mean reversion, θ is the long run level of volatility, σ_v is the 'volatility of volatility', λ is the market price of (volatility) risk, and $\kappa^* = \kappa + \lambda$ and $\theta^* = \kappa \theta / (\kappa + \lambda)$. The two Wiener processes, $dz_{s,t}$ and $dz_{v,t}$ have constant correlation ρ. Here κ^* is the *risk-neutral* mean reverting parameter and θ^* is the *risk-neutral* long run level of volatility. The parameter σ_v and ρ implicit in the risk-neutral process are the same as that in the real volatility process.

In the risk-neutral stochastic volatility process in (5.1), a low κ (or κ^*) corresponds to strong volatility persistence, volatility long memory and high kurtosis. A fast, mean reverting volatility will reduce the impact of stochastic volatility. The effect of low κ (or high volatility persistence) is most pronounced when θ the long run level is low but the initial 'instantaneous' volatility is high as shown in the table below. The table reports kurtosis of the simulated distribution when $\kappa = 0.1, \lambda = \rho = 0$. When the correlation coefficient ρ is zero, the distribution is symmetrical and has zero skewness.

$v_t \setminus \theta$	0.05	0.1	0.15	0.02	0.25	0.3
0.1	5.90	4.45	3.97	3.73	3.58	3.48
0.2	14.61	8.80	6.87	5.90	5.32	4.94
0.3	29.12	16.06	11.71	9.53	8.22	7.35
0.4	49.44	26.22	18.48	14.61	12.29	10.74
0.5	75.56	39.28	27.19	21.14	17.51	15.09

At low mean version κ, the option pricing impact crucially depends on the initial volatility, however. Figure 5.1 below presents the Black–Scholes implied volatility inverted from simulated option prices

Table 5.1 Sum of autocorrelation coefficients of the first 1000 lags for selected financial time series and simulated GARCH and GJR processes

	No. of obs	$\sum \rho(\lvert r \rvert)$	$\sum \rho(r^2)$	$\sum \rho(\ln\lvert r \rvert)$	$\sum \rho(\lvert Tr \rvert)$
Stock Market Indices:					
USA S&P500 Composite	9676	35.687	3.912	27.466	40.838
Germany DAX 30 Industrial	9634	75.571	37.102	41.890	79.186
Japan NIKKEI 225 Stock Average	8443	89.559	23.405	84.257	95.789
France CAC 40	8276	43.310	17.467	22.432	46.539
UK FTSE All Share and FTSE100	8714	30.817	12.615	18.394	33.199
Average STOCK INDICES		54.989	18.900	38.888	59.110
Stocks:					
Cadbury Schweppes	7418	48.607	19.236	85.288	50.235
Marks & Spencer Group	7709	40.635	17.541	67.480	42.575
Shell Transport	8115	38.947	20.078	44.711	40.035
FTSE Small Cap Index	4437	25.381	3.712	35.152	28.533
Average STOCKS		38.392	15.142	58.158	40.344
Exchange Rates:					
US $ to UK £	7942	56.308	24.652	84.717	57.432
Australian $ to UK £	7859	32.657	0.052	72.572	48.241
Mexican Peso to UK £	5394	9.545	1.501	13.760	14.932
Indonesian Rupiah to UK £	2964	20.819	4.927	31.509	21.753
Average EXCHANGE RATES		29.832	7.783	50.640	35.589
Interest Rates:					
US 1 month Eurodollar deposits	8491	281.799	20.782	327.770	331.877
UK Interbank 1-month	7448	12.699	0.080	22.901	25.657
Venezuela PAR Brady Bond	3279	19.236	9.944	32.985	19.800
South Korea Overnight Call	2601	54.693	12.200	57.276	56.648
Average INTEREST RATES		92.107	10.752	110.233	108.496

Table 5.1 (*Continued*)

Commodities:

Gold, Bullion, $/troy oz (London fixing) close	6536	125.309	39.305	140.747	133.880
Silver Fix (LBM), cash cents/troy oz	7780	45.504	8.275	88.706	52.154
Brent Oil (1 month forward) $/barrel	2389	11.532	5.469	9.882	11.81
Average COMMODITIES		60.782	17.683	79.778	65.948
Average ALL		54.931	14.113	65.495	61.555
1000 simulated GARCH : mean	10 000	1.045	1.206	0.478	1.033
standard deviation		(1.099)	(1.232)	(0.688)	(1.086)
1000 simulated GJR: mean	10 000	1.945	2.308	0.870	1.899
standard deviation		(1.709)	(2.048)	(0.908)	(1.660)

Note: 'Tr' denote trimmed returns whereby returns in the 0.01% tail take the value of the 0.01% quantile.
The simulated GARCH process is

$$\varepsilon_t = z_t \sqrt{h_t}, \qquad \varepsilon_t \sim N(0, 1)$$

$$h_t = (1 - 0.96 - 0.02) + 0.96 h_{t-1} + 0.02\varepsilon_{t-1}^2.$$

The simulated GJR process is

$$\varepsilon_t = z_t \sqrt{h_t}, \qquad \varepsilon_t \sim N(0, 1)$$

$$h_t = (1 - 0.9 - 0.03 - 0.5 \times 0.09) + 0.9 h_{t-1} + 0.03\varepsilon_{t-1}^2 + 0.09 D_{t-1}\varepsilon_{t-1}^2,$$

$$D_t = \begin{cases} 1 & \text{for } \varepsilon_t < 0 \\ 0 & \text{otherwise.} \end{cases}$$

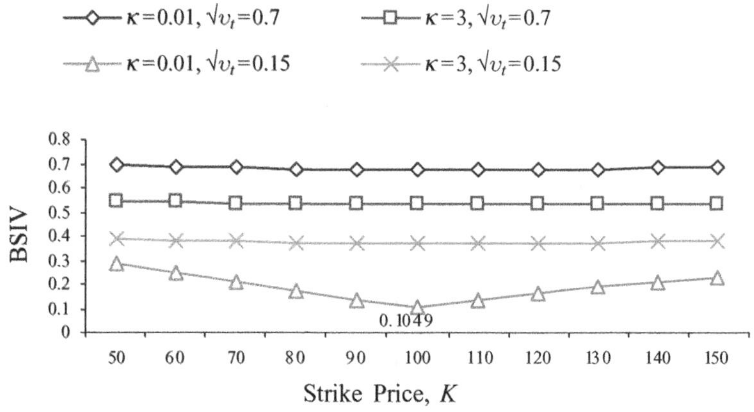

Figure 5.1 Effect of kappa
($S = 100$, $r = 0$, $T = 1$, $\lambda = 0$, $\sigma v = 0.6$, $\theta = 0.2$)

produced from a stochastic option pricing model. The Black–Scholes model is used here only to get the implied volatility which gives a clearer relative pricing relationship. The Black–Scholes implied volatility (BSIV) is directly proportional to option price. First we look at the high volatility state where $v_t = 0.7$. The implied volatility for $\kappa = 0.01$ is higher than that for $\kappa = 3.0$, which means that a long memory volatility (slow mean reversion and high volatility persistence) will lead to a higher option price. But, in reverse, long memory volatility will result in lower option prices, hence lower implied volatility at low volatility state, e.g. $\sqrt{v_t} = 0.15$. So unlike the conclusion in previous studies, long memory in volatility does not always lead to higher option prices. It is conditioned on the current level of volatility vis-à-vis the long run level of volatility.

5.3 FRACTIONALLY INTEGRATED MODEL

Both the historical volatility models and the ARCH models have been tested for fractional integration. Baillie, Bollerslev and Mikkelsen (1996) fitted FIGARCH to US dollar–Deutschemark exchange rates. Bollerslev and Mikkelsen (1996, 1999) used FIEGARCH to study S&P500 volatility and option pricing impact, and so did Taylor (2000). Vilasuso (2002) tested FIGARCH against GARCH and IGARCH for volatility prediction for five major currencies. In Andersen, Bollerslev, Diebold and Labys (2003), a vector autoregressive model with long distributed lags was built on the realized volatility of three exchange rates, which they called the VAR-RV model. In Zumbach (2002) the weights applied to the time series of realized volatility follow a power law, which he called the LM-ARCH model. Three other papers, viz. Li (2002), Martens and Zein (2004) and Pong, Shackleton, Taylor and Xu (2004), compared long memory volatility model forecasts with option implied volatility. Li (2002) used ARFIMA whereas the other two papers used log-ARFIMA. Hwang and Satchell (1998) studied the log-ARFIMA model also, but they forecast Black–Scholes 'risk-neutral' implied volatility of the equity option instead of the underlying asset.

5.3.1 FIGARCH

The FIGARCH$(1, d, 1)$ model below:

$$h_t = \omega + [1 - \beta_1 L - (1 - \phi_1 L)(1 - L)^d]\varepsilon_t^2 + \beta_1 h_{t-1}$$

was used in Baillie, Bollerslev and Mikkelsen (1996), and all the following specifications are equivalent:

$$
\begin{aligned}
(1 - \beta_1 L)h_t &= \omega + [1 - \beta_1 L - (1 - \phi_1 L)(1 - L)^d]\varepsilon_t^2, \\
h_t &= \omega(1 - \beta_1)^{-1} + (1 - \beta_1 L)^{-1} \\
&\quad \times [(1 - \beta_1 L) - (1 - \phi_1 L)(1 - L)^d]\varepsilon_t^2, \\
h_t &= \omega(1 - \beta_1)^{-1} + [1 - (1 - \beta_1 L)^{-1}(1 - \phi_1 L)(1 - L)^d]\varepsilon_t^2.
\end{aligned}
$$

For the one-step-ahead forecast

$$\widehat{h}_{t+1} = \omega(1 - \beta_1)^{-1} + [1 - (1 - \beta_1 L)^{-1}(1 - \phi_1 L)(1 - L)^d]\varepsilon_t^2,$$

and the multi-step-ahead forecast is

$$h_{T+\tau} = \omega(1 - \beta_1)^{-1} + [1 - (1 - \beta_1 L)^{-1}(1 - \phi_1 L)(1 - L)^d]\varepsilon_{T+\tau-1}^2.$$

The FIGARCH model is estimated based on the approximate maximum likelihood techniques using the truncated ARCH representation. We can transform the FIGARCH model to the ARCH model with infinite lags. The parameters in the lag polynomials

$$\lambda(L) = 1 - (1 - \beta_1 L)^{-1}(1 - \phi_1 L)(1 - L)^d$$

may be written as

$$
\begin{aligned}
\lambda_1 &= \phi_1 - \beta_1 + d, \\
\lambda_k &= \beta_1 \lambda_{k-1} + (\pi_k - \phi_1 \pi_{k-1}) \quad \text{for } k \geq 2,
\end{aligned}
$$

where

$$(1 - L)^d = \sum_{j=0}^{\infty} \pi_j L^j,$$

$$\pi_0 = 0.$$

In the literature, a truncation lag at $J = 1000$ is common.

5.3.2 FIEGARCH

Bollerslev and Mikkelsen (1996) find fractional integrated models provide better fit to S&P500 returns. Specifically, they find that fractionally integrated models perform better than GARCH(p, q) and IGARCH(p, q), and that FIEGARCH specification is better than FIGARCH. Bollerslev and Mikkelsen (1999) confirm that FIEGARCH beats EGARCH and IEGARCH in pricing options of S&P500 LEAPS (Long-term Equity Anticipation Securities) contracts. Specifically Bollerslev and Mikkelsen (1999) fitted an AR(2)-FIEGARCH($1, d, 1$) as shown below:

$$r_t = \mu + \left(\rho_1 L + \rho_2 L^2\right) r_t + z_t, \tag{5.2}$$
$$\ln \sigma_t^2 = \omega_t + (1 + \psi_1 L)(1 - \phi_1 L)^{-1}(1 - L)^{-d} g(\epsilon_t),$$
$$g(\epsilon_t) = \theta \epsilon_{t-1} + \gamma \left[|\epsilon_{t-1}| - E|\epsilon_{t-1}|\right],$$
$$\omega_t = \omega + \ln(1 + \delta N_t).$$

The FIEGARCH model in (5.2) is truly a model for absolute return. Since both EGARCH and FIEGARCH provide forecasts for $\ln \sigma$, to infer forecast for σ from $\ln \sigma$ requires adjustment for Jensen inequality which is not a straightforward task without the assumption of a normal distribution for $\ln \sigma$.

5.3.3 The positive drift in fractional integrated series

As Hwang and Satchell (1998) and Granger (2001) pointed out, positive I(d) process has a positive drift term or a time trend in volatility level which is not observed in practice. This is a major weakness of the fractionally integrated model for it to be adopted as a theoretically sound model for volatility.

All fractional integrated models of volatility have a nonzero drift. In practice the estimation of fractional integrated models require an arbitrary truncation of the infinite lags and as a result the mean will be biased. Zumbach's (2002) LM-ARCH will not have this problem because of the fixed number of lags and the way in which the weights are calculated. Hwang and Satchell's (1998) scaled-truncated log-ARFIMA model is mean adjusted to control for the bias that is due to this truncation and the log transformation. The FIGARCH has a positive mean in the conditional variance equation whereas FIEGARCH has no such problem because the lag-dependent terms have zero mean.

5.3.4 Forecasting performance

Vilasuso (2002) finds FIGARCH produces significantly better 1- and 10-day-ahead volatility forecasts for five major exchange rates than GARCH and IGARCH. Zumbach (2002) produces only one-day-ahead forecasts and find no difference among model performance. Andersen, Bollerslev, Diebold and Labys (2003) find the realized volatility constructed VAR model, i.e. VAR-RV, produces the best 1- and 10-day-ahead volatility forecasts. It is difficult to attribute this superior performance to the fractional integrated model alone because the VAR structure allows a cross series linkage that is absent in all other univariate models and we also know that the more accurate realized volatility estimates would result in improved forecasting performance, everything else being equal.

The other three papers that compare forecasts from LM models with implied volatility forecasts generally find implied volatility forecast to produce the highest explanatory power. Martiens and Zein (2004) find log-ARFIMA forecast beats implied in S&P500 futures but not in ¥/US$ and crude oil futures. Li (2002) finds implied produces better short horizon forecast whereas the ARFIMA provides better forecast for a 6-month horizon. However, when regression coefficients are constrained to be $\alpha = 0$ and $\beta = 1$, the regression R^2 becomes negative at long horizon. From our discussion in Section 2.4, this suggests that volatility at the 6-month horizon might be better forecast using the unconditional variance instead of model-based forecasts. Pong, Shackleton, Taylor and Xu (2004) find implied volatility to outperform time series volatility models including the log-ARFIMA model in forecasting 1- to 3-month-ahead volatility of the dollar-sterling exchange rate.

Many of the fractional integration papers were written more recently and used realized volatilities constructed from intraday high-frequency data. When comparison is made with option implied volatility, the implied volatility is usually extracted from daily closing option prices, however. Despite the lower data frequency, implied appears to outperform forecasts from LM models that use intraday information.

5.4 COMPETING MODELS FOR VOLATILITY LONG MEMORY

Fractionally integrated series is the simplest linear model that produces long memory characteristics. It is also the most commonly used and tested model in the literature for capturing long memory in volatility. There are many other nonlinear short memory models that exhibit spurious long memory in volatility, viz. break, volatility component and regime-switching models. These three models, plus the fractional integrated model, have very different volatility dynamics and produce very different volatility forecasts.

The volatility breaks model permits the mean level of volatility to change in a step function through time with some weak constraint on the number of breaks in the volatility level. It is more general than the volatility component model and the regime switching model. In the case of the volatility component model, the mean level is a slowly evolving process. For the regime-switching model, the mean level of volatility could differ according to regimes the total number of which is usually confined to a small number such as two or three.

5.4.1 Breaks

A break process can be written as

$$V_t = m_t + u_t,$$

where u_t is a noise variable and m_t represents occasional level shifts. m_t are controlled by q_t (a zero–one indicator for the presence of breaks) and η_t (the size of jump) such that

$$m_t = m_{t-1} + q_t \eta_t = m_0 + \sum_{i=1}^{t} q_i \eta_i,$$

$$q_t = \begin{cases} 0, & \text{with probability } 1 - p \\ 1, & \text{with probability } p \end{cases}.$$

The expected number of breaks for a given sample is Tp where T is the total number of observations. Provided that p converges to zero slowly as the sample size increases, i.e. $p \to 0$ as $T \to \infty$, such that $\lim_{T \to \infty} Tp$ is a nonzero constant, Granger and Hyung (2004) showed that the integrating parameter, $I(d)$, is a function of Tp. While d is bounded between 0 and 1, the expected value of d is proportionate to the number of breaks in the series.

One interesting empirical finding on the volatility break model comes from Aggarwal, Inclan and Leal (1999) who use the ICSS (integrated cumulative sums of squares) algorithm to identify sudden shifts in the variance of 20 stock market indices and the duration of such shifts. They find most volatility shifts are due to local political events. When dummy variables, indicating the location of sudden change in variance, were fitted to a GARCH(1,1) model, most of the GARCH parameters became statistically insignificant. The *GARCH(1,1) with occasional break model* can be written as follows:

$$h_t = \omega_1 D_1 + \cdots + \omega_{R+1} D_{R+1} + \alpha_1 \varepsilon_{t-1}^2 + \beta_1 h_{t-1},$$

where $D_1, \cdots, D_{R+1}$ are the dummy variables taking the value 1 in each regime of variance, and zero elsewhere. The one-step-ahead and multi-step-ahead forecasts are

$$\widehat{h}_{t+1} = \omega_{R+1} + \alpha_1 \varepsilon_t^2 + \beta_1 h_t,$$
$$h_{t+\tau} = \omega_{R+1} + (\alpha_1 + \beta_1) h_{t+\tau-1}.$$

In estimating the break points using the ICSS algorithms, a minimum length between breaks is needed to reduce the possibility of any temporary shocks in a series being mistaken as break.

5.4.2   Components model

Engle and Lee (1999) proposed the *component* GARCH (CGARCH) model whereby the volatility process is modelled as the sum of a permanent process, m_t, that has memory close to a unit root, and a transitory mean reverting process, u_t, that has a more rapid time decay. The model can be seen as an extension of the GARCH(1,1) model with the conditional variance mean-revert to a long term trend level, m_t, instead of a fixed position at σ. Specifically, m_t is permitted to evolve slowly in an autoregressive manner. The CGARCH(1,1) model has the following specification:

$$(h_t - m_t) = \alpha \left(\varepsilon_{t-1}^2 - m_{t-1}\right) + \beta \left(h_{t-1} - m_{t-1}\right) \equiv u_t, \quad (5.3)$$
$$m_t = \omega + \rho m_{t-1} + \varphi \left(\varepsilon_{t-1}^2 - h_{t-1}\right),$$

where $(h_t - m_t) = u_t$ represents the short-run transitory component and m_t represents a time-varying trend or permanent component in volatility which is driven by volatility prediction error $\left(\varepsilon_{t-1}^2 - h_{t-1}\right)$ and is integrated if $\rho = 1$.

For the one-step-ahead forecast

$$\widehat{h}_{t+1} = q_{t+1} + \alpha \left(\varepsilon_t^2 - q_t\right) + \beta \left(h_t - q_t\right),$$
$$q_{t+1} = \omega + \rho q_t + \varphi \left(\varepsilon_t^2 - h_t\right),$$

and for the multi-step-ahead forecast

$$h_{t+\tau} = q_{t+\tau} - (\alpha + \beta)q_{t+\tau-1} + (\alpha + \beta)h_{t+\tau},$$
$$q_{t+\tau} = \omega + \rho q_{t+\tau-1},$$

where $h_{t+\tau}$ and $q_{t+\tau-1}$ are calculated through repeat substitutions.

This model has various interesting properties: (i) both m_t and u_t are driven by $\left(\varepsilon_{t-1}^2 - h_{t-1}\right)$; (ii) the short-run volatility component mean-reverts to zero at a geometric rate of $(\alpha + \beta)$ if $0 < (\alpha + \beta) < 1$; (iii) the long-run volatility component evolves over time following an AR process and converge to a constant level defined by $\omega/(1 - \rho)$ if $0 < \rho < 1$; (iv) it is assumed that $0 < (\alpha + \beta) < \rho < 1$ so that the long-run component is more persistent than the short-run component.

This model was found to obey several economic and asset pricing relationships. Many have observed and proposed that the volatility persistence of large jumps is shorter than shocks due to ordinary news events. The component model allows large shocks to be transitory. Indeed Engle and Lee (1999) establish that the impact of the October 1987 crash on stock market volatility was temporary. The expected risk premium, as measured by the expected amount of returns in excess of the risk-free interest rate, in the stock market was found to be related to the long-run component of stock return volatility.[1] The authors suggested, but did not test, that such pricing relationship may have fundamental economic explanations. The well-documented 'leverage effect' (or volatility asymmetry) in the stock market (see Black, 1976; Christie, 1982; Nelson, 1991) is shown to have a temporary impact; the long-run volatility component shows no asymmetric response to market changes.

The reduced form of Equation (5.3) can be expressed as a GARCH(2,2) process below:

$$h_t = (1 - \alpha - \beta)\omega + (\alpha + \varphi)\varepsilon_{t-1}^2 + [-\varphi(\alpha + \beta) - \alpha\rho]\varepsilon_{t-2}^2$$
$$+ (\rho + \beta - \varphi)h_{t-1} + [\varphi(\alpha + \beta) - \beta\rho]h_{t-2},$$

---

[1] Merton (1980) and French, Schwert and Stambaugh (1987) also studied and measured the relationships between risk premium and 'total' volatility.

with all five parameters, α, β, ω, φ and ρ, constraint to be positive and real, $0 < (\alpha + \beta) < \rho < 1$, and $0 < \varphi < \beta$.

5.4.3   Regime-switching model

One approach for modelling changing volatility level and persistence is to use a Hamilton (1989) type regime-switching (RS) model, which like GARCH model is strictly stationary and covariance stationary. Both ARCH and GARCH models have been implemented with a Hamilton (1989) type regime-switching framework, whereby volatility persistence can take different values depending on whether it is in high or low volatility regimes. The most generalized form of regime-switching model is the RS-GARCH(1, 1) model used in Gray (1996) and Klaassen (1998)

$$h_{t,\,S_{t-1}} = \omega_{S_{t-1}} + \alpha_{S_{t-1}}\varepsilon_{t-1}^2 + \beta_{S_{t-1}}h_{t-1,\,S_{t-1}}$$

where S_t indicates the state of regime at time t.

It has long been argued that the financial market reacts to large and small shocks differently and the rate of mean reversion is faster for large shocks. Friedman and Laibson (1989), Jones, Lamont and Lumsdaine (1998) and Ederington and Lee (2001) all provide explanations and empirical support for the conjecture that volatility adjustment in high and low volatility states follows a twin-speed process: slower adjustment and more persistent volatility in the low volatility state and faster adjustment and less volatility persistence in the high volatility state.

The earlier RS applications, such as Pagan and Schwert (1990) and Hamilton and Susmel (1994) are more rigid, where conditional variance is state-dependent but not time-dependent. In these studies, only ARCH class conditional variance is entertained. Recent extensions by Gray (1996) and Klaassen (1998) allow GARCH-type heteroscedasticity in each state and the probability of switching between states to be time-dependent. More recent advancement is to allow more flexible switching probability. For example, Peria (2001) allowed the transition probabilities to vary according to economic conditions with the RS-GARCH model below:

$$r_t|\ \Phi_{t-1}\ \ N\,(\mu_i,\ h_{it})\quad \text{w.p. } p_{it},$$
$$h_{it} = \omega_i + \alpha_i\epsilon_{t-1}^2 + \beta_i h_{t-1}.$$

where i represents a particular regime, 'w.p.' stands for with probability, $p_{it} = \Pr(S_t = i|\ \Phi_{t-1})$ and $\sum p_{it} = 1$.

The STGARCH (*smooth transition* GARCH) model below was tested in Taylor, J. (2004)

$$h_t = \omega + (1 - F(\varepsilon_{t-1}))\alpha\varepsilon_{t-1}^2 + F(\varepsilon_{t-1})\delta\varepsilon_{t-1}^2 + \beta h_{t-1},$$

where

$$F(\varepsilon_{t-1}) = \frac{1}{1 + \exp(-\theta\varepsilon_{t-1})} \quad \text{for logistic STGARCH,}$$

$$F(\varepsilon_{t-1}) = 1 + \exp(-\theta\varepsilon_{t-1}^2) \quad \text{for exponential STGARCH.}$$

5.4.4 Forecasting performance

The TAR model used in Cao and Tsay (1992) is similar to a SV model with regime switching, and Cao and Tsay (1992) reported better forecasting performance from TAR than EGARCH and GARCH. Hamilton and Susmel (1994) find regime-switching ARCH with leverage effect produces better volatility forecast than the asymmetry version of GARCH. Hamilton and Lin (1996) use a bivariate RS model and find stock market returns are more volatile during a period of recession. Gray (1996) fits a RSGARCH (1,1) model to US 1-month T-Bill rates, where the rate of mean level reversion is permitted to differ under different regimes, and finds substantial improvement in forecasting performance. Klaassen (1998) also applies RSGARCH (1,1) to the foreign exchange market and finds a superior, though less dramatic, performance.

It is worth noting that interest rates are different to the other assets in that interest rates exhibit 'level' effect, i.e. volatility depends on the level of the interest rate. It is plausible that it is this level effect that Gray (1996) is picking up that result in superior forecasting performance. This level effect also appears in some European short rates (Ferreira, 1999). There is no such level effect in exchange rates and so it is not surprising that Klaassen (1998) did not find similar dramatic improvement. No other published forecasting results are available for break and component volatility models.

6
Stochastic Volatility

The stochastic volatility (SV) model is, first and foremost, a theoretical model rather than a practical and direct tool for volatility forecast. One should not overlook the developments in the stochastic volatility area, however, because of the rapid advancement in research, noticeably by Ole Barndorff-Nielsen and Neil Shephard. As far as implementation is concerned, the SV estimation still poses a challenge to many researchers. Recent publications indicate a trend towards the MCMC (Monte Carlo Markov Chain) approach. A good source of reference for the MCMC approach for SV estimation is Tsay (2002). Here we will provide only an overview. An early survey of SV work is Ghysels, Harvey and Renault (1996) but the subject is rapidly changing. A more recent SV book is Shephard (2003). The SV models and the ARCH models are closely related and many ARCH models have SV equivalence as continuous time diffusion limit (see Taylor, 1994; Duan, 1997; Corradi, 2000; Fleming and Kirby, 2003).

6.1 THE VOLATILITY INNOVATION

The discrete time SV model is

$$r_t = \mu + \varepsilon_t,$$
$$\varepsilon_t = z_t \exp(0.5h_t),$$
$$h_t = \omega + \beta h_{t-1} + \upsilon_t,$$

where υ_t may or may not be independent of z_t. We have already seen this continuous time specification in Section 5.2, and it will appear again in Chapter 9 when we discuss stochastic volatility option pricing models.

The SV model has an additional innovative term in the volatility dynamics and, hence, is more flexible than ARCH class models. It has been found to fit financial market returns better and has residuals closer to standard normal. Modelling volatility as a stochastic variable immediately leads to fat tail distributions for returns. The autoregressive term in the volatility process introduces persistence, and the correlation between the two innovative terms in the volatility process and the return process produces volatility asymmetry (Hull and White, 1987, 1988). Long memory SV models have also been proposed by allowing the volatility process to have a fractional integrated order (see Harvey, 1998).

The volatility noise term makes the SV model a lot more flexible, but as a result the SV model has no closed form, and hence cannot be estimated directly by maximum likelihood. The quasi-maximum likelihood estimation (QMLE) approach of Harvey, Ruiz and Shephard (1994) is inefficient if volatility proxies are non-Gaussian (Andersen and Sorensen, 1997). The alternatives are the generalized method of moments (GMM) approach through simulations (Duffie and Singleton, 1993), or analytical solutions (Singleton, 2001), and the likelihood approach through numerical integration (Fridman and Harris, 1998) or Monte Carlo integration using either importance sampling (Danielsson, 1994; Pitt and Shephard, 1997; Durbin and Koopman, 2000) or Markov chain (e.g. Jacquier, Polson and Rossi, 1994; Kim, Shephard and Chib, 1998). In the following section, we will describe the MCMC approach only.

6.2   THE MCMC APPROACH

The MCMC approach to modelling stochastic volatility was made popular by authors such as Jacquier, Polson and Rossi (1994). Tsay (2002) has a good description of how the algorithm works. Consider here the simplest case:

$$
\begin{aligned}
r_t &= a_t, \\
a_t &= \sqrt{h_t}\varepsilon_t, \\
\ln h_t &= \alpha_0 + \alpha_1 \ln h_{t-1} + v_t,
\end{aligned}
\tag{6.1}
$$

where $\varepsilon_t \sim N(0, 1)$, $v_t \sim N(0, \sigma_v^2)$ and ε_t and v_t are independent.

Let $w = (\alpha_0, \alpha_1, \sigma_v^2)'$. Let $R = (r_1, \cdots, r_n)'$ be the collection of n observed returns, and $H = (h_1, \cdots, h_n)'$ be the n-dimension unobservable conditional volatilities. Estimation of model (6.1) is made complicated because the likelihood function is a mixture over the n-dimensional H distribution as follows:

$$
f(R \mid w) = \int f(R \mid H) \cdot f(H \mid w) \, dH.
$$

The objective is still maximizing the likelihood of $\{a_t\}$, but the density of R is determined by H which in turn is determined by w.

Assuming that prior distributions for the mean and the volatility equations are independent, the Gibbs sampling approach to estimating model (6.1) involves drawing random samples from the following conditional posterior distributions:

$$f(\beta \mid R, X, H, w), \; f(H \mid R, X, \beta, w) \quad \text{and} \quad f(w \mid R, X, \beta, H)$$

This process is repeated with updated information till the likelihood tolerance or the predetermined maximum number of iterations is reached.

6.2.1 The volatility vector H

First, the volatility vector H is drawn element by element

$$f(h_t \mid R, H_{-t}, w)$$
$$\propto f(a_t \mid h_t, r_t) f(h_t \mid h_{t-1}, w) f(h_{t+1} \mid h_t, w)$$
$$\propto h_t^{-0.5} \exp\left(-\frac{r_t^2}{2h_t}\right) \cdot h_t^{-1} \exp\left[-\frac{(\ln h_t - \mu_t)^2}{2\sigma^2}\right] \qquad (6.2)$$

where

$$\mu_t = \left(\frac{1}{1+\alpha_1^2}\right)[\alpha_0(1-\alpha_1) + \alpha_1(\ln h_{t+1} + \ln h_{t-1})],$$
$$\sigma^2 = \frac{\sigma_v^2}{1+\alpha_1^2}$$

Equation (6.2) can be obtained using results for a missing value in an $AR(1)$ model. To see how this works, start from the volatility equation

$$\ln h_t = \alpha_0 + \alpha_1 \ln h_{t-1} + a_t,$$
$$\underbrace{\alpha_0 + \alpha_1 \ln h_{t-1}}_{y_t} = \underbrace{1}_{x_t} \times \ln h_t \; \underbrace{-a_t}_{b_t},$$
$$y_t = x_t \ln h_t + b_t, \qquad (6.3)$$

and for $t+1$

$$\ln h_{t+1} - \alpha_0 = \alpha_1 + \ln h_t + a_{t+1},$$
$$y_{t+1} = x_{t+1} \ln h_t + b_{t+1}. \qquad (6.4)$$

Given that b_t and b_{t+1} have the same distribution because a_t is also $N(0, \sigma_v^2)$, $\ln h_t$ can be estimated from (6.3) and (6.4) using the least squares principle,

$$\widehat{\ln h_t} = \frac{x_t y_t + x_{t+1} y_{t+1}}{x_t^2 + x_{t+1}^2}$$

$$= \frac{\alpha_0(1 - \alpha_1) + \alpha_1(\ln h_{t+1} + \ln h_{t-1})}{1 + \alpha_1^2}.$$

This is the conditional mean μ_t in Equation (6.2). Moreover, $\widehat{\ln h_t}$ is normally distributed

$$\widehat{\ln h_t} \sim N\left(\ln h_t, \frac{\sigma_v^2}{1 + \alpha_1^2}\right), \quad \text{or}$$

$$\sim N(\mu_t, \sigma^2)$$

6.2.2   The parameter w

First partition w as $\alpha = (\alpha_0, \alpha_1)'$ and σ_v^2. The conditional posterior distributions are:

(i) $f(\alpha \mid R, H, \sigma_v^2) = f(\alpha \mid H, \sigma_v^2)$. Note that $\ln h_t$ has an $AR(1)$ structure. Hence, if prior distribution of α is multivariate normal, $\alpha \sim MN(\alpha_0, C_0)$, then posterior distribution $f(\alpha \mid H, \sigma_v^2)$ is also multivariate normal with mean α_* and covariance C_*, where

$$C_*^{-1} = \frac{1}{\sigma_v^2}\left(\sum_{t=2}^{n} z_t z_t'\right) + C_0^{-1},$$

$$\alpha_* = C_*\left[\frac{1}{\sigma_v^2}\left(\sum_{t=2}^{n} z_t \ln h_t\right) + C_0^{-1}\alpha_0\right], \quad \text{and}$$

$$z_t = (1, \ln h_t)'. \tag{6.5}$$

(ii) $f(\sigma_v^2 \mid R, H, \alpha) = f(\sigma_v^2 \mid H, \alpha)$. If the prior distribution of σ_v^2 is $m\lambda/\sigma_v^2 \sim \chi_m^2$, then the conditional posterior distribution of σ_v^2 is an *inverted chi-squared* distribution with $m + n - 1$ degrees of freedom, i.e.

$$\frac{1}{\sigma_v^2}\left(m\lambda + \sum_{t=2}^{n} v_t^2\right) \sim \chi_{m+n-1}^2, \quad \text{and}$$

$$v_t = \ln h_t - \alpha_0 - \alpha_1 \ln h_{t-1} \quad \text{for } t = 2, \cdots, n. \tag{6.6}$$

Tsay (2002) suggested using the ARCH model parameter estimates as the starting value for the MCMC simulation.

6.3   FORECASTING PERFORMANCE

In a PhD thesis, Heynen (1995) finds SV forecast is best for a number of stock indices across several continents. There are only six other SV studies and the view about SV forecasting performance is by no means unanimous at the time of writing this book.

Heynen and Kat (1994) forecast volatility for seven stock indices and five exchange rates they find SV provides the best forecast for indices but produces forecast errors that are 10 times larger than EGARCH's and GARCH's for exchange rates. Yu (2002) ranks SV top for forecasting New Zealand stock market volatility, but the margin is very small, partly because the evaluation is based on variance and not standard deviation. Lopez (2001) finds no difference between SV and other time series forecasts using conventional error statistics. All three papers have the 1987s crash in the in-sample period, and the impact of the 1987 crash on the result is unclear.

Three other studies, Bluhm and Yu (2000), Dunis, Laws and Chauvin (2000) and Hol and Koopman (2002) compare SV and other time series forecasts with option implied volatility forecast. Dunis, Laws and Chauvin (2000) find combined forecast is the best for six exchange rates so long as the SV forecast is excluded. Bluhm and Yu (2000) rank SV equal to GARCH. Both Bluhm and Yu (2000) and Hol and Koopman (2002) conclude that implied is better than SV for forecasting stock index volatility.

7
Multivariate Volatility Models

At the time of writing this book, there was no volatility forecasting contest that is based on the multivariate volatility model. However, there have been a number of studies that examined cross-border volatility spillover in stock markets (Hamao, Masulis and Ng, 1989; King and Wadhwani, 1990; Karolyi, 1995; Koutmos and Booth, 1995), exchange rates (Baillie, Bollerslev and Redfearn, 1993; Hong, 2001), and interest rates (Tse and Booth, 1996). The volatility spillover relationships are potential source of information for volatility forecasting, especially in the very short term and during global turbulent periods. Several variants of multivariate ARCH models have existed for a long time while multivariate SV models are fewer and more recent. Truly multivariate volatility models (i.e. beyond two or three returns variables) are not easy to implement. The greatest challenges are parsimony, nonlinear relationships between parameters, and keeping the variance–covariance matrix positive definite. In the remainder of this short chapter, I will just illustrate one of the more recent multivariate ARCH models that I use a lot in my research. It is the asymmetric dynamic covariance (ADC) model due to Kroner and Ng (1998). I must admit that I have not used ADC to fit more than three variables! The ADC model encompasses many older multivariate ARCH models as we will explain later. Readers who are interested in multivariate SV models could refer to Liesenfeld and Richard (2003).

7.1 ASYMMETRIC DYNAMIC COVARIANCE MODEL

In implementing multivariate volatility of returns from different countries, the adjustment for time zone differences is important. In this section, I rely much on my joint work with Martin Martens that was published in the *Journal of Banking and Finance* in 2001. The model we used is presented below

$$r_t = \mu + \varepsilon_t + M\varepsilon_{t-1}, \quad \varepsilon_t \sim N(0, H_t),$$

$$h_{iit} = \theta_{iit},$$

$$h_{ijt} = \rho_{ijt}\sqrt{h_{iit}}\sqrt{h_{jjt}} + \phi_{ij}\theta_{ijt},$$

$$\theta_{ijt} = \omega_{ijt} + b_i' H_{t-1} b_j + a_i' \varepsilon_{t-1}\varepsilon_{t-1}' a_j + +g_i' \eta_{t-1}\eta_{t-1}' g_j.$$

The matrix M is used for adjusting nonsynchronous returns. It has nonzero elements only in places where one market closes before another, except in the case of the USA where the impact could be delayed till the next day. So Japan has an impact on the European markets but not the other way round. Europe has an impact on the USA market and the USA has an impact on the Japanese market on the next day. The conditional variance–covariance matrix H_t has different specifications for diagonal (conditional variance h_{iit}) and off-diagonal (conditional covariance h_{ijt}) elements.

Consider the following set of conditions:

(i) $a_i = \alpha_i e_i$ and $b_i = \beta_i e_i$ $\forall i$, where e_i is the ith column of an (n, n) identity matrix, and α_i and β_i, $i = 1, \cdots, n$, are scalars.
(ii) $A = \alpha(\omega\lambda')$ and $B = \beta(\omega\lambda')$ where $A = (a_1, \cdots, a_n)$, $B = (b_1, \cdots, b_n)$, ω and λ are $(n, 1)$ vectors and α and β are scalars.

The ADC model reduces to:

(i) a restricted VECH model of Bollerslev, Engle and Wooldridge (1988) if $\rho_{12} = 0$ and under condition (i) with the restrictions that $\beta_{ij} = \beta_i\beta_j$;
(ii) the constant correlation model of Bollerslev (1990) if $\phi_{12} = 0$ and under condition (i);
(iii) the BEKK model of Engle and Kroner (1995) if $\rho_{12} = 0$ and $\phi_{12} = 1$;
(iv) the factor ARCH (FARCH) model of Engle, Ng and Rothschild (1990) if $\rho_{12} = 0$, $\phi_{12} = 1$ and under condition (ii),

and, unlike most of its predecessors, it allows for volatility asymmetry in the spillover effect as well through the last term in θ_{ijt}.

7.2   A BIVARIATE EXAMPLE

Take a two-variable case as an example;

$$\varepsilon_t = \begin{bmatrix} \varepsilon_{1t} \\ \varepsilon_{2t} \end{bmatrix}, \quad \eta_t = \begin{bmatrix} \min(0, \varepsilon_{1t}) \\ \min(0, \varepsilon_{2t}) \end{bmatrix},$$

$$a_i = \begin{bmatrix} a_{1i} \\ a_{2i} \end{bmatrix}, \quad b_i = \begin{bmatrix} b_{1i} \\ b_{2i} \end{bmatrix}, \quad g_i = \begin{bmatrix} g_{1i} \\ g_{2i} \end{bmatrix}.$$

The condition variance of, for example, first return is

$$
\begin{aligned}
h_{11t} &= \omega_{11} + B_{11}h_{11,t-1} + a_1'\varepsilon_{t-1}\varepsilon_{t-1}'a_1 + g_1'\eta_{t-1}\eta_{t-1}'g_1 \\
&= \omega_{11} + B_{11}h_{11,t-1} + a_{11}^2\varepsilon_{1t-1}^2 + 2a_{11}a_{21}\varepsilon_{1t-1}\varepsilon_{2t-1} \\
&\quad + a_{21}^2\varepsilon_{2t-1}^2 + g_{11}^2\eta_{1t-1}^2 + 2g_{11}g_{21}\eta_{1t-1}\eta_{2t-1} + g_{21}^2\eta_{2t-1}^2,
\end{aligned}
$$

and similarly for the second return from, for example, another country. Here, we set $B_{11}h_{11,t-1}$ as a single element, although one could also have B as a matrix, bringing in previous day conditional variance of returns from the second country as $B_{21}h_{22,t-1}$. In the above specification, we only allow spillover to permeate through ε_{2t-1}^2 and assume that the impact will then be passed on 'internally' through $h_{11,t-1}$.

The conditional covariance $h_{ijt} = h_{12t}$ is slightly more complex. It accommodates both constant and time-varying components as follows:

$$
\begin{aligned}
h_{12t} &= \rho_{12}\sqrt{h_{11t}}\sqrt{h_{22t}} + \phi_{12}h_{12t}^*, \\
h_{12t}^* &= \omega_{12} + B_{12}h_{12,t-1} + a_1'\varepsilon_{t-1}\varepsilon_{t-1}'a_2 + g_1'\varepsilon_{t-1}\varepsilon_{t-1}'g_2 \\
&= \omega_{12} + B_{12}h_{12,t-1} + a_{11}a_{12}\varepsilon_{1t-1}^2 + a_{11}a_{22}\varepsilon_{1t-1}\varepsilon_{2t-1} \\
&\quad + a_{12}a_{21}\varepsilon_{1t-1}\varepsilon_{2t-1} + a_{21}a_{22}\varepsilon_{2t-1}^2 + g_{11}g_{12}\eta_{1t-1}^2 \\
&\quad + g_{11}g_{22}\eta_{1t-1}\eta_{2t-1} + g_{12}g_{21}\eta_{1t-1}\eta_{2t-1} + g_{21}g_{22}\eta_{2t-1}^2,
\end{aligned}
$$

with ρ_{12} capturing the constant correlation and h_{12t}^*, a time-varying covariance weighted by ϕ_{12}. In Martens and Poon (2001), we calculate time-varying correlation as

$$\rho_{12t} = \frac{h_{12t}}{\sqrt{h_{11t}}\sqrt{h_{22t}}}.$$

In the implementation, we first estimate all returns as univariate GJR-GARCH and estimate the MA parameters for synchronization correction independently. These parameter estimates are fed into the ADC model as starting values.

7.3 APPLICATIONS

The future of multivariate volatility models very much depends on their use. Their use in long horizon forecasting is restricted unless one adopts a more parsimonious factor approach (see Sentana, 1998; Sentana and Fiorentini, 2001). For capturing volatility spillover, multivariate volatility models will continue to be useful for short horizon forecast and univariate risk management. The use of multivariate volatility models for estimating conditional correlation and multivariate risk management will be restrictive because correlation is a linear concept and a poor measure of dependence, especially among large values (Poon, Rockinger and Tawn, 2003, 2004). There are a lot of important details in the modelling of multivariate extremes of financial asset returns and we hope to see some new results soon. It will suffice to illustrate here some of these issues with a simple example on linear relationship alone.

Let Y_t be a stock return and X_t be the returns on the stock market portfolio or another stock return from another country. The stock returns regression gives

$$Y_t = \alpha + \beta X_t + \varepsilon_t, \tag{7.1}$$
$$\beta = \frac{Cov\,(Y_t, X_t)}{Var\,(X_t)} = \frac{\rho_{xy}\sigma_y}{\sigma_x}, \quad \text{or}$$
$$\rho_{xy} = \frac{\beta\sigma_x}{\sigma_y}.$$

If the factor loading, β, in (7.1) remains constant, then ρ_{xy} could increase simply because σ_x/σ_y increases during the high-volatility state. This is the main point in Forbes and Rigobon (2002) who claim findings in many contagion studies are being driven by high volatility.

However, β, the factor loading, need not remain constant. One common feature in financial crisis is that many returns will move together and jointly become more volatile. This means that indiosyncratic risk will be small $\sigma_\varepsilon^2 \to 0$, and from (7.1)

$$\sigma_y^2 = \beta^2\sigma_x^2,$$
$$\beta = \frac{\sigma_y}{\sigma_x}, \quad \text{and} \quad \rho_{xy} \to 1.$$

The difficulty in generalizing this relationship is that there are crises that are local to a country or a region that have no worldwide impact or impact on the neighbouring country. We do not yet have a model that will make such a distinction, let alone one that will predict it.

The study of univariate jump risk in option pricing is a hot topic just now. The study of the joint occurrence of jumps and multivariate volatility models will probably 'meet up' in the not so-distant future. Before we understand how the large events jointly occur, the use of the multivariate volatility model on its own in portfolio risk management will be very dangerous. The same applies to asset allocation and portfolio formation, although the impact here is over a long horizon, and hence will be less severely affected by joint-tail events.

8

Black–Scholes

A European-style call (put) option is a right, but not an obligation, to purchase (sell) an asset at the agreed strike price on option maturity date, T. An American-style option is a European option that can be exercised prior to T.

8.1 THE BLACK–SCHOLES FORMULA

The Black–Scholes (BS) formula below is for pricing *European* call and put options:

$$c = S_0 N(d_1) - K e^{-rT} N(d_2), \tag{8.1}$$
$$p = K e^{-rT} N(-d_2) - S_0 N(-d_1),$$
$$d_1 = \frac{\ln(S_0/K) + \left(r + \frac{1}{2}\sigma^2\right) T}{\sigma \sqrt{T}}, \tag{8.2}$$
$$d_2 = d_1 - \sigma \sqrt{T},$$
$$N(d_1) = \frac{1}{\sqrt{2\pi}} \int_{-\infty}^{d_1} e^{-0.5 z^2} dz,$$

where c (p) is the price of the European call (put), S_0 is the current price of the underlying assset, K is the strike or exercise price, r is the continuously compounded risk-free interest rate, and T is the time to option maturity. $N(d_1)$ is the cumulative probability distribution of a standard normal distribution for the area below d_1, and $N(-d_1) = 1 - N(d_1)$.

As $T \to 0$,

$$d_1 \quad \text{and} \quad d_2 \to \infty,$$
$$N(d_1) \quad \text{and} \quad N(d_2) \to 1,$$
$$N(-d_1) \quad \text{and} \quad N(-d_2) \to 0,$$

which means

$$c \geq S_0 - K, \quad p \geq 0 \qquad \text{for } S_0 > K, \tag{8.3}$$
$$c \geq 0, \qquad p \geq K - S_0 \qquad \text{for } S_0 < K. \tag{8.4}$$

As $\sigma \to 0$, again

$$N(d_1) \quad \text{and} \quad N(d_2) \to 1,$$
$$N(-d_1) \quad \text{and} \quad N(-d_2) \to 0.$$

This will lead to

$$c \geq S_0 - Ke^{-rT}, \quad \text{and} \tag{8.5}$$
$$p \geq Ke^{-rT} - S_0. \tag{8.6}$$

The conditions (8.3), (8.4), (8.5) and (8.6) are the boundary conditions for checking option prices before using them for empirical tests. These conditions need not be specific to Black–Scholes. Options with market prices (transaction or quote) violating these boundary conditions should be discarded.

8.1.1 The Black–Scholes assumptions

  (i) For constant μ and σ, $dS = \mu S dt + \sigma S dz$.

 (ii) Short sale is permitted with full use of proceeds.

(iii) No transaction costs or taxes; securities are infinitely divisible.

(iv) No dividend before option maturity.

 (v) No arbitrage (i.e. market is at equilibrium).

(vi) Continuous trading (so that rebalancing of portfolio is done instantaneously).

(vii) Constant risk-free interest rate, r.

(viii) Constant volatility, σ.

Empirical findings suggest that option pricing is not sensitive to the assumption of a constant interest rate. There are now good approximating solutions for pricing American-style options that can be exercised early and options that encounter dividend payments before option maturity. The impact of stochastic volatility on option pricing is much more profound, an issue which we shall return to shortly. Apart from the constant volatility assumption, the violation of any of the remaining assumptions will result in the option price being traded within a band instead of at the theoretical price.

8.1.2   Black–Scholes implied volatility

Here, we first show that

$$\frac{\partial C_{BS}}{\partial \sigma} > 0,$$

which means that C_{BS} is a monotonous function in σ and there is a one-to-one correspondence between C_{BS} and σ.

From (8.1)

$$\frac{\partial C_{BS}}{\partial \sigma} = S\frac{\partial N}{\partial d_1}\frac{\partial d_1}{\partial \sigma} - Ke^{-r(T-t)}\frac{\partial N}{\partial d_2}\frac{\partial d_2}{\partial \sigma}, \qquad (8.7)$$

$$\frac{\partial N(x)}{\partial x} = \frac{1}{\sqrt{2\pi}}e^{-\frac{1}{2}x^2},$$

$$\frac{\partial d_1}{\partial \sigma} = \sqrt{T-t} - \frac{d_1}{\sigma},$$

$$\frac{\partial d_2}{\partial \sigma} = \sqrt{T-t} - \frac{d_1}{\sigma} - \sqrt{T-t} = -\frac{d_1}{\sigma}.$$

Substitute these results into (8.7) and get

$$\frac{\partial C_{BS}}{\partial \sigma} = \frac{S}{\sqrt{2\pi}}e^{-\frac{1}{2}d_1^2}\left(\sqrt{T-t} - \frac{d_1}{\sigma}\right) + \frac{Ke^{-r(T-t)}}{\sqrt{2\pi}}e^{-\frac{1}{2}d_2^2}\frac{d_1}{\sigma}$$

$$= \frac{Se^{-\frac{1}{2}d_1^2}\sqrt{T-t}}{\sqrt{2\pi}} + \frac{d_1}{\sigma\sqrt{2\pi}}$$

$$\times \left[-Se^{-\frac{1}{2}d_1^2} + Ke^{-r(T-t)}e^{-\frac{1}{2}\left(d_1 - \sigma\sqrt{T-t}\right)^2}\right]$$

$$= \frac{Se^{-\frac{1}{2}d_1^2}\sqrt{T-t}}{\sqrt{2\pi}} + \frac{d_1}{\sigma\sqrt{2\pi}}$$

$$\times \left[-Se^{-\frac{1}{2}d_1^2} + Ke^{-r(T-t)}e^{\left(-\frac{1}{2}d_1^2 + d_1\sigma\sqrt{T-t} - \frac{1}{2}\sigma^2(T-t)\right)}\right]$$

$$= \frac{Se^{-\frac{1}{2}d_1^2}\sqrt{T-t}}{\sqrt{2\pi}} + \frac{d_1 e^{-\frac{1}{2}d_1^2}}{\sigma\sqrt{2\pi}}$$

$$\times \left[-S + Ke^{\left(-r(T-t) + d_1\sigma\sqrt{T-t} - \frac{1}{2}\sigma^2(T-t)\right)}\right]. \qquad (8.8)$$

Also from (8.2)

$$d_1\sigma\sqrt{T-t} - \frac{1}{2}\sigma^2(T-t) - r(T-t) = \log\left(\frac{S}{K}\right) \qquad (8.9)$$

and substituting this result into (8.8), we get

$$
\frac{\partial C_{BS}}{\partial \sigma} = \frac{Se^{-\frac{1}{2}d_1^2}\sqrt{T-t}}{\sqrt{2\pi}} + \frac{d_1 e^{-\frac{1}{2}d_1^2}}{\sigma\sqrt{2\pi}} \left[-S + K\frac{S}{K} \right]
$$

$$
= \frac{Se^{-\frac{1}{2}d_1^2}\sqrt{T-t}}{\sqrt{2\pi}} > 0
$$

8.1.3 Black–Scholes implied volatility smile

Given an observed European call option price C^{obs} for a contract with strike price K and expiration date T, the implied volatility σ_{iv} is defined as the input value of the volatility parameter to the Black–Scholes formula such that

$$
C_{BS}(t, S; K, T; \sigma_{iv}) = C^{obs}. \tag{8.10}
$$

The option implied volatility σ_{iv} is often interpreted as a market's expectation of volatility over the option's maturity, i.e. the period from t to T. We have shown in the previous section that there is a one-to-one correspondence between prices and implied volatilities. Since $\partial C_{BS}/\partial \sigma > 0$, the condition

$$
C^{obs} = C_{BS}(t, S; K, T; \sigma_{iv}) > C_{BS}(t, S; K, T; 0)
$$

means $\sigma_{iv} > 0$; i.e. implied volatility is always greater than zero. The implied volatilities from put and call options of the same strike price and time to maturity are the same because of put–call parity. Traders often quote derivative prices in terms of σ_{iv} rather than dollar prices, the conversion to price being made through the Black–Scholes formula.

Given the true (unconditional) volatility is σ over period T. If Black–Scholes is correct, then

$$
C_{BS}(t, S; K, T; \sigma_{iv}) = C_{BS}(t, S; K, T; \sigma)
$$

for all strikes. That is the function (or graph) of $\sigma_{iv}(K)$ against K for fixed t, S, T and r, observed from market option prices is supposed to be a straight horizontal line. But, it is well known that the Black–Scholes σ_{iv}, differ across strikes. There is plenty of documented empirical evidence to suggest that implied volatilities are different across options of different strikes, and the shape is like a smile when we plot Black–Scholes implied volatility σ_{iv} against strike price K, the shape is anything but a straight line. Before the 1987 stock market crash, $\sigma_{iv}(K)$ against

K was often observed to be U-shaped, with the minimum located at or near at-the-money options, $K = Se^{-r(T-t)}$. Hence, this gives rise to the term 'smile effect'. After the stock market crash in 1987, $\sigma_{iv}(K)$ is typically downward sloping at and near the money and then curves upward at high strikes. Such a shape is now known as a 'smirk'. The smile/smirk usually 'flattens' out as T gets longer. Moreover, implied volatility from option is typically higher than historical volatility and often decreases with time to maturity.

Since $\partial C_{BS}/\partial \sigma > 0$, the smile/smirk curve, tells us that there is a premium charged for options at low strikes (OTM puts and ITM calls see footnote 2) above their BS price as compared with the ATM options. Although the market uses Black–Scholes implied volatility, σ_{iv}, as pricing units, the market itself prices options as though the constant volatility lognormal model fails to capture the probabilities of large downward stock price movements and so supplement the Black–Scholes price to account for this.

8.1.4   Explanations for the 'smile'

There are at least two theoretical explanations (viz. distributional assumption and stochastic volatility) for this puzzle. Other explanations that are based on market microstructure and measurement errors (e.g. liquidity, bid–ask spread and tick size) and investor risk preference (e.g. model risk, lottery premium and portfolio insurance) have also been proposed. In the next chapter on option pricing using stochastic volatility, we will explain how violation of distributional assumption and stochastic volatility could induce BS implied volatility smile. Here, we will concentrate on understanding how Black–Scholes distributional assumption produces volatility smile. Before we proceed, we need to make use of the positive relationship between volatility and option price, and the put–call parity[1]

$$c_t + Ke^{r(T-t)} = p_t + S_t \qquad (8.11)$$

which establishes the positive relationship between call and put option prices. Since implied volatility is positively related to option price, Equation (8.11) suggests there is also a positive relationship between implied volatilities derived from call and put options that have the same strike price and the same time to maturity.

---

[1] The discussion here is based on Hull (2002).

As mentioned before, Black–Scholes requires stock price to follow a lognormal distribution or the logarithmic stock returns to have a normal distribution. There is now widely documented empirical evidence that risky financial asset returns have leptokurtic tails. In the case where the strike price is very high, the call option is deep-out-of-the-money[2] and the probability for this option to be exercised is very low. Nevertheless, a leptokurtic right tail will give this option a higher probability, than that from a normal distribution, for the terminal asset price to exceed the strike price and the call option to finish in the money. This higher probability leads to a higher call price and a higher Black–Scholes implied volatility at high strike.

Next, we look at the case when the strike price is low. First note that option value has two components: intrinsic value and time value. Intrinsic value reflects how deep the option is in the money. Time value reflects the amount of uncertainty before the option expires, hence it is most influenced by volatility. A deep-in-the-money call option has high intrinsic value and little time value, and a small amount of bid–ask spread or transaction tick size is sufficient to perturb the implied volatility estimation. We could, however, make use of the previous argument but apply it to an out-of-the-money (OTM) put option at low strike price. An OTM put option has a close to nil intrinsic value and the put option price is due mainly to time value. Again because of the thicker tail on the left, we expect the probability that the OTM put option finishes in the money to be higher than that for a normal distribution. Hence the put option price (and hence the call option price through put–call parity) should be greater than that predicted by Black–Scholes. If we use Black–Scholes to invert volatility estimates from these option prices, the Black–Scholes implied will be higher than actual volatility. This results in volatility smile where implied volatility is much higher at very low and very high strikes.

The above arguments apply readily to the currency market where exchange rate returns exhibit thick tail distributions that are approximately symmetrical. In the stock market, volatility skew (i.e. low implied at high strike but high implied at low strike) is more common than volatility smile after the October 1987 stock market crash. Since the distribution

---

[2] In option terminology, an option is *out of the money* when it is not profitable to exercise the option. For a call option, this happens when $S < X$, and in the case of a put, the condition is $S > X$. The reverse is true for an *in-the-money* option. A call or a put is said to be *at the money* (ATM) when $S = X$. A *near-the-money* option is an option that is not exactly ATM, but close to being ATM. Sometimes, discounted values of S and X are used in the conditions.

is skewed to the far left, the right tail can be thinner than the normal distribution. In this case implied volatility at high strike will be lower than that expected from a volatility smile.

8.2 BLACK–SCHOLES AND NO-ARBITRAGE PRICING

8.2.1 The stock price dynamics

The Black–Scholes model for pricing European equity options assumes the stock price has the following dynamics:

$$dS = \mu S dt + \sigma S dz, \tag{8.12}$$

and for the growth rate on stock:

$$\frac{dS}{S} = \mu dt + \sigma dz. \tag{8.13}$$

From Ito's lemma, the logarithm of the stock price has the following dynamics:

$$d \ln S = \left(\mu - \frac{1}{2}\sigma^2 \right) dt + \sigma dz, \tag{8.14}$$

which means that the stock price has a lognormal distribution or the logarithm of the stock price has a normal distribution. In discrete time

$$d \ln S = \left(\mu - \frac{1}{2}\sigma^2 \right) dt + \sigma dz,$$

$$\Delta \ln S = \left(\mu - \frac{1}{2}\sigma^2 \right) \Delta t + \sigma \, \varepsilon \sqrt{\Delta t},$$

$$\ln S_T - \ln S_0 \sim N \left[\left(\mu - \frac{1}{2}\sigma^2 \right) T, \ \sigma \sqrt{T} \right],$$

$$\ln S_T \sim N \left[\ln S_0 + \left(\mu - \frac{1}{2}\sigma^2 \right) T, \ \sigma \sqrt{T} \right]. \tag{8.15}$$

8.2.2 The Black–Scholes partial differential equation

The derivation of the Black–Scholes partial differential equation (PDE) is based on the fundamental fact that the option price and the stock price depend on the same underlying source of uncertainty. A portfolio can then be created consisting of the stock and the option which eliminates this source of uncertainty. Given that this portfolio is riskless, it must therefore earn the risk-free rate of return. Here is how the logic works:

$$\Delta S = \mu S \Delta t + \sigma S \Delta z, \tag{8.16}$$

$$\Delta f = \left[\frac{\partial f}{\partial S} \mu S + \frac{\partial f}{\partial t} + \frac{1}{2} \frac{\partial^2 f}{\partial S^2} \sigma^2 S^2 \right] \Delta t + \frac{\partial f}{\partial S} \sigma S \Delta z. \tag{8.17}$$

We set up a hedged portfolio, Π, consisting of $\partial f / \partial S$ number of shares and short one unit of the derivative security. The change in portfolio value is

$$\begin{aligned}
\Delta \Pi &= -\Delta f + \frac{\partial f}{\partial S} \Delta S \\
&= -\left[\frac{\partial f}{\partial S} \mu S + \frac{\partial f}{\partial t} + \frac{1}{2} \frac{\partial^2 f}{\partial S^2} \sigma^2 S^2 \right] \Delta t - \frac{\partial f}{\partial S} \sigma S \Delta z \\
&\quad + \frac{\partial f}{\partial S} \mu S \Delta t + \frac{\partial f}{\partial S} \sigma S \Delta z \\
&= -\left[\frac{\partial f}{\partial t} + \frac{1}{2} \frac{\partial^2 f}{\partial S^2} \sigma^2 S^2 \right] \Delta t.
\end{aligned}$$

Note that uncertainty due to Δz is cancelled out and μ, the premium for risk (returns on S), is also cancelled out. Not only has $\Delta \Pi$ no uncertainty, it is also preference-free and does not depend on μ, a parameter controlled by the investor's risk aversion.

If the portfolio value is fully hedged, then no arbitrage implies that it must earn only a risk-free rate of return

$$r \Pi \Delta t = \Delta \Pi,$$

$$r \Pi \Delta t = -\Delta f + \frac{\partial f}{\partial S} \Delta S,$$

$$\begin{aligned}
r \left(-f + \frac{\partial f}{\partial S} S \right) \Delta t &= -\left[\frac{\partial f}{\partial S} \mu S + \frac{\partial f}{\partial t} + \frac{1}{2} \frac{\partial^2 f}{\partial S^2} \sigma^2 S^2 \right] \Delta t - \frac{\partial f}{\partial S} \sigma S \Delta z \\
&\quad + \frac{\partial f}{\partial S} [\mu S \Delta t + \sigma S \Delta z],
\end{aligned}$$

$$\begin{aligned}
r(-f) \Delta t &= -r S \frac{\partial f}{\partial S} \Delta t - \frac{\partial f}{\partial S} \mu S \Delta t - \frac{\partial f}{\partial t} \Delta t - \frac{1}{2} \frac{\partial^2 f}{\partial S^2} \sigma^2 S^2 \Delta t \\
&\quad - \frac{\partial f}{\partial S} \sigma S \Delta z + \frac{\partial f}{\partial S} \mu S \Delta t + \frac{\partial f}{\partial S} \sigma S \Delta z,
\end{aligned}$$

and finally we get the well-known Black–Scholes PDE

$$rf = r S \frac{\partial f}{\partial S} + \frac{\partial f}{\partial t} + \frac{1}{2} \frac{\partial^2 f}{\partial S^2} \sigma^2 S^2 \tag{8.18}$$

8.2.3 Solving the partial differential equation

There are many solutions to (8.18) corresponding to different derivatives, f, with underlying asset S. In other words, without further constraints, the PDE in (8.18) does not have a unique solution. The particular security being valued is determined by its boundary conditions of the differential equation. In the case of an European call, the value at expiry $c(S, T) = \max(S - K, 0)$ serves as the final condition for the Black–Scholes PDE. Here, we show how BS formula can be derived using the risk-neutral valuation relationship. We need the following facts:

(i) From (8.15),

$$\ln S \sim N\left(\ln S_0 + \mu - \frac{1}{2}\sigma^2, \sigma\right).$$

Under risk-neutral valuation relationship, $\mu = r$ and

$$\ln S \sim N\left(\ln S_0 + r - \frac{1}{2}\sigma^2, \sigma\right).$$

(ii) If y is a normally distributed variable,

$$\int_a^\infty e^y f(y)\, dy = N\left(\frac{\mu_y - a}{\sigma_y} + \sigma_y\right) e^{\mu_y + \frac{1}{2}\sigma_y^2}.$$

(iii) From the definition of cumulative normal distribution,

$$\int_a^\infty f(y)\, dy = 1 - N\left(\frac{a - \mu_y}{\sigma_y}\right) = N\left(\frac{\mu_y - a}{\sigma_y}\right).$$

Now we are ready to solve the BS formula. First, the terminal value of a call is

$$c_T = E\left[\max(S - K, 0)\right]$$
$$= \int_K^\infty (S - K) f(S)\, dS$$
$$= \int_{\ln K}^\infty e^{\ln S} f(\ln S)\, d\ln S - K \int_{\ln K}^\infty f(\ln S)\, d\ln S.$$

Substituting facts (ii) and (iii) and using information from (i) with

$$\mu_y = \ln S_0 + r - \frac{1}{2}\sigma^2,$$
$$\sigma_y = \sigma,$$
$$a = \ln K,$$

we get

$$
\begin{aligned}
c_T &= S_0 e^r N \left(\frac{\ln S_0 + r + \frac{1}{2}\sigma^2 - \ln K}{\ln K} \right) \\
&\quad - K N \left(\frac{\ln S_0 + r - \frac{1}{2}\sigma^2 - \ln K}{\ln K} \right) \\
&= S_0 e^r N (d_1) - K N (d_2),
\end{aligned}
\tag{8.19}
$$

where

$$
d_1 = \frac{\ln S_0/K + r - \frac{1}{2}\sigma^2}{\sigma},
$$
$$
d_2 = d_1 - \sigma.
$$

The present value of the call option is derived by applying e^{-r} to both sides. The put option price can be derived using put–call parity or using the same argument as above. The σ in the above formula is volatility over the option maturity. If we use σ as the annualized volatility then we replace σ with $\sigma\sqrt{T}$ in the formula.

There are important insights from (8.19), all valid only in a 'risk-neutral' world:

  (i) $N(d_2)$ is the probability that the option will be exercised.
 (ii) Alternatively, $N(d_2)$ is the probability that call finishes in the money.
(iii) $X N(d_2)$ is the expected payment.
 (iv) $S_0 e^{rT} N(d_1)$ is the expected value $E[S_T - X]^+$, where $E[\cdot]^+$ is expectation computed for positive values only.
  (v) In other words, $S_0 e^{rT} N(d_1)$ is the risk-neutral expectation of S_T, $E^Q[S_T]$ with $S_T > X$.

8.3 BINOMIAL METHOD

In a highly simplified example, we assume a stock price can only move up by one node or move down by one node over a 3-month period as shown below. The option is a call option for the right to purchase the share at $21 at the end of the period (i.e. in 3 month's time).

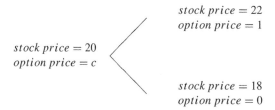

Construct a portfolio consisting of Δ amount of shares and short one call option. If we want to make sure that the value of this portfolio is the same whether it is up state or down state, then

$$\$22 \times \Delta - \$1 = \$18 \times \Delta + \$0,$$
$$\Delta = 0.25.$$

stock price $= 20$

portfolio value
$= 4.5e^{-0.12 \times 3/12}$
$= 4.367$

stock price $= 22$
portfolio value $= 22 \times 0.25 - 1 = 4.5$

stock price $= 18$
portfolio value $= 18 \times 0.25 = 4.5$

Given that the portfolio's value is \$4.367, this means that

$$\$20 \times 0.25 - f = \$4.367$$
$$f = \$0.633.$$

This is the value of the option under no arbitrage.

From the above simple example, we can make the following generalization;

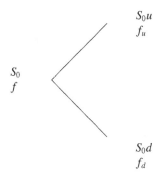

The amount Δ is calculated using

$$S_0 u \times \Delta - f_u = S_0 d \times \Delta - f_d,$$

$$\Delta = \frac{f_u - f_d}{S_0 u - S_0 d}. \tag{8.20}$$

Since the terminal value of the 'riskless' portfolio is the same in the up state and in the down state, we could use any one of the values (say the up state) to establish the following relationship

$$S_0 \times \Delta - f = (S_0 u \times \Delta - f_u) e^{-rT},$$

$$f = S_0 \times \Delta - (S_0 u \times \Delta - f_u) e^{-rT}. \tag{8.21}$$

Substituting the value of Δ from (8.20) into (8.21), we get

$$f = S_0 \times \frac{f_u - f_d}{S_0 u - S_0 d} - \left(S_0 u \times \frac{f_u - f_d}{S_0 u - S_0 d} - f_u \right) e^{-rT}$$

$$= \frac{f_u - f_d}{u - d} - \left(u \times \frac{f_u - f_d}{u - d} - f_u \right) e^{-rT}$$

$$= \left(\frac{e^{rT} (f_u - f_d)}{u - d} - \frac{u (f_u - f_d)}{u - d} + \frac{u f_u - d f_u}{u - d} \right) e^{-rT}$$

$$= \left(\frac{e^{rT} f_u - e^{rT} f_d}{u - d} + \frac{u f_d - d f_u}{u - d} \right) e^{-rT}$$

$$= \left(\frac{e^{rT} - d}{u - d} f_u + \frac{u - e^{rT}}{u - d} f_d \right) e^{-rT}.$$

By letting $p = (e^{rT} - d)/(u - d)$, we get

$$f = e^{-rT} [p f_u + (1 - p) f_d] \tag{8.22}$$

and

$$1 - p = \frac{u - d - e^{rT} + d}{u - d} = \frac{u - e^{rT}}{u - d}.$$

We can see from (8.22) that although p is not the real probability distribution of the stock price, it has all the characteristics of a probability measure (viz. sum to one and nonnegative). Moreover, when the expectation is calculated based on p, the expected terminal payoff is discounted using the risk-free interest. Hence, p is called the risk-neutral probability measure.

We can verify that the underlying asset S also produces a risk-free rate of returns under this risk-neutral measure.

$$S_0 e^{\mu T} = \left(\frac{e^{rT} - d}{u - d} \right) S_0 u + \left(\frac{u - e^{rT}}{u - d} \right) S_0 d,$$

$$e^{\mu T} = \frac{u e^{rT} - ud + ud - d e^{rT}}{u - d},$$

$$= \frac{(u - d) e^{rT}}{u - d} = e^{rT},$$

$$\mu = r.$$

The actual return of the stock is no longer needed and neither is the actual distribution of the terminal stock price. (This is a rather amazing discovery in the study of derivative securities!!!)

8.3.1   Matching volatility with u and d

We have already seen in the previous section and Equation (8.22) that the risk-neutral probability measure is set such that the expected growth rate is the risk-free rate, r.

$$f = \left(\frac{e^{rT} - d}{u - d} f_u + \frac{u - e^{rT}}{u - d} f_d \right) e^{-rT}$$

$$= [p f_u + (1 - p) f_d] e^{-rT},$$

$$p = \frac{e^{rT} - d}{u - d}.$$

This immediately leads to the question of how does one set the values of u and d? The key is that u and d are jointly determined such that the volatility of the binomial process equal to σ which is given or can be estimated from prices of the asset underlying the option contract. Given that there are two unknowns and there is only one constant σ, there are a number of ways to specify u and d. The good or better ways are those that guarantee the nodes recombined after an upstate followed by a downstate, and *vice versa*. In Cox, Ross and Rubinstein (1979), u and d are defined as follows:

$$u = e^{\sigma \sqrt{\delta t}}, \quad \text{and} \quad d = e^{-\sigma \sqrt{\delta t}}.$$

It is easy to verify that the nodes recombine since $ud = du = 1$. So after each up move and down move (and *vice versa*), the stock price will return to S_0.

To verify that the volatility of stock *returns* is approximately $\sigma \sqrt{\delta t}$ under the risk-neutral measure, we note that

$$Var = E\left[x^2\right] - [E(x)]^2,$$
$$\ln u = \sigma \sqrt{\delta t}, \text{ and } \ln d = -\sigma \sqrt{\delta t}.$$

The expected stock returns is

$$E(x) = p \ln \frac{S_0 u}{S_0} + (1-p) \ln \frac{S_0 d}{S_0}$$
$$= p\sigma \sqrt{\delta t} - (1-p)\sigma \sqrt{\delta t}$$
$$= (2p-1)\sigma \sqrt{\delta t},$$

and

$$E\left[x^2\right] = p \left(\ln \frac{S_0 u}{S_0} \right)^2 + (1-p) \left(\ln \frac{S_0 d}{S_0} \right)^2$$
$$= p\sigma^2 \delta t + (1-p)\sigma^2 \delta t$$
$$= \sigma^2 \delta t.$$

Hence

$$Var = \sigma^2 \delta t - (2p-1)^2 \sigma^2 \delta t$$
$$= \sigma^2 \delta t \left(1 - 4p^2 + 4p - 1\right)$$
$$= \sigma^2 \delta t \times 4p(1-p).$$

It has been shown elsewhere that as $\delta t \to 0$, $p \to 0.5$ and $Var \to \sigma^2 \delta t$.

8.3.2 A two-step binomial tree and American-style options

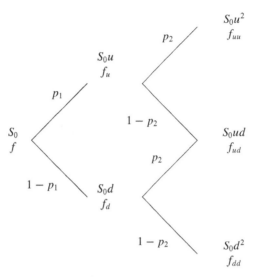

The binomial tree is often constructed in such a way that the branches recombine. If the volatilities in period 1 and period 2 are different, then, in order to make the binomial tree recombine, $p_1 \neq p_2$. (This is a more advanced topic in option pricing.) Here, we take the simple case where volatility is constant, and $p_1 = p_2 = p$. Hence, to price a European option, we simply take the expected terminal value under the *risk-neutral* measure and discount it with a risk-free interest rate, as follows:

$$f = e^{-r \times 2\delta t} \left[p^2 f_{uu} + 2p\left(1 - p\right) f_{ud} + \left(1 - p\right)^2 f_{dd} \right]. \qquad (8.23)$$

Note that the hedge ratio for state 2 will be different depending on whether state 1 is an up state or a down state

$$\Delta_0 = \frac{f_u - f_d}{S_0 u - S_0 d},$$

$$\Delta_{1,u} = \frac{f_{uu} - f_{ud}}{S_0 u^2 - S_0 ud},$$

$$\Delta_{1,d} = \frac{f_{ud} - f_{dd}}{S_0 ud - S_0 d^2}.$$

This also means that, for such a model to work in practice, one has to be able to *continuously and costlessly rebalance* the composition of the portfolio of stock and option. This is a very important assumption and should not be overlooked.

We can see from (8.23) that the intermediate nodes are not required for the pricing of European options. What are required are the range of possible values for the terminal payoff and the risk-neutral probability density for each node. This is not the case for the American option and all the nodes in the intermediate stages are needed because of the possibility of early exercise. As the number of nodes increases, the binomial tree converges to a lognormal distribution for stock price.

8.4   TESTING OPTION PRICING MODEL IN PRACTICE

Let $C = f(K, S, r, \sigma, T - t)$ denote the theoretical (or model) price of the option and f is some option pricing model, e.g. f_{BS} denotes the Black–Scholes formula. At any one time, we have options of many different strikes, K, and maturities, $T - t$. (Here we use t and T as dates; t is now and T is option maturity date. So the time to maturity is $T - t$.) Since σ_{t_1} and σ_{t_2} need not be the same for $t_1 \neq t_2$, we tend to use only options with the same maturity $T - t$ because volatility itself has a term structure. Assuming that there are C_1^{obs}, C_2^{obs} and C_3^{obs} observed option prices (possibly these are market-traded option prices) associated with three exercise prices K_1, K_2 and K_3. To find the theoretical option price C, we need the five parameters K, S, r, σ and $T - t$. Except for σ, the other four parameters K, S, r and $T - t$ can be determined accurately and easily. We could estimate σ from historical stock prices. The problem with this approach is that when $C \neq C^{obs}$ (i.e. the model price is not the same as the market price), we do not know if this is because we did not estimate σ properly or because the option pricing model $f(\cdot)$ is wrong. A better approach is to use 'backward induction', i.e. use an iterative procedure to find the σ that minimizes the pricing errors

$$C_1 - C_1^{obs}, \quad C_2 - C_2^{obs}, \quad \text{and} \quad C_3 - C_3^{obs}.$$

The above is usually done by minimizing the unsigned errors

$$\sum_{i=1}^{n} W_i \left| C_i - C_i^{obs} \right|^m \tag{8.24}$$

with an optimization routine searching over all possible values of σ; n is the number of observed option prices (three in this case), and W_i is the weight applied to observation i.

In the simplest case, $W_i = 1$ for all i. To give the greatest weight to the ATM option, we could set

$$
W_i = \begin{cases} 10{,}000 & \text{for } S = Ke^{-r(T-t)} \\ \dfrac{1}{\left| \dfrac{S}{Xe^{-r(T-t)}} - 1 \right|} & \text{for } S \neq Ke^{-r(T-t)} \end{cases}.
$$

$W_i = 10\,000$ is equivalent to an option price that is 0.0001 away from being at the money.

The power term, m, is the control for large pricing error. The larger the value of m, the greater the emphasis placed on large errors for errors > 1. If a very large error is due to data error, then a large m means the entire estimation will be driven by this data error. Typically, m is set equal to 1 or 2 corresponding to 'absolute errors' and 'squared errors'.

Since the option price is much greater for an ITM option than for an OTM option, the pricing error is likely to be of a greater magnitude for an ITM option. Hence, for an ITM option and an OTM option that are an equal distance from being ATM, the procedure in (8.24) will place a greater weight on pricing an ITM option correctly and pay little or negligible attention to OTM options. One way to overcome this is to minimize their Black–Scholes implied volatilities instead. Here, we are using BS as a conversion tool. So long as $\partial C^{BS}/\partial \sigma > 0$ and there is a one-to-one correspondence between option price and BS implied volatility. Such a procedure does not require the assumption that the BS model is correct.

To implement the new procedure, we start with an initial value σ^* and get C_1, C_2 and C_3 from f, the option pricing model that we wish to test. f could even be Black–Scholes, if it is our intention to test Black–Scholes. Use the Black–Scholes model f_{BS} to invert BS implied volatility IV_1, IV_2 and IV_3 from the theoretical prices C_1, C_2 and C_3 calculated in the previous step. If f in the previous step is indeed Black–Scholes, then $IV_1 = IV_2 = IV_3 = \sigma^*$. Use the Black–Scholes model f_{BS} to invert BS implied volatility IV_1^{obs}, IV_2^{obs} and IV_3^{obs} from the market observed option prices C_1^{obs}, C_2^{obs} and C_3^{obs}.

Finally, minimize the function

$$
\sum_{i=1}^{n} W_i \left| IV_i - IV_i^{obs} \right|^m
$$

using the algorithm and logic as before.

8.5 DIVIDEND AND EARLY EXERCISE PREMIUM

As option holders are not entitled to dividends, the option price should be adjusted for known dividends to be distributed during the life of the option and the fact that the option holder may have the right to exercise early to receive the dividend.

8.5.1 Known and finite dividends

Assume that there is only one dividend at τ. Should the call option holder decide to exercise the option, she will receive $S_\tau - K$ at time τ and if she decides not to exercise the option, her option value will be worth $c(S_\tau - D_\tau, K, r, T, \sigma)$. The Black (1975) approximation involves making such comparisons for each dividend date. If the decision is not to exercise, then the option is priced now at $c\left(S_t - D_\tau e^{-r(\tau - t)}, K, r, T, \sigma\right)$. If the decision is to exercise, then the option is priced according to $c(S_t, K, r, \tau, \sigma)$. We note that if the decision is not to exercise, the American call option will have the same value as the European call option calculated by removing the discounted dividend from the stock price.

A more accurate formula that takes into account of the probability of early exercise is that by Roll (1977), Geske (1979), and Whaley (1981), and presented in Hull (2002, appendix 11). These formulae (even the Black-approximation) work quite well for American calls. In the case of an American put, a better solution is to implement the Barone-Adesi and Whaley (1987) formula (see Section 8.5.3).

8.5.2 Dividend yield method

When the dividend is in the form of yield it can be easily 'netted off' from the risk-free interest rate as in the case of a currency option. To calculate the dividend yield of an index option, the dividend yield, q, is the average annualized yield of dividends distributed during the life of the option:

$$q = \frac{1}{t} \ln \left(\frac{S + \sum_{i=1}^{n} D_i e^{r(t-t_i)}}{S} \right)$$

where D_i and t_i are the amount and the timing of the ith dividend on the index with t_i should also be annualized in a similar fashion as t. The dividend yield rate computed here is thus from the actual dividends paid during the option's life which will therefore account for the monthly seasonality in dividend payments.

8.5.3   Barone-Adesi and Whaley quadratic approximation

Define $M = \frac{2r}{\sigma^2}$ and $N = 2(r - q)/\sigma^2$, then[3] for an American call option

$$C(S) = \begin{cases} c(S) + A_2 \left(\dfrac{S}{S^*}\right)^{q_2} & \text{when} \quad S < S^* \\ S - K & \text{when} \quad S \geq S^*. \end{cases} \tag{8.25}$$

The variable S^* is the critical price of the index above which the option should be exercised. It is estimated by solving the equation,

$$S^* - K = c(S^*) + \left\{1 - e^{-qt}\mathrm{N}\left[d_1(S^*)\right]\right\}\frac{S^*}{q_2},$$

iteratively. The other variables are

$$q_2 = \frac{1}{2}\left[1 - N + \sqrt{(N-1)^2 + \frac{4M}{1 - e^{-rt}}}\right],$$

$$A_2 = \frac{S^*}{q_2}\left\{1 - e^{-qt}\mathrm{N}\left[d_1(S^*)\right]\right\},$$

$$d_1(S^*) = \frac{\ln(S^*/K) + (r - q + 0.5\sigma^2)t}{\sigma\sqrt{t}}. \tag{8.26}$$

To compute delta and vega for hedging purposes[4]:

$$\Delta_C = \frac{\partial C}{\partial S} = \begin{cases} e^{-qt}\mathrm{N}(d_1(S)) + \frac{A_2 q_2}{S^*}\left(\dfrac{S}{S^*}\right)^{(q_2-1)} & \text{when} \quad S < S^* \\ 1 & \text{when} \quad S \geq S^*, \end{cases}$$

$$\Lambda_C = \frac{\partial C}{\partial \sigma} = \begin{cases} S\sqrt{t}\,\mathrm{N}'(d_1)\,e^{-qt} & \text{when} \quad S < S^* \\ 0 & \text{when} \quad S \geq S^*. \end{cases} \tag{8.27}$$

---

[3] Note that in Barone-Adesi and Whaley (1987), $K(t)$ is $\left(1 - e^{-rt}\right)$, and b is $(r - q)$.

[4] Vega for the American options cannot be evaluated easily because C partly depends on S^*, which itself is a complex function of σ. The expression for vega in the case when $S < S^*$ in Equation (8.27) represents the vega for the European component only. Vega for the American option could be derived using numerical methods.

For an American put option, the valuation formula is:

$$P(S) = \begin{cases} p(S) + A_1 \left(\frac{S}{S^{**}}\right)^{q_1} & \text{when} \quad S > S^{**} \\ K - S & \text{when} \quad S \leq S^{**}. \end{cases} \qquad (8.27a)$$

The variable S^{**} is the critical index price below which the option should be exercised. It is estimated by solving the equation,

$$K - S^{**} = p\left(S^{**}\right) - \left\{1 - e^{-qt} N\left[-d_1\left(S^{**}\right)\right]\right\} \frac{S^{**}}{q_1},$$

iteratively. The other variables are

$$q_1 = \frac{1}{2}\left[1 - N - \sqrt{(N-1)^2 + \frac{4M}{1-e^{-rt}}}\right],$$

$$A_1 = -\frac{S^{**}}{q_1}\left\{1 - e^{-qt} N\left[-d_1\left(S^{**}\right)\right]\right\},$$

$$d_1\left(S^{**}\right) = \frac{\ln\left(S^{**}/K\right) + (r - q + 0.5\sigma^2)t}{\sigma\sqrt{t}}.$$

To compute delta and vega for hedging purposes:

$$\Delta_P = \frac{\partial P}{\partial S} = \begin{cases} -e^{-qt} N(d_1(S)) + \frac{A_1 q_1}{S^{**}}\left(\frac{S}{S^{**}}\right)^{(q_1-1)} & \text{when} \quad S > S^{**} \\ -1 & \text{when} \quad S \leq S^{**}, \end{cases}$$

$$\Lambda_P = \frac{\partial P}{\partial \sigma} = \begin{cases} \frac{\partial C}{\partial \sigma} = S\sqrt{t}\, N'(d_1)\, e^{-qt} & \text{when} \quad S > S^{**} \\ 0 & \text{when} \quad S \leq S_*^{*}. \end{cases}$$

8.6   MEASUREMENT ERRORS AND BIAS

Early studies of option implied volatility suffered many estimation problems,[5] such as the improper use of the Black–Scholes model for an American style option, the omission of dividend payments, the option price and the underlying asset prices not being recorded at the same time, or stale prices being used. Since transactions may take place at bid or ask prices, transaction prices of the option and the underlying assets are subject to bid–ask bounce making the implied volatility estimation

---

[5] Mayhew (1995) gives a detailed discussion on such complications involved in estimating implied volatility from option prices, and Hentschel (2001) provides a discussion of the confidence intervals for implied volatility estimates.

unstable. Finally, in the case of an S&P100 OEX option, the privilege of a wildcard option is often omitted.[6] In more recent studies, many of these measurement errors have been taken into account. Many studies use futures and options futures because these markets are more active than the cash markets and hence there is a smaller risk of prices being stale.

Conditions in the Black–Scholes model include: no arbitrage, transaction cost is zero and continuous trading. As mentioned before, the lack of such a trading environment will result in options being traded within a band around the theoretical price. This means that implied volatility estimates extracted from market option prices will also lie within a band even without the complications described in Chapter 10. Figlewski (1997) shows that implied volatility estimates can differ by several percentage points due to bid–ask spread and discrete tick size alone. To smooth out errors caused by bid–ask bounce, Harvey and Whaley (1992) use a nonlinear regression of ATM option prices, observed in a 10-minute interval before the market close, on model prices.

Indication of nonideal trading environment is usually reflected in poor trading volume. This means implied volatility of options written on different underlying assets will have different forecasting power. For most option contracts, ATM option has the largest trading volume. This supports the popularity of ATM implied volatility referred to later in Chapter 10.

8.6.1 Investor risk preference

In the Black–Scholes world, investor risk preference is irrelevant in pricing options. Given that some of the Black–Scholes assumptions have been shown to be invalid, there is now a model risk. Figlewski and Green (1999) simulate option writers positions in the S&P500, DM/$, US LIBOR and T-Bond markets using actual cash data over a 25-year period. The most striking result from the simulations is that delta hedged short maturity options, with no transaction costs and a perfect knowledge of realized volatility, finished with losses on average in all four markets. This is clear evidence of Black–Scholes model risk. If option writers are aware of this model risk and mark up option prices accordingly, the Black–Scholes implied volatility will be greater than the true volatility.

---

[6] This wildcard option arises because the stock market closes later than the option market. The option trader is given the choice to decide, before the stock market closes, whether or not to trade on an option whose price is fixed at an earlier closing time.

In some situations, investor risk preference may override the risk-neutral valuation relationship. Figlewski (1997), for example, compares the purchase of an OTM option to buying a lottery ticket. Investors are willing to pay a price that is higher than the fair price because they like the potential payoff and the option premium is so low that mispricing becomes negligible. On the other hand, we also have fund managers who are willing to buy comparatively expensive put options for fear of the collapse of their portfolio value. Both types of behaviour could cause the market price of options to be higher than the Black–Scholes price, translating into a higher Black–Scholes implied volatility. Arbitrage arguments do not apply here because these are unique risk preferences (or aversions) associated with some groups of individuals. Franke, Stapleton and Subrahmanyam (1998) provide a theoretical framework in which such option trading behaviour may be analysed.

8.7   APPENDIX: IMPLEMENTING BARONE-ADESI AND WHALEY'S EFFICIENT ALGORITHM

The determination of S^* and S^{**} in Equations (8.25) and (8.27a) are not exactly straightforward. We have some success in solving S^* and S^{**} using NAG routing C05NCF. Barone-Adesi and Whaley (1987), however, have proposed an efficient method for determining S^*, details of which can be found in Barone-Adesi and Whaley (1987, hereafter referred to as BAW) pp. 309 to 310. BAW claimed that convergence of S^* and S^{**} can be achieved with three or fewer iterations.

American calls

The following are step-by-step procedures for implementing BAW's efficient method for estimating S^* of the American call.

Step 1. Make initial guess of σ and denote this initial guess as σ_j with $j = 1$.

Step 2. Make initial guess of S^*, S_i (with $i = 1$), as follow; denoting S^* at $T = +\infty$ as $S^*(\infty)$:

$$S_1 = X + \left[S^*(\infty) - K\right]\left[1 - e^{h_2}\right], \qquad (8.28)$$

where

$$S^*(\infty) = \frac{K}{1 - \dfrac{1}{q_2(\infty)}}, \qquad (8.29)$$

$$q_2(\infty) = \frac{1}{2}\left[1 - N + \sqrt{(N-1)^2 + 4M}\right], \qquad (8.30)$$

$$h_2 = -\left((r-q)t + 2\sigma\sqrt{t}\right)\left\{\frac{K}{S^*(\infty) - K}\right\}. \quad (8.31)$$

Note that the lower bound of S^* is K. So if $S_1 < K$, reset $S_1 = K$. However, the condition $S^* < K$ rarely occurs.

Step 3. Compute the l.h.s. and r.h.s. of Equation (8.25a) as follows:

$$\text{l.h.s.}(S_i) = S_i - X, \quad \text{and} \qquad (8.32)$$
$$\text{r.h.s.}(S_i) = c(S_i) + \{1 - e^{-qt}N[d_1(S_i)]\}S_i/q_2. \quad (8.33)$$

Compute starting value of $c(S_i)$ using the simple Black–Scholes Equation (8.25) and $d_1(S_i)$ using Equation (8.26). It will be useful to set up a function (or subroutine variable) for d_1.

Step 4. Check tolerance level,

$$|\text{l.h.s.}(S_i) - \text{r.h.s.}(S_i)|/K < 0.00001. \qquad (8.34)$$

Step 5. If Equation (8.34) is not satisfied; compute the slope of Equation (8.33), b_i, and the next guess of S^*, S_{i+1}, as follows:

$$b_i = e^{-qt}N[d_1(S_i)](1 - 1/q_2)$$
$$+[1 - e^{-qt}n\left[d_1(S_i)]/\sigma\sqrt{t}\right]/q_2, \qquad (8.35)$$
$$S_{i+1} = [X + \text{r.h.s.}(S_i) - b_i S_i]/(1 - b_i), \qquad (8.36)$$

where $n(.)$ is the univariate normal density function. Repeat from step 3.

Step 6. When Equation (8.34) is satisfied, compute $C(S)$ according to Equation (8.25). If $C(S)$ is greater than the observed American call price, try a smaller σ_{j+1}, otherwise try a larger σ_{j+1}. Repeat steps 1 to 5 until $C(S)$ is the same as the observed American call price. Step 6 could be handled by a NAG routine such as C05ADF for a quick solution.

American puts

To approximate S^{**} for American puts, steps 2, 3 and 5 have to be modified.

Step 1. Make initial guess of σ and denote this initial guess as σ_j with $j = 1$.

Step 2. Make initial guess of S^{**}, S_i (with $i = 1$), as follows, denoting S^{**} at $T = +\infty$ as $S^{**}(\infty)$:

$$S_1 = S^{**}(\infty) + \left[K - S^{**}(\infty)\right]e^{h_1}, \qquad (8.37)$$

where

$$S^{**}(\infty) = \frac{K}{1 - \dfrac{1}{q_1(\infty)}},$$

$$q_1(\infty) = \frac{1}{2}\left[1 - N - \sqrt{(N-1)^2 + 4M}\right],$$

$$h_1 = \left((r - q)t - 2\sigma\sqrt{t}\right)\left\{\frac{K}{K - S^{**}(\infty)}\right\}. \qquad (8.38)$$

Note that the upper bound of S^{**} is K. So if $S_1 > K$, reset $S_1 = K$. Again, the condition $S^{**} > X$ rarely occurs. According to Barone-Adesi and Whaley (1987, footnote 9), the influence of $(r - q)$ must be bounded in the put exponent to ensure critical prices monotonically decrease in t, for very large values of $(r - q)$ and t. A reasonable bound on $(r - q)$ is $0.6\sigma\sqrt{t}$, so the critical stock price declines with a minimum velocity $e^{-1.4\sigma\sqrt{t}}$. This check is required before computing h_1, in Equation (8.38).

Step 3. Compute the l.h.s. and r.h.s. of Equation (8.37) as follows:

$$\text{l.h.s.}(S_i) = K - S_i, \quad \text{and}$$
$$\text{r.h.s.}(S_i) = p(S_i) - \left\{1 - e^{-qt}N\left[-d_1(S_i)\right]\right\}S_i/q_1. \qquad (8.39)$$

Step 4. Check tolerance level, as before,

$$\left|\text{l.h.s.}(S_i) - \text{r.h.s.}(S_i)\right|/K < 0.00001. \qquad (8.40)$$

Step 5. If Equation (8.40) is not satisfied; compute the slope of Equation (8.39), b_i, and the next guess of S^{**}, S_{i+1}, as follows:

$$b_i = -e^{-qt}N\left[-d_1(S_i)\right](1 - 1/q_1)$$
$$\quad - \left[1 + e^{-qt}n\left[d_1(S_i)\right]/\sigma\sqrt{t}\right]/q_1,$$
$$S_{i+1} = \left[X - \text{r.h.s.}(S_i) + b_i S_i\right]/(1 + b_i).$$

Repeat from step 3 above.

Step 6. When Equation (8.40) is satisfied, compute $P(S)$ using Equation (8.27a). If $P(S)$ is greater than the observed American call price, try a larger σ_{j+1}, otherwise try a smaller σ_{j+1}. Then repeat steps 1 to 5 until $P(S)$ is the same as the observed American put price. Similarly the case for the American call, step 6 could be handled by a NAG routine such as C05ADF for a quick solution.

9
Option Pricing with Stochastic Volatility

If Black–Scholes (BS) is the correct option pricing model, then there can only be one BS implied volatility regardless of the strike price of the option, or whether the option is a call or a put. BS implied volatility smile and skew are clear evidence that market option prices are not priced according to the BS formula. This raises the important question about the relationship between BS implied volatility and the true volatility.

The BS option price is a positive function of the volatility of the underlying asset. If the BS model is correct, then market option price should be the same as the BS option price and the BS implied volatility derived from market option price will be the same as the true volatility. If the BS price is incorrect and is lower than the market price, then BS implied volatility overstates the true volatility. The reverse is true if the BS price is higher than the market price. The problem is complicated by the fact that BS implied volatility differs across strike prices. All the theories that predict the relationship between BS price and the market option price are all contingent on the proposed alternative option pricing model or the proposed alternative pricing dynamic being correct. Given that the BS implied volatility, despite all its shortcomings, has been proven overwhelmingly to be the best forecast of volatility, it will be useful to understand the links between BS implied volatility bias and the true volatility. This is the objective of this chapter.

There have been a lot of efforts made to solve the BS anomalies. The stochastic volatility (SV) option pricing model is one of the most important extensions of Black–Scholes. The SV option pricing model is motivated by the widespread evidence that volatility is stochastic and that the distribution of risky asset returns has tail(s) longer than that of a normal distribution. An SV model with correlated price and volatility innovations can address both anomalies. The SV option pricing model was developed roughly over a decade with contributions from Johnson and Shanno (1987), Wiggins (1987), Hull and White (1987, 1988), Scott (1987), Stein and Stein (1991) and Heston (1993). It was in Heston (1993) that a closed form solution was derived using the characteristic function of the price distribution. Section 9.1 presents this landmark Heston SV option pricing model while some details of the derivation are presented in the Appendix to this chapter (Section 9.5). In Section 9.2, we simulate a series of Heston option prices from a range of parameters. Then we use these option prices as if they were the market option prices to back out the corresponding BS implied volatilities. If market option prices are priced according to the Heston formula, the simulations in this section will give us some insight into the relationship between BS implied volatility bias and the true volatility. In Section 9.3, we analyse the usefulness and practicality of the Heston model by looking at the impact of Heston model parameters on skewness and kurtosis range and sensitivity, and some empirical tests of Heston model. Finally, Section 9.4 analyses empirical findings on the the predictive power of Heston implied volatility as a volatility forecast.

9.1   THE HESTON STOCHASTIC VOLATILITY OPTION PRICING MODEL

Heston (1993) specifies the stock price and volatility price processes as follows:

$$dS_t = \mu S dt + \sqrt{v_t} S dz_{s,t},$$
$$dv_t = \kappa \left[\theta - v_t\right] dt + \sigma_v \sqrt{v_t} dz_{v,t},$$

where v_t is the instantaneous variance, κ is the speed of mean reversion, θ is the long-run level of volatility and σ_v is the 'volatility of volatility'. The two Wiener processes, $dz_{s,t}$ and $dz_{v,t}$ have constant correlation ρ. The assumption that consumption growth has a constant correlation with spot-asset returns generates a risk premium proportional to v_t. Given the volatility risk premium, the risk-neutral volatility process can be written as

$$dv_t = \kappa \left[\theta - v_t\right] dt - \lambda v_t dt + \sigma_v \sqrt{v_t} dz_{v,t}^*$$
$$= \kappa^* \left[\theta^* - v_t\right] dt + \sigma_v \sqrt{v_t} dz_{v,t}^*,$$

where λ is the market price of (volatility) risk, and $\kappa^* = \kappa + \lambda$ and $\theta^* = \kappa\theta/(\kappa + \lambda)$. Here κ^* is the *risk-neutral* mean reverting parameter and θ^* is the *risk-neutral* long-run level of volatility. The parameter σ_v and ρ implicit in the risk-neutral process are the same as that in the real volatility process. Given the price and the volatility dynamics, the

Heston (1993) formula for pricing European calls is

$$c = SP_1 - Ke^{-r(T-t)}P_2,$$

$$P_j = \frac{1}{2} + \frac{1}{\pi} \int_0^\infty \text{Re} \left[\frac{e^{-i\phi \ln K} f_i}{i\phi} \right] d\phi, \quad \text{for } j = 1, 2$$

$$f_i = \exp\{C(T-t;\phi) + D(T-t;\phi)v + i\phi x\},$$

where

$$x = \ln S, \quad \tau = T - t,$$

$$C(\tau;\phi) = r\phi i\tau + \frac{a}{\sigma_v^2}\left\{(b_j - \rho\sigma_v\phi i + d)\tau - 2\ln\left[\frac{1 - ge^{d\tau}}{1 - g}\right]\right\},$$

$$D(\tau;\phi) = \frac{b_j - \rho\sigma_v\phi i + d}{\sigma_v^2}\left[\frac{1 - e^{d\tau}}{1 - ge^{d\tau}}\right],$$

$$g = \frac{b_j - \rho\sigma_v\phi i + d}{b_j - \rho\sigma_v\phi i - d},$$

$$d = \sqrt{(\rho\sigma_v\phi i - b_j)^2 - \sigma_v^2(2\mu\phi i - \phi^2)},$$

$$\mu_1 = 1/2, \ \mu_2 = -1/2, \ a = \kappa\theta = \kappa^*\theta^*,$$

$$b_1 = \kappa + \lambda - \rho\sigma_v = \kappa^* - \rho\sigma_v, \ b_2 = \kappa + \lambda = \kappa^*.$$

9.2   HESTON PRICE AND BLACK–SCHOLES IMPLIED

In this section, we analyse possible BS implied bias by simulating a series of Heston option prices with parameter values similar to those in Bakshi, Cao and Chen (1997), Nandi (1998), Das and Sundaram (1999), Bates (2000), Lin, Strong and Xu (2001), Fiorentini, Angel and Rubio (2002) and Andersen, Benzoni and Lund (2002). For the simulations, we set the asset price as 100, interest rate as zero, time to maturity is 1 year, and strike prices ranging from 50 to 150. In most simulations, and unless otherwise stated, the current 'instantaneous' volatility, σ_t, is set equal to the long-run level, θ, at 20%. There are five other parameters used in the Heston formula, namely, κ, the speed of mean reversion, θ, the long-run volatility level, λ, the market price of risk, σ_v, volatility of volatility, and ρ, the correlation between the price and the volatility processes. If we set $\lambda = 0$, then the volatility process becomes risk-neutral, and κ and θ become κ^* and θ^* respectively.

The first set of simulations presented in Figure 9.1(a) involves replicating the Black–Scholes prices as a special case. Here we set $\sigma_v = 0$.

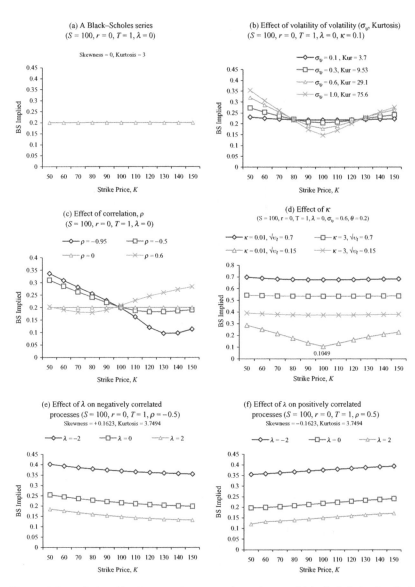

Figure 9.1 Relationships between Heston option prices and Black–Scholes implied volatility

Since there is no volatility risk, $\lambda = 0$. This is a special case where the Heston price and the Black–Scholes price are identical and the BS implied volatility is the same across strike prices. In this special case, BS implied volatility (at any strike price) is a perfect representation of true volatility.

In the second set of simulations presented in Figure 9.1(b), we alter σ_v, the volatility of volatility, and keep all the other parameters the same and constant. The effect of an increase in σ_v is to increase the unconditional volatility and kurtosis of *risk-neutral* price distribution. It is the risk-neutral distribution because λ, the market price of risk, is set equal to zero. As σ_v increases and without appropriate compensation for volatility risk premium, ATM (at-the-money) implied volatility underestimates true volatility while OTM (out-of-the-money) implied volatility overestimates it. This is the same outcome as Hull and White (1987) where the price and the volatility processes are not correlated and there is no risk premium for volatility risk. With appropriate adjustment for volatility (which will require a volatility risk premium input), the ATM implied volatility will be at the right level, but Black–Scholes will continue to underprice OTM options (and OTM BS implied overestimates true volatility) because of the BS lognormal thin tail assumptions. Assuming that $\rho = 0$ or at least is constant over time, and that σ_v and λ are relatively stable, a time series regression of historical 'actual volatility' on historical 'implied volatility' at a particular strike will be sufficient to correct for these biases. This is basically the Ederington and Guan (1999) approach. We will show in the next section that ρ is not likely to be stable. When ρ is not constant, the analysis below and Figure 9.1(c) show that ATM implied volatility is least affected by changing ρ. This explains why ATM implied volatility is the most robust and popular choice of volatility forecast.

In Figure 9.1(c), it is clear that changing the correlation coefficient alone has no impact on ATM implied volatility. Correlation has the greatest impact on skewness of the price distribution and determines the shape of volatility smile or skew. Its impact on kurtosis is less marked when compared with σ_v, the volatility of volatility.

Figure 9.1(d) highlights the impact of κ, the mean reversion parameter which we have already briefly touched on in relation to the long memory of volatility in Chapter 5. The higher the rate of mean reversion, the more likely the return distribution will be normal even when the volatility of volatility, σ_v, and the initial volatility, $\sqrt{v_t}$, are both high. When this is the case, there is no strike price bias in BS implied (i.e. there will not be volatility smile). When κ is low, this is when the problem starts. A low κ corresponds with volatility persistence where BS implied volatility will be sensitive to the current state of volatility level. At high volatility state, high $\sqrt{v_t}$ compensates for the low κ and the strike price bias is less severe. Strike price effect or the volatility smile is the most acute when initial volatility level $\sqrt{v_t}$ is low. ATM options will be overpriced vis-à-vis

OTM options.[1] (Note that we have set $\lambda = 0$ in this set of simulations.) When $\sigma_v = 0.6$, $\theta = 0.2$, $\sqrt{v_t} = 0.15$ and $\kappa = 0.01$, the ATM BS implied is only 0.1049 much lower than any of the volatility parameters.

Figure 9.1(e) and 9.1(f) can be used to infer the impacts of parameter estimates above when the volatility risk premium λ is omitted. In the literature, we often read '... volatility risk premium is negative reflecting the negative correlation between the price and the volatility dynamics ...' (Buraschi and Jackwerth, 2001; Bakshi and Kapadia, 2003. All series in Figure 9.1(e) have correlation $\rho = -0.5$ and all series in Figure 9.1(f) have correlation $\rho = +0.5$. A negative λ (volatility risk premium) produces higher Heston price and higher BS implied volatility. The impact is the same whether the correlation ρ is negative or positive. We will see later in the next section that empirical evidence indicates that Figure 9.1(f) is just as likely a scenario as Figure 9.1(e). As $\kappa^* = \kappa + \lambda$ and $\theta^* = \kappa\theta/(\kappa + \lambda)$, a negative λ has the effect of reducing κ^* (resulting in a smaller option price) and increasing θ^* (resulting in a bigger option price). Simulations, not reported here, show that the price impact of θ^* is much greater than that of κ^*, so the outcome will be a higher option price due to the negative λ. Hence, a 'negative risk premium' is to be expected whether the price and the volatility processes are positively or negatively correlated.[2] This also means that, without accounting for the volatility risk premium, the BS option price will be too low and the BS implied will always overstate true volatility. Both volatility and volatility risk premium have positive impact on option price. The omission of volatility risk premium will cause the volatility risk premium component to be 'translated' into higher BS implied volatility.

9.3 MODEL ASSESSMENT

In this section, we evaluate the Heston model using simulations. In particular, we examine the skewness and kurtosis planes covered by a range of Heston parameter values. We have no information on the volatility risk premium. Hence, to avoid an additional dimension of complexity, we will evaluate the risk-neutral parameters κ^* and θ^* instead of κ and θ for the true volatility process.

---

[1] When BS overprice options, the BS implied volatility will understate volatility because BS implied is inverted from market price, which is lower than the BS price.

[2] This is really a misnomer: while the λ parameter is negative, it actually results in a higher option price. So strictly speaking the volatility risk premium is positive!

9.3.1   Zero correlation

We learn from the simulations in Section 9.2 and from Figure 9.1 that, according to the Heston model, skewness in stock returns distribution and BS implied volatility asymmetry are determined completely by the correlation parameter, ρ. When the correlation parameter is equal to zero, we get zero skewness and both the returns distribution and BS implied volatility will be symmetrical. Figure 9.2 presents the kurtosis values produced by different combinations of κ, θ and σ_v. One important pattern emerged that highlights the importance of the mean reversion parameter, κ. When κ is low we have high volatility persistence, and *vice versa* for high value of κ.

At high value of κ, kurtosis is close to 3, regardless of the value of θ and σ_v. This is, unfortunately, the less likely scenario for a financial market time series that typically has high volatility persistence and low value of κ. At low value of κ, the kurtosis is the highest at low level of σ_v, the parameter for volatility of volatility. At high level of σ_v, kurtosis drops to 3 very consistently, regardless of the value of the other parameters. At low level of σ_v, the long-term level of volatility, θ, comes into effect. The higher the value of θ, the lower the kurtosis value, even though it is still much greater than 3.

When skewness is zero and kurtosis is low (i.e. relatively flat BS implied volatility), it will be difficult to differentiate whether it is due to a high κ, a high σ_v or both. This also reflects the underlying property that a high κ, a high σ_v or both make the stochastic volatility structure less important and the BS model will be adequate in this case.

9.3.2   Nonzero correlation

In Figures 9.3 and 9.4, we illustrate skewness and kurtosis, respectively, for the case when the correlation coefficient, ρ, is greater than 0. The case for $\rho < 0$ will not be discussed here as it is the reflective image of $\rho > 0$ (e.g. instead of positive skewness, we get negative skewness etc.).

Figure 9.3 shows that skewness is first 'triggered' by a nonzero correlation coefficient, after which κ and σ_v combine to drive skewness. High skewness occurs when σ_v is high and κ is low (i.e. high volatility persistence). At relatively low skewness level, there is a huge range of high κ, low σ_v or both that produce similar values of skewness. A low θ

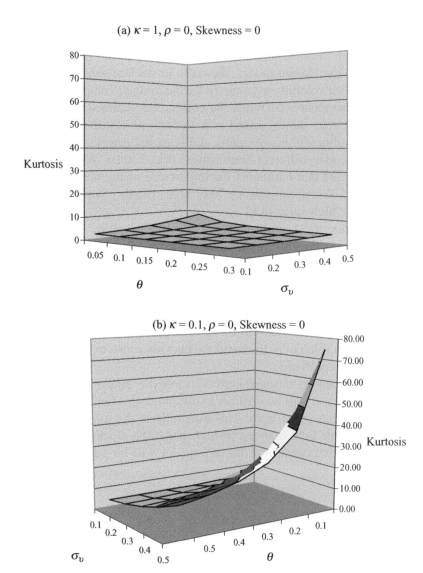

Figure 9.2 Impact of Heston parameters on kurtosis for symmetrical distribution with zero correlation and zero skewness

and high ρ produces high skewness, but at low level of σ_v, skewness is much less sensitive to these two parameters.

Figure 9.4 gives a similar pattern for kurtosis. Except when σ_v is very high and κ is low, the plane for kurtosis is very flat and not sensitive to θ or ρ.

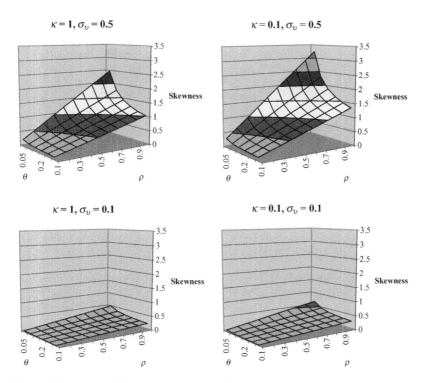

Figure 9.3   Impact of Heston parameters on skewness

9.4   VOLATILITY FORECAST USING THE HESTON MODEL

The thick tail and nonsymmetrical distribution found empirically could be a result of volatility being stochastic. The simulation results in the previous section suggest that σ_v, the volatility of volatility, is the main driving force for kurtosis and skewness (if correlation is not equal to zero). At high κ, volatility mean reversion will cancel out much of the σ_v impact on kurtosis and some of that on skewness. Correlation between the price and the volatility processes, ρ, determines the sign of the skewness. But beyond that its impact on the magnitude of skewness is much less compared with σ_v and κ. Correlation has negligible impact on kurtosis. The long-run volatility level, θ, has very little impact on skewness and kurtosis, except when σ_v is very high and κ is very low. So a stochastic volatility pricing model is useful and will outperform Black–Scholes only when volatility is truly stochastic (i.e. high σ_v) and volatility is persistent (i.e. low κ). The difficulty with the Heston model is that, once

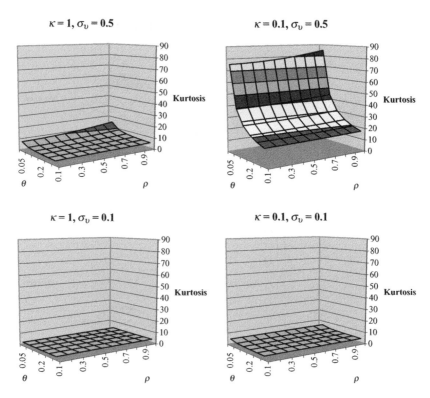

Figure 9.4   Impact of Heston parameters on kurtosis

we move away from the high σ_v and low κ region, a large combination of parameter values can produce similar skewness and kurtosis. This contributes to model parameter instability and convergence difficulty during estimation.

Through simulation results we can predict the degree of Black–Scholes pricing bias as a result of stochastic volatility. In the case where volatility is stochastic and $\rho = 0$, Black–Scholes overprices near-the-money (NTM) or at-the-money (ATM) options and the degree of over-pricing increases with maturity. On the other hand, Black–Scholes underprices both in- and out-of-the-money options. In term of implied volatility, ATM implied volatility will be lower than actual volatility while implied volatility of far-from-the-money options (i.e. either very high or very low strikes) will be higher than actual volatility. The pattern of pricing bias will be much harder to predict if ρ is not zero, when there is a premium for bearing volatility risk, and if either or both values vary through time.

Some of the early work on option implied volatility focuses on finding an optimal weighting scheme to aggregate implied volatility of options across strikes. (See Bates (1996) for a comprehensive survey of these weighting schemes.) Since the plot of implied volatility against strikes can take many shapes, it is not likely that a single weighting scheme will remove all pricing errors consistently. For this reason and together with the liquidity argument, ATM option implied volatility is often used for volatility forecast but not implied volatilities at other strikes.

9.5   APPENDIX: THE MARKET PRICE OF VOLATILITY RISK

9.5.1   Ito's lemma for two stochastic variables

Given two stochastic processes,[3]

$$dS_1 = \mu_1 (S_1, S_2, t) \, dt + \sigma_1 (S_1, S_2, t) \, dX_1,$$
$$dS_2 = \mu_2 (S_1, S_2, t) \, dt + \sigma_2 (S_1, S_2, t) \, dX_2,$$
$$E\{dX_1 dX_2\} = \rho dt,$$

where X_1 and X_2 are two related Brownian motions.

From Ito's lemma, the derivative function $V(S_1, S_2, t)$ will have the following process:

$$dV = \left\{ V_t + \frac{1}{2}\sigma_1^2 V_{S_1 S_1} + \rho\sigma_1\sigma_2 V_{S_1 S_2} + \frac{1}{2}\sigma_2^2 V_{S_2 S_2} \right\} dt$$
$$+ V_{S_1} dS_1 + V_{S_2} dS_2,$$

where

$$V_t = \frac{\partial V}{\partial t}, \quad V_{S_1 S_1} = \frac{\partial^2 V}{\partial S_1^2} \quad \text{and} \quad V_{S_1 S_2} = \frac{\partial}{\partial S_1}\left(\frac{\partial V}{\partial S_2}\right).$$

9.5.2   The case of stochastic volatility

Here, we assume S_1 is the underlying asset and S_2 is the stochastic volatility σ_1 as follows:

$$dS_1 = \mu_1 (S_1, \sigma, t) \, dt + \sigma_1 (S_1, \sigma, t) \, dX_1, \qquad (9.1)$$
$$d\sigma_1 = p (S_1, \sigma, t) \, dt + q (S_1, \sigma, t) \, dX_2,$$
$$E\{dX_1 dX_2\} = \rho dt,$$

---

[3] I am grateful to Konstantinos Vonatsos for helping me with materials presented in this section.

and from Ito's lemma, we get:

$$dV = \left\{ V_t + \frac{1}{2}\sigma_1^2 V_{S_1 S_1} + pq\sigma_1 V_{S_1\sigma} + \frac{1}{2}q^2 V_{S_2\sigma} \right\} dt \qquad (9.2)$$
$$+ V_{S_1} dS_1 + V_\sigma d\sigma.$$

In the following stochastic volatility derivation, $\mu_1 = \mu S_t$ is the mean drift of the stock price process. The volatility of S_1, $\sigma_1 = f(\sigma) S_1$ is stochastic and is level-dependent. The mean drift of the volatility process is more complex as volatility cannot become negative and should be stationary in the long run. Hence an OU (Ornstein–Uhlenbeck) process is usually recommended with $p(S_1, \sigma, t) = \alpha(m - \sigma)$ and $q(S_1, \sigma, t) = \beta$:

$$d\sigma_1 = \alpha(m - \sigma_1) dt + \beta dX_2.$$

Here, $p = \alpha(m - \sigma)$ is the mean drift of the volatility process, m is the long-term mean level of the volatility, and α is the speed at which volatility reverts to m, and β is the *volatility of volatility*.

9.5.3   Constructing the risk-free strategy

To value an option $V(S_1, \sigma, t)$ we must form a risk-free portfolio using the underlying asset to hedge the movement in S_1 and use another option $\overline{V}(S_1, \sigma, t)$ to hedge the movement in σ. Let the risk-free portfolio be:

$$\Pi = V - \Delta_1 \overline{V} - \Delta S_1.$$

Applying Ito's lemma from (9.2) on the risk-free portfolio Π,

$$d\Pi = \left\{ V_t + \frac{1}{2}\sigma_1^2 V_{S_1 S_1} + \frac{1}{2}q^2 V_{\sigma\sigma} + pq\sigma_1 V_{S_1\sigma} \right\} dt$$
$$- \Delta_1 \left\{ \overline{V}_t + \frac{1}{2}\sigma_1^2 \overline{V}_{S_1 S_1} + \frac{1}{2}q^2 \overline{V}_{\sigma\sigma} + pq\sigma_1 \overline{V}_{S_1\sigma} \right\} dt$$
$$+ \left\{ V_{S_1} - \Delta_1 \overline{V}_{S_1} - \Delta \right\} dS_1$$
$$+ \left\{ V_\sigma - \Delta_1 \overline{V}_\sigma \right\} d\sigma.$$

To eliminate $d\sigma$, set

$$V_\sigma - \Delta_1 \overline{V}_\sigma = 0,$$
$$\Delta_1 = \frac{V_\sigma}{\overline{V}_\sigma},$$

and, to eliminate dS_1, set

$$V_{S_1} - \frac{V_\sigma}{\overline{V}_\sigma}\overline{V}_{S_1} - \Delta = 0,$$

$$\Delta = V_{S_1} - \frac{V_\sigma}{\overline{V}_\sigma}\overline{V}_{S_1}.$$

This results in:

$$d\Pi = \left\{ V_t + \frac{1}{2}\sigma_1^2 V_{S_1 S_1} + \frac{1}{2}q^2 V_{\sigma\sigma} + \rho q\sigma_1 V_{S_1\sigma} \right\} dt$$

$$- \frac{V_\sigma}{\overline{V}_\sigma}\left\{ \overline{V}_t + \frac{1}{2}\sigma_1^2 \overline{V}_{S_1 S_1} + \frac{1}{2}q^2 \overline{V}_{\sigma\sigma} + \rho q\sigma_1 \overline{V}_{S_1\sigma} \right\} dt$$

$$= r\Pi dt$$

$$= r\left\{ V - \frac{V_\sigma}{\overline{V}_\sigma}\overline{V} - \left[V_{S_1} - \frac{V_\sigma}{\overline{V}_\sigma}\overline{V}_{S_1} \right] S_1 \right\} dt.$$

Dividing both sides by V_σ, we get:

$$\frac{1}{V_\sigma}\left\{ V_t + \frac{1}{2}\sigma_1^2 V_{S_1 S_1} + \frac{1}{2}q^2 V_{\sigma\sigma} + \rho q\sigma_1 V_{S_1\sigma} \right\}$$

$$- \frac{1}{\overline{V}_\sigma}\left\{ \overline{V}_t + \frac{1}{2}\sigma_1^2 \overline{V}_{S_1 S_1} + \frac{1}{2}q^2 \overline{V}_{\sigma\sigma} + \rho q\sigma_1 \overline{V}_{S_1\sigma} \right\}$$

$$= r\frac{V}{V_\sigma} - r\frac{\overline{V}}{\overline{V}_\sigma} - r\frac{V_{S_1}S_1}{V_\sigma} + r\frac{\overline{V}_{S_1}S_1}{\overline{V}_\sigma}.$$

Now we separate the two options by moving $\overline{V}$ to one side and V to the other:

$$\frac{1}{V_\sigma}\left\{ V_t + \frac{1}{2}\sigma_1^2 V_{S_1 S_1} + \frac{1}{2}q^2 V_{\sigma\sigma} + \rho q\sigma_1 V_{S_1\sigma} - rV + rV_{S_1}S_1 \right\}$$

$$= \frac{1}{\overline{V}_\sigma}\left\{ \overline{V}_t + \frac{1}{2}\sigma_1^2 \overline{V}_{S_1 S_1} + \frac{1}{2}q^2 \overline{V}_{\sigma\sigma} + \rho q\sigma_1 \overline{V}_{S_1\sigma} - r\overline{V} + r\overline{V}_{S_1}S_1 \right\}.$$

Each side of the equation is a function of S_1, σ and t, and is independent of the other option. So we may write:

$$\frac{1}{V_\sigma}\left\{ V_t + \frac{1}{2}\sigma_1^2 V_{S_1 S_1} + \frac{1}{2}q^2 V_{\sigma\sigma} + \rho q\sigma_1 V_{S_1\sigma} - rV + rV_{S_1}S_1 \right\}$$

$$= f(S_1, \sigma, t),$$

$$V_t + \frac{1}{2}\sigma_1^2 V_{S_1 S_1} + \frac{1}{2}q^2 V_{\sigma\sigma} + \rho q\sigma_1 V_{S_1\sigma} - rV + rV_{S_1}S_1$$

$$= f(S_1, \sigma, t) V_\sigma, \qquad (9.3)$$

and similarly for the RHS. In order to solve the PDE, we need to understand the function $f(S_1, \sigma, t)$ which depends on whether or not dS_1 and $d\sigma$ are correlated.

9.5.4 Correlated processes

If two Brownian motions dX_1 and dX_2 are correlated with correlation coefficient ρ, then we may write:

$$dX_2 = \rho dX_1 + \sqrt{1 - \rho^2}d\epsilon_t,$$

where $d\epsilon_t$ is the part of dX_2 that is not related to dX_1.

Now consider the hedged portfolio,

$$\Pi = V - \Delta S_1, \tag{9.4}$$

where only the risk that is due to the underlying asset and its correlated volatility risk are hedged. Volatility risk orthogonal to dS_1 is not hedged. From Ito's lemma, we get:

$$
\begin{aligned}
d\Pi &= dV - \Delta dS_1 \\
&= \left\{ V_t + \frac{1}{2}\sigma_1^2 V_{S_1 S_1} + \rho q \sigma_1 V_{S_1 \sigma} + \frac{1}{2}q^2 V_{\sigma\sigma} \right\} dt \\
&\quad + V_{S_1} dS_1 + V_\sigma d\sigma - \Delta dS_1.
\end{aligned} \tag{9.5}
$$

Now write:

$$
\begin{aligned}
dS_1 &= \mu_1 dt + \sigma_1 dX_1, \quad \text{and} \\
d\sigma &= p dt + q dX_2 \\
&= p dt + q \left[\rho dX_1 + \sqrt{1 - \rho^2}d\epsilon_t \right].
\end{aligned}
$$

Substitute this result into (9.5) and get:

$$
\begin{aligned}
d\Pi &= \left\{ V_t + \frac{1}{2}\sigma_1^2 V_{S_1 S_1} + \rho q \sigma_1 V_{S_1 \sigma} + \frac{1}{2}q^2 V_{\sigma\sigma} \right\} dt \\
&\quad + V_{S_1}\{\mu_1 dt + \sigma_1 dX_1\} + V_\sigma \left\{ p dt + q \left[\rho dX_1 + \sqrt{1 - \rho^2}d\epsilon_t \right] \right\} \\
&\quad - \Delta\{\mu_1 dt + \sigma_1 dX_1\} \\
&= \left\{ V_t + \frac{1}{2}\sigma_1^2 V_{S_1 S_1} + \rho q \sigma_1 V_{S_1 \sigma} + \frac{1}{2}q^2 V_{\sigma\sigma} \right\} dt \\
&\quad + \left(V_{S_1}\mu_1 + V_\sigma p - \Delta\mu_1 \right) dt + \left(V_{S_1}\sigma_1 + V_\sigma q \rho - \Delta\sigma_1 \right) dX_1 \\
&\quad + V_\sigma q \sqrt{1 - \rho^2}d\epsilon_t.
\end{aligned} \tag{9.6}
$$

So to get rid of dX_1, the hedge ratio should be:

$$V_{S_1}\sigma_1 + V_\sigma q\rho - \Delta\sigma_1 = 0,$$

$$\Delta = V_{S_1} + \frac{V_\sigma q\rho}{\sigma_1}.$$

With this hedge ratio, only the uncorrelated volatility risk, $V_\sigma q\sqrt{1 - \rho^2}d\epsilon_t$, is left in the portfolio. If $\rho = 1$, the portfolio Π would be risk-free.

Now substitute value of Δ into (9.6). We get:

$$\begin{aligned}
d\Pi &= \left\{ V_t + \frac{1}{2}\sigma_1^2 V_{S_1 S_1} + \rho q\sigma_1 V_{S_1\sigma} + \frac{1}{2}q^2 V_{\sigma\sigma} \right\} dt \\
&\quad + \left(V_{S_1}\mu_1 + V_\sigma p - V_{S_1}\mu_1 - \frac{V_\sigma q\rho\mu_1}{\sigma_1} \right) dt + V_\sigma q\sqrt{1 - \rho^2}d\epsilon_t \\
&= \left\{ V_t + \frac{1}{2}\sigma_1^2 V_{S_1 S_1} + \rho q\sigma_1 V_{S_1\sigma} + \frac{1}{2}q^2 V_{\sigma\sigma} \right\} dt \\
&\quad + \left(V_\sigma p - \frac{V_\sigma q\rho\mu_1}{\sigma_1} \right) dt + V_\sigma q\sqrt{1 - \rho^2}d\epsilon_t.
\end{aligned} \tag{9.7}$$

9.5.5 The market price of risk

Next we made the assumption that the partially hedged portfolio Π in (9.4) will earn a risk-free return plus a premium for unhedged volatility risk, Ω, such that

$$\begin{aligned}
d\Pi &= r\Pi dt + \Omega \\
&= r(V - \Delta S_1)dt + \Omega \\
&= r\left(V - V_{S_1}S_1 - \frac{V_\sigma q\rho}{\sigma_1}S_1 \right) dt + \Omega.
\end{aligned} \tag{9.8}$$

Substituting $d\Pi$ from (9.7), we get:

$$\begin{aligned}
&\left\{ V_t + \frac{1}{2}\sigma_1^2 V_{S_1 S_1} + \rho q\sigma_1 V_{S_1\sigma} + \frac{1}{2}q^2 V_{\sigma\sigma} \right\} dt \\
&\quad + \left(V_\sigma p - \frac{V_\sigma q\rho\mu_1}{\sigma_1} \right) dt + V_\sigma q\sqrt{1 - \rho^2}d\epsilon_t \\
&= rV dt - r V_{S_1}S_1 dt - r\frac{V_\sigma q\rho}{\sigma_1}S_1 dt + \Omega,
\end{aligned}$$

$$\Omega = \left\{ V_t + \frac{1}{2}\sigma_1^2 V_{S_1 S_1} + \rho q \sigma_1 V_{S_1 \sigma} + \frac{1}{2}q^2 V_{\sigma\sigma} - rV + rV_{S_1} S_1 \right\} dt$$
$$+ \left[V_\sigma p + \frac{V_\sigma q \rho}{\sigma_1}(rS_1 - \mu_1) \right] dt + V_\sigma q \sqrt{1 - \rho^2} d\epsilon_t.$$

Now replace the {} term with $f(S_1, \sigma, t)$ in (9.3) we get:

$$\Omega = \left(fV_\sigma + V_\sigma p + \frac{V_\sigma q \rho}{\sigma_1}(rS_1 - \mu_1) \right) dt + V_\sigma q \sqrt{1 - \rho^2} d\epsilon_t$$
$$= V_\sigma q \sqrt{1 - \rho^2} \left\{ \left[\frac{f + p + \frac{q\rho}{\sigma_1}(rS_1 - \mu_1)}{q\sqrt{1 - \rho^2}} \right] dt + d\epsilon_t \right\}.$$

Now define 'market price of risk' $\tilde{\gamma}$:

$$\tilde{\gamma} = \frac{f + p + \frac{q\rho}{\sigma_1}(rS_1 - \mu_1)}{q\sqrt{1 - \rho^2}}, \tag{9.9}$$

where $\tilde{\gamma}$ is the 'returns' associated with each unit of risk that is due to $d\epsilon_t$ (i.e. the unhedged volatility risk), hence, the denominator $q\sqrt{1 - \rho^2}$.
From (9.9), we can get an expression for f:

$$f = -p + \frac{q\rho}{\sigma_1}(\mu_1 - rS_1) + \tilde{\gamma}q\sqrt{1 - \rho^2}.$$

Substituting $p = \alpha(m - \sigma)$, $q = \beta$, $\mu_1 = \mu S_1$, and $\sigma_1 = f(\sigma)S_1$:

$$f = -\alpha(m - \sigma) + \frac{\beta\rho}{f(\sigma)S_1}(\mu S_1 - rS_1) + \tilde{\gamma}\beta\sqrt{1 - \rho^2}.$$
$$= -\alpha(m - \sigma) + \frac{\beta\rho(\mu - r)}{f(\sigma)} + \tilde{\gamma}\beta\sqrt{1 - \rho^2}.$$

We can now price the option with stochastic volatility in (9.3) using the expression for f above and get:

$$0 = V_t + \frac{1}{2}f^2 S_t^2 V_{S_1 S_1} + \frac{1}{2}\beta^2 V_{\sigma\sigma} + \rho\beta f S_t V_{S_1 \sigma} - rV + rV_{S_1} S_1$$
$$+ \left[\alpha(m - \sigma) - \beta \left(\frac{\rho(\mu - r)}{f(\sigma)} + \tilde{\gamma}\sqrt{1 - \rho^2} \right) \right] V_\sigma \tag{9.10}$$

Now write

$$\Lambda(S_1, \sigma, t) = \frac{\rho(\mu - r)}{f(\sigma)} + \tilde{\gamma}\sqrt{1 - \rho^2}.$$

We write (9.10) as

$$\underbrace{V_t + \frac{1}{2}f^2 S_1^2 V_{S_1 S_1} + r\left(V_{S_1} S_1 - V\right)}_{\text{Black–Scholes}} + \underbrace{\rho\beta f S_1 V_{S_1 \sigma}}_{\text{correlation}}$$

$$\underbrace{+\frac{1}{2}\beta^2 V_{\sigma\sigma} + \alpha\left(m - \sigma\right) V_\sigma}_{L_{\text{ou}}} - \underbrace{\beta\Lambda V_\sigma}_{\text{premium}} = 0 \quad (9.11)$$

or, on rearrangement,[4]

$$\underbrace{V_t + \frac{1}{2}f^2 S_1^2 V_{S_1 S_1} + r V_{S_1} S_1}_{\text{Black–Scholes}} + \underbrace{\rho\beta f S_1 V_{S_1 \sigma}}_{\text{correlation}} + \underbrace{\frac{1}{2}\beta^2 V_{\sigma\sigma} + \alpha\left(m - \sigma\right) V_\sigma}_{L_{\text{ou}}}$$

$$= \underbrace{rV}_{\text{risk-free return as in BS}} + \underbrace{\beta\Lambda V_\sigma}_{\text{premium for volatility risk}}$$

This analysis show that when volatility is stochastic in the form in (9.1), the option price will be higher. The additional risk premium is related to the correlation between volatility and the stock price processes and the mean-reverting dynamic of the volatility process.

---

[4] This result is shown in Fouque, Papanicolaou and Sircar (2000).

10
Option Forecasting Power

Option implied volatility has always been perceived as a market's expectation of future volatility and hence it is a market-based volatility forecast. It makes use of a richer and more up-to-date information set, and arguably it should be superior to time series volatility forecast. On the other hand, we showed in the previous two chapters that option model-based forecast requires a number of assumptions to hold for the option theory to produce a useful volatility estimate. Moreover, option implied also suffers from many market-driven pricing irregularities. Nevertheless, the volatility forecasting contests show overwhelmingly that option implied volatility has superior forecasting capability, outperforming many historical price volatility models and matching the performance of forecasts generated from time series models that use a large amount of high-frequency data.

10.1 USING OPTION IMPLIED STANDARD DEVIATION TO FORECAST VOLATILITY

Once an implied volatility estimate is obtained, it is usually scaled by $\sqrt{n}$ to get an n-day-ahead volatility forecast. In some cases, a regression model may be used to adjust for historical bias (e.g. Ederington and Guan, 2000b), or the implied volatility may be parameterized within a GARCH/ARFIMA model with or without its own persistence adjustment (e.g. Day and Lewis, 1992; Blair, Poon and Taylor, 2001; Hwang and Satchell, 1998).

Implied volatility, especially that of stock options, can be quite unstable across time. Beckers (1981) finds taking a 5-day average improves the forecasting power of stock option implied. Hamid (1998) finds such an intertemporal averaging is also useful for stock index option during very turbulent periods. On a slightly different note, Xu and Taylor (1995) find implied estimated from a sophisticated volatility term structure model produces similar forecasting performance as implied from the shortest maturity option.

In contrast to time series volatility forecasting models, the use of implied volatility as a volatility forecast involves some extra complexities. A test on the forecasting power of option implied standard deviation (ISD) is a joint test of option market efficiency and a correct option pricing model. Since trading frictions differ across assets, some options are easier to replicate and hedge than the others. It is therefore reasonable to expect different levels of efficiency and different forecasting power for options written on different assets.

While each historical price constitutes an observation in the sample used in calculating volatility forecast, each option price constitutes a volatility forecast over the option maturity, and there can be many option prices at any one time. The problem of volatility smile and volatility skew means that options of different strike prices produce different Black–Scholes implied volatility estimates.

The issue of a correct option pricing model is more fundamental in finance. Option pricing has a long history and various extensions have been made since Black–Scholes to cope with dividend payments, early exercise and stochastic volatility. However, none of the option pricing models (except Heston (1993)) that appeared in the volatility forecasting literature allows for a premium for bearing volatility risk. In the presence of a volatility risk premium, we expect the option price to be higher which means implied volatility derived using an option pricing model that assumes zero volatility risk premium (such as the Black–Scholes model) will also be higher, and hence automatically be more biased as a volatility forecast. Section 10.3 examines the issue of biasedness of ISD forecasts and evaluates the extent to which implied biasedness is due to the omission of volatility risk premium.

10.2   AT-THE-MONEY OR WEIGHTED IMPLIED?

Since options of different strikes have been known to produce different implied volatilities, a decision has to be made as to which of these implied volatilities should be used, or which weighting scheme should be adopted, that will produce a forecast that is most superior. The most common strategy is to choose the implied derived from an ATM option based on the argument that an ATM option is the most liquid and hence ATM implied is least prone to measurement errors. The analysis in Chapter 9 shows that, omitting volatility risk premium, ATM implied is also least likely to be biased.

If ATM implied is not available, then an NTM (nearest-to-the-money) option is used instead. Sometimes, to reduce measurement errors and the effect of bid–ask bounce, an average is taken from a group of NTM implied volatilities. Weighting schemes that also give greater weight to ATM implied are vega (i.e. the partial derivative of option price w.r.t. volatility) weighted or trading volume weighted, weighted least squares (WLS) and some multiplicative versions of these three. The WLS method, first appeared in Whaley (1982), aims to minimize the sum of squared errors between the market and the theoretical prices of a group of options. Since the ATM option has the highest trading volume and the ATM option price is the most sensitive to volatility input, all three weighting schemes (and the combinations thereof) have the effect of placing the greatest weight on ATM implied. Other less popular weighting schemes include equally weighted, and weight based on the elasticity of option price to volatility.

The forecasting power of individual and composite implied volatilities has been tested in Ederington and Guan (2000b), Fung, Lie and Moreno (1990), Gemmill (1986), Kroner, Kneafsey and Claessens (1995), Scott and Tucker (1989) and Vasilellis and Meade (1996). The general consensus is that among the weighted implied volatilities, those that favour the ATM option such as the WLS and the vega weighted implied are better. The worst performing ones are equally weighted and elasticity weighted implied using options across all strikes. Different findings emerged as to whether an individual implied volatility forecasts better than a composite implied. Beckers (1981) Feinstein (1989b), Fung, Lie and Moreno (1990) and Gemmill (1986) find evidence to support individual implied although they all prefer a different implied (viz. ATM, Just-OTM, OTM and ITM respectively for the four studies). Kroner, Kneafsey and Claessens find composite implied volatility forecasts better than ATM implied. On the other hand, Scott and Tucker (1989) conclude that when emphasis is placed on ATM implied, which weighting scheme one chooses does not really matter.

A series of studies by Ederington and Guan have reported some interesting findings. Ederington and Guan (1999) report that the information content of implied volatility of S&P500 futures options exhibits a frown shape across strikes with options that are NTM and have moderately high strike (i.e. OTM calls and ITM puts) possess the largest information content with R^2 equal to 17% for calls and 36% for puts.

10.3   IMPLIED BIASEDNESS

Usually, forecast unbiasedness is not an overriding issue in any forecasting exercise. Forecast bias can be estimated and corrected if the degree of bias remains stable through time. Testing for biasedness is usually carried out using the regression equation (2.3), where $\widehat{X}_i = \widehat{X}_t$ is the implied forecast of period t volatility. For a forecast to be unbiased, one would require $\alpha = 0$ and $\beta = 1$. Implied forecast is upwardly biased if $\alpha > 0$ and $\beta = 1$, or $\alpha = 0$ and $\beta > 1$. In the case where $\alpha > 0$ and $\beta < 1$, which is the most common scenario, implied underforecasts low volatility and overforecasts high volatility.

It has been argued that implied bias will persist only if it is difficult to perform arbitrage trades that are needed to remove the mispricing. This is more likely in the case of stock index options and less likely for futures options. Stocks and stock options are traded in different markets. Since trading of a basket of stocks is cumbersome, arbitrage trades in relation to a mispriced stock index option may have to be done indirectly via index futures. On the other hand, futures and futures options are traded alongside each other. Trading in these two contracts are highly liquid. Despite these differences in trading friction, implied biasedness is reported in both the S&P100 OEX market (Canina and Figlewski, 1993; Christensen and Prabhala, 1998; Fleming, Ostdiek and Whaley, 1995; Fleming, 1998) and the S&P500 futures options market (Feinstein, 1989b; Ederington and Guan, 1999, 2002).

Biasedness is equally widespread among implied volatilities of currency options (see Guo, 1996b; Jorion, 1995; Li, 2002; Scott and Tucker, 1989; Wei and Frankel, 1991). The only exception is Jorion (1996) who cannot reject the null hypothesis that the one-day-ahead forecasts from implied are unbiased. The five studies listed earlier use implied to forecast exchange rate volatility over a much longer horizon ranging from one to nine months.

Unbiasedness of implied forecast was not rejected in the Swedish market (Frennberg and Hansson, 1996). Unbiasedness of implied forecast was rejected for UK stock options (Gemmill, 1986), US stock options (Lamoureux and Lastrapes, 1993), options and futures options across a range of assets in Australia (Edey and Elliot, 1992) and for 35 futures options contracts traded over nine markets ranging from interest rate to livestock futures (Szakmary, Ors, Kim and Davidson, 2002). On the other hand, Amin and Ng (1997) find the hypothesis that $\alpha = 0$ and $\beta = 1$ cannot be rejected for the Eurodollar futures options market.

Where unbiasedness was rejected, the bias in all but two cases was due to $\alpha > 0$ and $\beta < 1$. These two exceptions are Fleming (1998) who reports $\alpha = 0$ and $\beta < 1$ for S&P100 OEX options, and Day and Lewis (1993) who find $\alpha > 0$ and $\beta = 1$ for distant-term oil futures options contracts.

Christensen and Prabhala (1998) argue that implied is biased because of error-in-variable caused by measurement errors. Using last period implied and last period historical volatility as instrumental variables to correct for these measurement errors, Christensen and Prabhala (1998) find unbiasedness cannot be rejected for implied volatility of the S&P100 OEX option. Ederington and Guan (1999, 2002) find bias in S&P500 futures options implied also disappeared when similar instrument variables were used.

10.4   VOLATILITY RISK PREMIUM

It has been suggested that implied biasedness could not have been caused by model misspecification or measurement errors because this has relatively small effects for ATM options, used in most of the studies that report implied biasedness. In addition, the clientele effect cannot explain the bias either because it only affects OTM options. The volatility risk premium analysed in Chapter 9 is now often cited as an explanation.

Poteshman (2000) finds half of the bias in S&P500 futures options implied was removed when actual volatility was estimated with a more efficient volatility estimator based on intraday 5-minute returns. The other half of the bias was almost completely removed when a more sophisticated and less restrictive option pricing model, i.e. the Heston (1993) model, was used. Further research on option volatility risk premium is currently under way in Benzoni (2001) and Chernov (2001). Chernov (2001) finds, similarly to Poteshman (2000), that when implied volatility is discounted by a volatility risk premium and when the errors-in-variables problems in historical and realized volatility are removed, the unbiasedness of the S&P100 index option implied volatility cannot be rejected over the sample period from 1986 to 2000. The volatility risk premium debate continues if we are able to predict the magnitude and the variations of the volatility premium and if implied from an option pricing model that permits a nonzero market price of risk will outperform time series models when all forecasts (including forecasts of volatility risk premium) are made in an *ex ante* manner.

Ederington and Guan (2000b) find that using regression coefficients produced from in-sample regression of forecast against realized volatility is very effective in correcting implied forecasting bias. They also find that after such a bias correction, there is little to be gained from averaging implied across strikes. This means that ATM implied together with a bias correction scheme could be the simplest, and yet the best, way forward.

11
Volatility Forecasting Records

11.1 WHICH VOLATILITY FORECASTING MODEL?

Our JEL survey has concentrated on two questions: is volatility forecastable? If it is, which method will provide the best forecasts? To consider these questions, a number of basic methodological viewpoints need to be discussed, mostly about the evaluation of forecasts. What exactly is being forecast? Does the time interval (the observation interval) matter? Are the results similar for different speculative markets? How does one measure predictive performance?

Volatility forecasts are classified in this section as belonging in one of the following four categories:

- HISVOL: for historical volatility, which include random walk, historical averages of squared returns, or absolute returns. Also included in this category are time series models based on historical volatility using moving averages, exponential weights, autoregressive models, or even fractionally integrated autoregressive absolute returns, for example. Note that HISVOL models can be highly sophisticated. The multivariate VAR realized volatility model in Andersen, Bollerslev, Diebold and Labys (2001) is classified here as a 'HISVOL' model. All models in this group model volatility directly, omitting the goodness of fit of the returns distribution or any other variables such as option prices.
- GARCH: any member of the ARCH, GARCH, EGARCH and so forth family is included.
- SV: for stochastic volatility model forecasts.
- ISD: for option implied standard deviation, based on the Black–Scholes model and various generalizations.

The survey of papers includes 93 studies, but 25 of them did not involve comparisons between methods from at least two of these groups, and so were not helpful for comparison purposes.

Table 11.1 involves just pairwise comparisons. Of the 66 studies that were relevant, some compared just one pair of forecasting techniques,

Table 11.1 Pair-wise comparisons of forecasting performance
of various volatility models

	Number of studies	Studies percentage
HISVOL > GARCH	22	56%
GARCH > HISVOL	17	44%
HISVOL > ISD	8	24%
ISD > HISVOL	26	76%
GARCH > ISD	1	6%
ISD > GARCH	17	94%
SV > HISVOL	3	
SV > GARCH	3	
GARCH > SV	1	
ISD > SV	1	

Note: "A > B" means model A's forecasting performance is better than
that of model B's

other compared several. For those involving both HISVOL and GARCH
models, 22 found HISVOL better at forecasting than GARCH (56% of
the total), and 17 found GARCH superior to HISVOL (44%).

The combination of forecasts has a mixed picture. Two studies find it
to be helpful but another does not.

The overall ranking suggests that ISD provides the best forecasting
with HISVOL and GARCH roughly equal, although possibly HISVOL
does somewhat better in the comparisons. The success of the implied
volatility should not be surprising as these forecasts use a larger, and
more relevant, information set than the alternative methods as they use
option prices. They are also less practical, not being available for all
assets.

Among the 93 papers, 17 studies compared alternative version of
GARCH. It is clear that GARCH dominates ARCH. In general, models that incorporate volatility asymmetry such as EGARCH and GJR-
GARCH, perform better than GARCH. But certain specialized specifications, such as fractionally integrated GARCH (FIGARCH) and regime
switching GARCH (RSGARCH) do better in some studies. However,
it seems clear that one form of study that is included is conducted just
to support a viewpoint that a particular method is useful. It might not
have been submitted for publication if the required result had not been
reached. This is one of the obvious weaknesses of a comparison such as
this: the papers being reported have been prepared for different reasons

and use different data sets, many kinds of assets, various intervals and a variety of evaluation techniques. Rarely discussed is if one method is significantly better than another. Thus, although a suggestion can be made that a particular method of forecasting volatility is the best, no statement is available about the cost–benefit from using it rather than something simpler or how far ahead the benefits will occur.

Financial market volatility is clearly forecastable. The debate is on how far ahead one can accurately forecast and to what extent volatility changes can be predicted. This conclusion does not violate market efficiency since accurate volatility forecast is not in conflict with underlying asset and option prices being correct. The option implied volatility, being a market-based volatility forecast, has been shown to contain most information about future volatility. The supremacy among historical time series models depends on the type of asset being modelled. But, as a rule of thumb, historical volatility methods work equally well compared with more sophisticated ARCH class and SV models. Better reward could be gained by making sure that actual volatility is measured accurately. These are broad-brush conclusions, omitting the fine details that we outline in this book. Because of the complex issues involved and the importance of volatility measure, volatility forecasting will continue to remain a specialist subject and to be studied vigorously.

11.2   GETTING THE RIGHT CONDITIONAL VARIANCE AND FORECAST WITH THE 'WRONG' MODELS

Many of the time series volatility models, including the GARCH models, can be thought of as approximating a deeper time-varying volatility construction, possibly involving several important economic explanatory variables. Since time series models involve only lagged returns it seems likely that they will provide an adequate, possibly even a very good, approximation to actuality for long periods but not at all times. This means that they will forecast well on some occasions, but less well on others, depending on fluctuations in the underlying driving variables.

Nelson (1992) proves that if the true process is a diffusion or near-diffusion model with no jumps, then even when misspecified, appropriately defined sequences of ARCH terms with a large number of lagged residuals may still serve as consistent estimators for the volatility of the true underlying diffusion, in the sense that the difference between the true instantaneous volatility and the ARCH estimates converges to zero in probability as the length of the sampling frequency diminishes. Nelson (1992) shows that such ARCH models may misspecify both the conditional mean and the dynamic of the conditional variance; in fact the misspecification may be so severe that the models make no sense as data-generating processes, they could still produce consistent one-step-ahead conditional variance estimates and short-term forecasts.

Nelson and Foster (1995) provide further conditions for such mis-specified ARCH models to produce consistent forecasts over the medium and long term. They show that forecasts by these misspecified models will converge in probability to the forecast generated by the true diffusion or near-diffusion process, provided that all unobservable state variables are consistently estimated and that the conditional mean and conditional covariances of all state variables are correctly specified. An example of a true diffusion process given by Nelson and Foster (1995) is the stochastic volatility model described in Chapter 6.

These important theoretical results confirm our empirical observations that under normal circumstances, i.e. no big jumps in prices, there may be little practical difference in choosing between volatility models, provided that the sampling frequency is small and that, whichever model one has chosen, it must contain sufficiently long lagged residuals. This might be an explanation for the success of high-frequency and long memory volatility models (e.g. Blair, Poon and Taylor, 2001; Andersen, Bollerslev, Diebold and Labys, 2001).

11.3 PREDICTABILITY ACROSS DIFFERENT ASSETS

Early studies that test the forecasting power of option ISD are fraught with many estimation deficiencies. Despite these complexities, option ISD has been found empirically to contain a significant amount of information about future volatility and it often beats volatility forecasts produced by sophisticated time series models. Such a superior performance appears to be common across assets.

11.3.1 Individual stocks

Latane and Rendleman (1976) were the first to discover the forecasting capability of option ISD. They find actual volatilities of 24 stocks calculated from in-sample period and extended partially into the future are more closely related to implied than historical volatility. Chiras and Manaster (1978) and Beckers (1981) find prediction from implied can explain a large amount of the cross-sectional variations of individual stock volatilities. Chiras and Manaster (1978) document an R^2 of 34–70% for a large sample of stock options traded on CBOE whereas Beckers (1981) reports an R^2 of 13–50% for a sample that varies from 62 to 116 US stocks over the sample period. Gemmill (1986) produces an R^2 of 12–40% for a sample of 13 UK stocks. Schmalensee and Trippi (1978) find implied volatility rises when stock price falls and that implied volatilities of different stocks tend to move together. From a time series perspective, Lamoureux and Lastrapes (1993) and Vasilellis and Meade (1996) find implied volatility could also predict time series variations of equity volatility better than forecasts produced from time series models.

The forecast horizons of this group of studies that forecast equity volatility are usually quite long, ranging from 3 months to 3 years. Studies that examine incremental information content of time series forecasts find volatility historical average provides significant incremental information in both cross-sectional (Beckers, 1981; Chiras and Manaster, 1978; Gemmill, 1986) and time series settings (Lamoureux and Lastrapes, 1993) and that combining GARCH and implied volatility produces the best forecast (Vasilellis and Meade, 1996). These findings have been interpreted as an evidence of stock option market inefficiency since option implied does not subsume all information. In general, stock option implied volatility exhibits instability and suffers most from measurement errors and bid–ask spread because of the lower liquidity.

11.3.2   Stock market index

There are 22 studies that use index option ISD to forecast stock index volatility; seven of these forecast volatility of S&P100, ten forecast volatility of S&P500 and the remaining five forecast index volatility of smaller stock markets. The S&P100 and S&P500 forecasting results make an interesting contrast as almost all studies that forecast S&P500 volatility use S&P500 futures options which is more liquid and less prone to measurement errors than the OEX stock index option written on S&P100. We have dealt with the issue of measurement errors in the discussion of biasness in Section 10.3.

All but one study (viz. Canina and Figlewski, 1993) conclude that implied volatility contains useful information about future volatility. Blair, Poon and Taylor (2001) and Poteshman (2000) record the highest R^2 for S&P100 and S&P500 respectively. About 50% of index volatility is predictable up to a 4-week horizon when actual volatility is estimated more accurately using very high-frequency intraday returns.

Similar, but less marked, forecasting performance emerged from the smaller stock markets, which include the German, Australian, Canadian and Swedish markets. For a small market such as the Swedish market, Frennberg and Hansson (1996) find seasonality to be prominent and that implied volatility forecast cannot beat simple historical models such as the autoregressive model and random walk. Very erratic and unstable forecasting results were reported in Brace and Hodgson (1991) for the Australian market. Doidge and Wei (1998) find the Canadian Toronto index is best forecast with GARCH and implied volatility combined, whereas Bluhm and Yu (2000) find VDAX, the German version of VIX, produces the best forecast for the German stock index volatility.

A range of forecast horizons were tested among this group of studies, though the most popular choice is 1 month. There is evidence that the S&P implied contains more information after the 1987 crash (see Christensen and Prabhala (1998) for S&P100 and Ederington and Guan (2002) for S&P500). Some described this as the 'awakening' of the S&P option markets.

About half of the papers in this group test if there is incremental information contained in time series forecasts. Day and Lewis (1992), Ederington and Guan (1999, 2004), and Martens and Zein (2004) find ARCH class models and volatility historical average add a few percentage points to the R^2, whereas Blair, Poon and Taylor (2001), Christensen and Prabhala (1998), Fleming (1998), Fleming, Ostdiek and Whaley (1995), Hol and Koopman (2001) and Szakmary, Ors, Kim and Davidson (2002) all find option implied dominates time series forecasts.

11.3.3 Exchange rate

The strong forecasting power of implied volatility is again confirmed in the currency markets. Sixteen papers study currency options for a number of major currencies, the most popular of which are DM/US$ and ¥/US$. Most studies find implied volatility to contain information about future volatility for a short horizon up to 3 months. Li (2002) and Scott and Tucker (1989) find implied volatility forecast well for up to a 6–9-month horizon. Both studies register the highest R^2 in the region of 40–50%.

A number of studies in this group find implied volatility beats time series forecasts including volatility historical average (see Fung, Lie and

Moreno, 1990; Wei and Frankel, 1991) and ARCH class models (see Guo, 1996a, 1996b; Jorion, 1995, 1996; Martens and Zein, 2004; Pong, Shackleton, Taylor and Xu, 2002; Szakmary, Ors, Kim and Davidson, 2002; Xu and Taylor, 1995). Some studies find combined forecast is the best choice (see Dunis, Law and Chauvin, 2000; Taylor and Xu, 1997).

Two studies find high-frequency intraday data can produce more accurate time series forecast than implied. Fung and Hsieh (1991) find one-day-ahead time series forecast from a long-lag autoregressive model fitted to 15-minutes returns is better than implied volatility. Li (2002) finds the ARFIMA model outperformed implied in long-horizon forecasts while implied volatility dominates over shorter horizons. Implied volatility forecasts were found to produce higher R^2 than other long memory models, such as the Log-ARFIMA model in Martens and Zein (2004) and Pong, Shackleton, Taylor and Xu (2004). All these long memory forecasting models are more recent and are built on volatility compiled from high-frequency intraday returns, while the implied volatility remains to be constructed from less frequent daily option prices.

11.3.4   Other assets

The forecasting power of implied volatility from interest rate options was tested in Edey and Elliot (1992), Fung and Hsieh (1991) and Amin and Ng (1997). Interest rate option models are very different from other option pricing models because of the need to price the whole term structure of interest rate derivatives consistently all at the same time in order to rule out arbitrage opportunities. Trading in interest rate instruments is highly liquid as trading friction and execution cost are negligible. Practitioners are more concerned about the term structure fit than the time series fit, as millions of pounds of arbitrage profits could change hands instantly if there is any inconsistency in contemporaneous prices.

Earlier studies such as Edey and Elliot (1992) and Fung and Hsieh (1991) use the Black model (a modified version of Black–Scholes) that prices each interest rate option without cross-referencing to prices of other interest rate derivatives. The single factor Heath–Jarrow–Morton model, used in Amin and Ng (1997) and fitted to short rate only, works in the same way, although the authors have added different constraints to the short-rate dynamics as the main focus of their paper is to compare different variants of short-rate dynamics. Despite the complications, all three studies find significant forecasting power is implied of interest rate (futures) options. Amin and Ng (1997) in particular report an R^2 of 21%

for 20-day-ahead volatility forecasts, and volatility historical average adds only a few percentage points to the R^2.

Implied volatilities from options written on nonfinancial assets were examined in Day and Lewis (1993, crude oil), Kroner, Kneafsey and Claessens (1995, agriculture and metals), Martens and Zein (2004, crude oil) and a recent study (Szakmary, Ors, Kim and Davidson, 2002) that covers 35 futures options contracts across nine markets including S&P500, interest rates, currency, energy, metals, agriculture and livestock futures. All four studies find implied volatility dominates time series forecasts although Kroner, Kneafsey and Claessens (1995) find combining GARCH and implied produces the best forecast.

12
Volatility Models in Risk Management

The volatility models described in this book are useful for estimating value-at-risk (VaR), a measure introduced by the Basel Committee in 1996. In many countries, it is mandatory for banks to hold a minimum amount of capital calculated as a function of VaR. Some financial institutions other than banks also use VaR voluntarily for internal risk management. So volatility modelling and forecasting has a very important role in the finance and banking industries. In Section 12.1, we give a brief background of the Basel Committee and the Basel Accords. In Section 12.2, we define VaR and explain how the VaR estimate is tested according to regulations set out in the Basel Accords. Section 12.3 describes how volatility models can be combined with extreme value theory to produce, hitherto the most accurate, VaR estimate. The content in this section is largely based on McNeil and Frey (2000) in the context where there is only one asset (or one risk factor). A multivariate extension is possible but is still under development. Section 12.4 describes various ways to evaluate the VaR model based on Lopez (1998).

Market risk and VaR represent only one of the many types of risk discussed in the Basel Accords. We have specifically omitted credit risk and operational risk as volatility models have little use in predicting these risks. Readers who are interested in risk management in a broader context could refer to Jorion (2001) or Banks (2004).

12.1 BASEL COMMITTEE AND BASEL ACCORDS I & II

The Basel Accords have been in place for a number of years. They set out an international standard for minimum capital requirement among international banks to safeguard against credit, market and operational risks. The Bank for International Settlements (BIS) based at Basel, Switzerland, hosts the Basel Committee who in turn set up the Basel Accords. While Basel Committee members are all from the G10 countries and have no formal supranational supervisory authority, the Basel

Accords have been adopted by almost all countries that have active international banks. Many financial institutions that are not regulated by the national Banking Acts also pay attention to the risk management procedures set out in the Basel Accords for internal risk monitoring purposes. The IOSCO (International Organization of Securities Commissions), for example, has issued several parallel papers containing guidelines similar to the Basel Accords for the risk management of derivative securities.

The first Basel Accord, which was released in 1988 and which became known as the Capital Accord, established a minimum capital standard at 8% for assets subject to credit risk:

$$\frac{\text{Liquidity-weighted assets}}{\text{Risk-weighted assets}} \geq 8\%. \tag{12.1}$$

Detailed guidelines were set for deriving the denominator according to some predefined risk weights; typically a very risky loan will be given a 100% weight. The numerator consists of bank capital weighted the liquidity of the assets according to a list of weights published by the Basel Committee.

In April 1995, an amendment was issued to include capital charge for assets that are vulnerable to '*market risk*', which is defined as the *risk of loss arising from adverse changes in market prices. Specifically, capital charges are to be supplied: (i) to the current market value of open positions (including derivative positions) in interest rate related instruments and equities in banks' trading books, and (ii) to banks' total currency and commodities position in respect of foreign exchange and commodities risk respectively.* A detailed 'Standardised Measurement Method' was prescribed by the Basel Committee for calculating the capital charge for each market risk category.

If we rearrange Equation (12.1) such that

Liquidity-weighted assets $\geq 8\% \times$ Risk-weighted assets, $\qquad$ (12.2)

then the market risk related capital charge is added to credit risk related 'Liquidity-weighted assets' in the l.h.s. of Equation (12.2). This effectively increases the 'Risk-weighted assets' in the r.h.s. by 12.5 times the additional market risk related capital charge.

In January 1996, another amendment was made to allow banks to use their internal proprietary model together with the VaR approach for calculating market risk related risk capital. This is the area where volatility models could play an important role because, by adopting the internal approach, the banks are given the flexibility to specify model parameters and to take into consideration the correlation (and possible diversification) effects across as well as within broad risk factor categories. The condition for the use of the internal model is that it is subject to regular backtesting procedures using at least one year's worth of historical data. More about VaR estimation and backtesting will be provided in the next sections.

In June 2004, Basel II was released with two added dimensions, viz. *supervisory review* of an institution's internal assessment process and capital adequacy, and *market discipline* through information disclosure. Basel II also saw the introduction of operational risk for the first time in the calculation of risk capital to be included in the denominator in Equation (12.1). '*Operational risk*' is defined as *the risk of losses resulting from inadequate or failed internal processes, people and systems, or external events*. The Basel Committee admits that assessments of operational risk are imprecise and it will accept a crude approximation that is based on applying a multiplicative factor to the bank's gross income.

12.2   VaR AND BACKTEST

In this section, we discuss market risk related VaR only, since this is the area where volatility models can play an important role. The computation of VaR is needed only if the bank chooses to adopt its own internal model for calculating market risk related capital requirement.

12.2.1   VaR

'*Value-at-risk*' *(VaR)* is defined as *the 1% quantile of the lower tail distribution of the trading book held over a 10-day period*.[1] The capital charge will then be the higher of the previous day's VaR or three times the average daily VaR of the preceding 60 business days. The multiplicative factor of three was used as a cushion for cumulative losses arising from adverse market conditions and to account for potential weakness in the modelling process.[2] Given that today's portfolio value is known, the prediction of losses over a 10-day period amounts to predicting the rate of change (or portfolio returns) over the 10-day period (Figure 12.1).

---

[1] A separate VaR will be calculated for each risk factor. So there will be separate VaR for interest rate related instruments, equity, foreign exchange risk and commodities risk. If correlations among the four risk factors are not considered, then the total VaR will be the sum of the four VaR estimates.

[2] While one may argue that such a multiplicative factor is completely arbitrary, it is nevertheless mandatory.

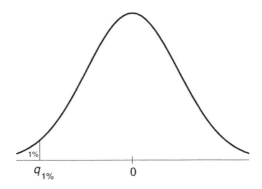

Figure 12.1   Returns distribution and VaR

The VaR estimate for tomorrow's trading position is then calculated as today's portfolio value times the 1% quantile value if it is a negative return. (A positive return will not attract any risk capital.)

The discovery of stochastic volatility has led to the common practice of modelling returns distribution conditioned on volatility level at a specific point in time. Volatility dynamic has been extensively studied since the seminal work of Engle (1982). It is now well known that a volatile period in the financial markets tends to be followed by another volatile period, whereas a tranquil period tends to be followed by another tranquil period. VaR as defined by the Basel Committee is a short-term forecast. Hence a good VaR model should fully exploit the dynamic of volatility structure.

12.2.2 Backtest

For banks who decide to use their own internal models, they have to perform a backtest procedure at least at a quarterly interval. The backtest procedure involves comparing the bank's daily profits and losses with model-generated VaR measures in order to gauge the quality and accuracy of their risk measurement systems. Specifically, this is done by counting from the record of the last 12 months (or 250 trading days) the number of times when actual losses are greater than the predicted risk measure. The proportion actually covered can then be checked to see if it is consistent with a 99% level of confidence.

In the 1996 backtest document, the Basel Committee was unclear about whether the exceptional losses should take into account fee income and changes in portfolio position. Hence the long discussion about the choice of 10-day, 1-day or intraday intervals for calculating exceptional losses, and the discussion of whether actual or simulated trading results should be tested. Before we discuss these two issues, it is important to note that (i) *actual* VaR violations could be due to an inadequate (volatility) model or a bad decision (e.g. a decision to change portfolio composition at the wrong time); (ii) financial market volatility often does not obey the scaling law, i.e. variance of 10-day return is not equal to 1-day variance times $\sqrt{10}$.

To test model adequacy, the backtest should be based on a simulated portfolio assuming that the bank has been holding the same portfolio for the last 12 months. This will help to separate a bad model from a bad decision. Given that the VaR used for calculating the capital requirement is for a 10-day holding period, the backtest should also be performed using a 10-day window to accumulate profits/losses. The current rules, which require the VaR test to be calculated for a 1-day profits/losses, fail to recognize the volatility dynamics over the 10-day period is vastly different from the 1-day volatility dynamic.

The Basel Committee recommends that backtest also be conducted on actual trading outcomes in addition to the simulated portfolio position. Specifically, it recommends a comprehensive approach that involves a detailed attribution of income by source, including fees, spreads, market movements and intraday trading results. This is very useful for uncovering risks that are not captured in the volatility model.

12.2.3   The three-zone approach to backtest evaluation

The Basel Committee then specifies a three-zone approach to evaluate the outcome of the backtest. To understand the rationale of the three-zone approach, it is important to recognize that all appropriately implemented control systems are subject to random errors. On the other hand, there are cases where the control system is a bad one and yet there are no failures. The objective of the backtest is to distinguish the two situations which are known as type I (rejecting a system when it is working) and type II (accepting a bad system) errors respectively.

Given that the confidence level set for the VaR measure is 99%, there is a 1% chance of exceptional losses that are tolerated. For 250 trading days, this translates into 2.5 occurrences where the VaR estimate will be violated. Figure 12.2 shows the outcome of simulations involving a system with 99% coverage and 95% coverage as reported in the Basel document (January 1996, Table 1). We can see that the number of exceptions under the true 99% coverage can range from 0 to 9, with

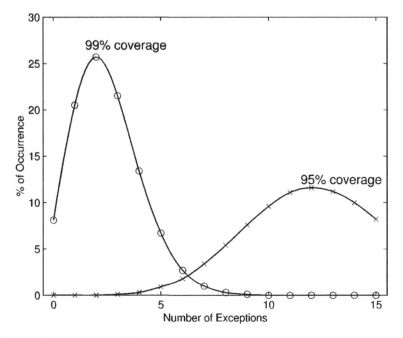

Figure 12.2   Type I and II backtest errors

most of the instances centred around 2. If the true coverage is 95%, we
might get four or more exceptions with the mean centred around 12. If
only these two coverages are possible then one may conclude that if the
number of exceptions is four or below, then the 99% coverage is true. If
there are ten or more exceptions it is more likely that the 99% coverage
is not true. If the number of exceptions is between five and nine, then it
is possible that the true coverage might be from either the 99% or the
95% population and it is impossible to make a conclusion.

The difficulty one faces in practice is that there could potentially be an
endless range of possible coverages (i.e. 98%, 97%, 96%, ..., etc). So
while we are certain about the range of type I errors (because we know
that our objective is to have a 99% coverage), we cannot be precise about
the possible range of type II errors (because we do not know the true
coverage). The three-zone approach and the recommended increase in
scaling factors (see Table 12.1) is the Basel Committee's effort to seek
a compromise in view of this statistical uncertainty. From Table 12.1,
if the backtest reveals that in the last trading year there are 10 or more
VaR violations, for example, then the capital charge will be four times
VaR, instead of three times VaR.

Table 12.1 Three-zone approach to internal backtesting of VaR

Zones	No. of exceptions	Increase in scaling factor	Cumulative probability
Green	0–4	0	8.11 to 89.22%
Yellow	5	+0.40	95.88%
	6	+0.50	98.63%
	7	+0.65	99.60%
	8	+0.75	99.89%
	9	+0.85	99.97%
Red	10 or more	+1	99.99%

Note: The table is based on a sample of 250 observations. The cumulative probability is the probability of obtaining a given number of or fewer exceptions in a sample of 250 observations when the true coverage is 99%. (Source: Basel 1996 Amendment, Table 2).

When the backtest signals a red zone, the national supervisory body will investigate the reasons why the bank's internal model produced such a large number of misses, and may demand the bank to begin working on improving its model immediately.

12.3   EXTREME VALUE THEORY AND VaR ESTIMATION

The extreme value approach to VaR estimation is a response to the finding that standardized residuals of many volatility models have longer tails than the normal distribution. This means that a VaR estimate produced from the standard volatility model without further adjustment will underestimate the 1% quantile. Using GARCH-t, where the standardized residuals are assumed to follow a Student-t distribution, partially alleviates the problem, but GARCH-t is inadequate when the left tail and the right tail are not symmetrical. The EVT-GARCH method proposed by McNeil and Frey (2000) is to model conditional volatility and marginal distribution of the left tail separately. We need to model only the left tail since the right tail is not relevant as far as VaR computation is concerned.

Tail event is by definition rare and a long history of data is required to uncover the tail structure. For example, one would not just look into the last week's or the last year's data to model and forecast the next earthquake or the next volcano eruption. The extreme value theory (EVT) is best suited for studying rare extreme events of this kind where sound statistical theory for maximal has been well established. There is a problem, however, in using a long history of data to produce a short-term forecast. The model is not sensitive enough to current market condition. Moreover, one important assumption of EVT is that the tail events are independent and identically distributed (*iid*). This assumption is likely to be violated because of stochastic volatility and volatility persistence in particular. Volatility persistence suggests one tail event is likely to be followed by another tail event. One way to overcome this violation of the *iid* assumption is to filter the data with a volatility model and study the volatility filtered *iid* residuals using EVT. This is exactly what McNeil and Frey (2000) proposed. In order to produce a VaR estimate in the original return scale to conform with the Basel requirement, we then trace back the steps by first producing the 1% quantile estimate for the volatility filtered return residuals, and convert the 1% quantile estimate to the original return scale using the conditional volatility forecast for the next day.

12.3.1 The model

Following the GARCH literature, let us write the return process as

$$r_t = \mu + z_t \sqrt{h_t}. \tag{12.3}$$

In the process above, we assume there is no serial correlation in daily return. (Otherwise, an AR(1) or an MA(1) term could be added to the r.h.s. of (12.3).) Equation (12.3) is estimated with some appropriate specification for the volatility process, h_t (see Chapter 4 for details). For stock market returns, h_t typically follows an EGARCH(1,1) or a GJR-GARCH(1,1) process. The GARCH model in (12.3) is estimated using quasi-maximum likelihood with a Gaussian likelihood function, even though we know that z_t is not normally distributed. QME estimators are unbiased and since the standardized residuals will be modelled using an extreme value distribution, such a procedure is deemed appropriate.

The standardized residuals z_t are obtained by rearranging (12.3)

$$z_t = \frac{r_t - \mu}{\sqrt{h_t}}.$$

Since our main concern is about losses, we could multiply z_t by -1 so that we are always working with positive values for convenience. The z_t variable is then ranked in descending order, such that $z_{(1)} \geq z_{(2)} \geq \cdots \geq z_{(n)}$ where n is the number of observations.

The next stage involves estimating the generalized Pareto distribution (GPD) to all z that are greater than a high threshold u. The GPD distribution has density function

$$f(z) = \begin{cases} 1 - \left[1 + \dfrac{\xi(z-u)}{\beta}\right]^{-1/\xi} & \text{for } \xi \neq 0 \\[2ex] 1 - e^{-(z-u)/\beta} & \text{for } \xi = 0 \end{cases}.$$

The parameter ξ is called the tail index and β is the scale parameter.

The estimation of the model parameters (the tail index ξ in particular) and the choice of the threshold u are not independent processes. As u becomes larger, there will be fewer and fewer observations being included in the GPD estimation. This makes the estimation of ξ very unstable with a large standard error. But, as u decreases, the chance of an observation that does not belong to the tail distribution being included in the GPD estimation increases. This increases the risk of the ξ estimate being biased. The usual advice is to estimate ξ (and β) at different levels of u. Then starting from the highest value of u, a lower value of u is preferred unless there is a change in the level of ξ estimate, which indicates there may be a possible bias caused by the inclusion of too many observations in the GPD estimation.

Once the parameters ξ and β are estimated, the 1% quantile is obtained by inverting the cumulative density function

$$F(z) = 1 - \frac{k}{n}\left[1 + \widehat{\xi}\left(\frac{z-u}{\widehat{\beta}}\right)\right]^{-1/\xi},$$

$$z_q = u + \frac{\widehat{\beta}}{\widehat{\xi}}\left[\left(\frac{1-q}{k/n}\right)^{-\xi} - 1\right],$$

where $q = 0.01$ and k is the number of z exceeding the threshold u.

We are now ready to calculate the VaR estimate using (12.3) and the volatility forecast for the next day:

$$VaR_{t+1} = \text{current position} \times \left(\mu - z_q\sqrt{\widehat{h}_{t+1}}\right).$$

12.3.2 10-day VaR

It is well-known that the variance of a Gaussian variable follows a simple scaling law and the Basel Committee, in its 1996 Amendment, states that it will accept a simple $\sqrt{T}$ scaling of 1-day VaR for deriving the 10-day VaR required for calculating the market risk related risk capital.

The stylized facts of financial market volatility and research findings have repeatedly shown that a 10-day VaR is not likely to be the same as $\sqrt{10} \times$ 1-day VaR. First, the dynamic of a stationary volatility process suggests that if the current level of volatility is higher than unconditional volatility, the subsequent daily volatility forecasts will decline and converge to unconditional volatility, and vice versa for the case where the initial volatility is lower than the unconditional volatility. The rate of convergence depends on the degree of volatility persistence. In the case where initial volatility is higher than unconditional volatility, the scaling factor will be less than $\sqrt{10}$. In the case where initial volatility is lower than unconditional volatility, the scaling factor will be more than $\sqrt{10}$. In practice, due to volatility asymmetry and other predictive variables that might be included in the volatility model, it is always best to calculate $\widehat{h}_{t+1}, \widehat{h}_{t+2}, \cdots, \widehat{h}_{t+10}$ separately. The 10-day VaR is then produced using the 10-day volatilty estimate calculated from the sum of $\widehat{h}_{t+1}, \widehat{h}_{t+2}, \cdots, \widehat{h}_{t+10}$.

Secondly, financial asset returns are not normally distributed. Danielsson and deVries (1997) show that the scaling parameter for quantile derived using the EVT method increases at the approximate rate of T^ξ, which is typically less than the square-root-of-time adjustment. For a typical value of $\xi \, (= 0.25)$, $T^\xi = 1.778$, which is less than $10^{0.5} \, (= 3.16)$. McNeil and Frey (2000) on the other hand dispute this finding and claim the exponent to be greater than 0.5. The scaling factor of $10^{0.5}$ produced far too many VaR violations in the backtest of five financial series, except for returns on gold. In view of the conflicting empirical findings, one possible solution is to build models using 10-day returns data. This again highlights the difficulty due to the inconsistency in the rule applies to VaR for calculating risk capital and that applies to VaR for backtesting.

12.3.3 Multivariate analysis

The VaR computation described above is useful for the single asset case and cases where there is only one risk factor. The cases for multi-asset and multi-risk-factor are a lot more complex which require multivariate extreme theories and a better understanding of the dependence structure between the variables of interest. Much research in this area is still ongoing. But it is safe to say that correlation coefficient, the key measure used in portfolio diversification, can produce very misleading information about the dependence structure of extreme events in financial markets (Poon, Rockinger and Tawn, 2004). The VaR of a portfolio is not a simple function of the weighted sum of the VaR of the individual assets. Detailed coverage of multivariate extreme value theories and applications is beyond the scope of this book. The simplest solution we could offer here is to treat portfolio returns as a univariate variable and apply the procedures above. Such an approach does not provide insight about the tail relationship between assets and that between risk factors, but it will at least produce a sensible estimate of portfolio VaR.

12.4   EVALUATION OF VaR MODELS

In practice, there will be many different models for calculating VaR, many of which will satisfy Basel's backtest requirement. The important questions are 'Which model should one use?' and 'If there are exceptions, how do we know if the model is malfunctioning?'. Lopez (1998) proposes two statistical tests and a supplementary evaluation that is based on the user specifying a loss function.

The first statistical test involves modelling the number of exceptions as independent draws from a binomial distribution with a probability of occurrence equal to 1%. Let x be the actual number of exceptions observed for a sample of 250 trading outcomes. The probability of observing x exceptions from a 99 % coverage is

$$\Pr(x) = C_x^{250} \times 0.01^x \times 0.99^{250-x}.$$

The likelihood ratio statistic for testing if the actual unconditional coverage $\alpha = x/250 = 0.01$ is

$$LR_{uc} = 2 \left[\log \left(\alpha^x \times (1 - \alpha)^{250-x} \right) - \log \left(0.01^x \times 0.99^{250-x} \right) \right].$$

The LR_{uc} test statistic has an asymptotic χ^2 distribution with one degree of freedom.

The second test makes use of the fact that VaR is the interval forecast of the lower 1% tail of the one-step-ahead conditional distribution of returns. So given a set of VaR_t, the indicator variable I_{t+1} is constructed as

$$I_{t+1} = \begin{cases} 1 & \text{for } r_{t+1} \leq \text{VaR}_t \\ 0 & \text{for } r_{t+1} > \text{VaR}_t \end{cases}.$$

If VaR_t provides correct conditional coverage, ΣI_{t+1} must equal unconditional coverage, and I_{t+1} must be serially independent. The LR_{cc} test is a joint test of these two properties. The relevant test statistic is

$$LR_{cc} = LR_{uc} + LR_{ind},$$

which has an asymptotic χ^2 distribution with two degrees of freedom. The LR_{ind} statistic is the likelihood ratio statistic for the null hypothesis of serial independence against first-order serial dependence.

The LR_{uc} test and the LR_{cc} test are formal statistical tests for the distribution of VaR exceptions. It is useful to supplement these formal tests with some numerical scores that are based on the loss function of the decision maker. The loss fuction is specified as the cost of various outcomes below:

$$C_{t+1} = \begin{cases} f\,(r_{t+1}, VaR_t) & \text{for } r_{t+1} \leq VaR_t \\ g\,(r_{t+1}, VaR_t) & \text{for } r_{t+1} > VaR_t \end{cases}.$$

Since this is a cost function and the prevention of VaR exception is of paramount importance, $f\,(x, y) \geq g\,(x, y)$ for a given y. The best VaR model is one that provides the smallest total cost, ΣC_{t+1}.

There are many ways to specify f and g depending on the concern of the decision maker. For example, for the regulator, the concern is principally about VaR exception where $r_{t+1} \leq VaR_t$ and not when $r_{t+1} > VaR_t$. So the simplest specification for f and g will be $f = 1$ and $g = 0$ as follows:

$$C_{t+1} = \begin{cases} 1 & \text{for } r_{t+1} \leq VaR_t \\ 0 & \text{for } r_{t+1} > VaR_t \end{cases}.$$

If the exception as well as the magnitude of the exception are both important, one could have

$$C_{t+1} = \begin{cases} 1 + (r_{t+1} - VaR_t)^2 & \text{for } r_{t+1} \leq VaR_t \\ 0 & \text{for } r_{t+1} > VaR_t \end{cases}.$$

The expected shortfall proposed by Artzner, Delbaen, Eber and Heath (1997, 1999) is similar in that the magnitude of loss above VaR is weighted by the probability of occurrence. This is equivalent to

$$C_{t+1} = \begin{cases} |r_{t+1} - VaR_t| & \text{for } r_{t+1} \leq VaR_t \\ 0 & \text{for } r_{t+1} > VaR_t \end{cases}.$$

For banks who implement the VaR model and has to set aside capital reserves, $g = 0$ is not appropriate because liquid assets do not provide good returns. So one cost function that will take into account the opportunity cost of money is

$$C_{t+1} = \begin{cases} |r_{t+1} - \text{VaR}_t|^{\gamma} & \text{for } r_{t+1} \leq \text{VaR}_t \\ |r_{t+1} - \text{VaR}_t| \times i & \text{for } r_{t+1} > \text{VaR}_t \end{cases},$$

where γ reflects the seriousness of large exception and i is a function of interest rate.

13
VIX and Recent Changes in VIX

The volatility index (VIX) compiled by the Chicago Board of Option Exchange has always been shown to capture financial turmoil and produce good forecast of S&P100 volatility (Fleming, Ostdiek and Whaley, 1995; Ederington and Guan, 2000a; Blair, Poon and Taylor, 2001; Hol and Koopman, 2002). It is compiled on a real-time basis aiming to reflect the volatility over the next 30 calendar days. In September 2003, the CBOE revised the way in which VIX is calculated and in March 2004 it started futures trading on VIX. This is to be followed by options on VIX and another derivative product may be variance swap. The old version of VIX, now renamed as VXO, continued to be calculated and released during the transition period.

13.1 NEW DEFINITION FOR VIX

There are three important differences between VIX and VXO:

 (i) The new VIX uses information from *out-of-the-money* call and put options of a wide range of strike prices, whereas VXO uses eight at- and near-the-money options.
 (ii) The new VIX is model-free whereas VXO is a weighted average of Black–Scholes implied volatility.
 (iii) The new VIX is based on S&P500 index options whereas VXO is based on S&P100 index options.

The VIX is calculated as the aggregate value of a weighted strip of options using the formula below:

$$\sigma_{vix}^2 = \frac{2}{T} \sum_i \frac{\Delta K_i}{K_i^2} e^{rT} Q(K_i) - \frac{1}{T}\left[\frac{F}{K_0} - 1\right]^2, \qquad (13.1)$$

$$F = K_0 + e^{rT}(c_0 - p_0), \qquad (13.2)$$

$$\Delta K_i = \frac{K_{i+1} + K_{i-1}}{2}, \qquad (13.3)$$

where r is the continuously compounded risk-free interest rate to expiration, T is the time to expiration (in minutes!), F is the forward price of the index calculated using put–call parity in (13.2), K_0 is the first strike just below F, K_i is the strike price of ith *out-of-the-money* options (i.e. call if $K_i > F$ and put if $K_i < F$), $Q(K_i)$ is the midpoint of the bid–ask spread for option at strike price K_i, ΔK_i in (13.3) is the interval between strike prices. If i is the lowest (or highest) strike, then $\Delta K_i = K_{i+1} - K_i$ (or $\Delta K_i = K_i - K_{i-1}$).

Equations (13.1) to (13.3) are applied to two sets of options contracts for the near term T_1 and the next near term T_2 to derive a constant 30-day volatility index VIX:

$$VIX = 100 \times \sqrt{\left\{ T_1 \sigma_1^2 \left(\frac{N_{T_2} - N_{30}}{N_{T_2} - N_{T_1}} \right) + T_2 \sigma_2^2 \left(\frac{N_{30} - N_{T_1}}{N_{T_2} - N_{T_1}} \right) \right\} \times \frac{N_{365}}{N_{30}}},$$

where N_τ is the number of minutes ($N_{30} = 30 \times 1400 = 43,200$ and $N_{365} = 365 \times 1400 = 525,600$).

13.2   WHAT IS THE VXO?

VXO, the predecessor of VIX, was released in 1993 and replaced by the new VIX in September 2003. VXO is an implied volatility composite compiled from eight options written on the S&P100. It is constructed in such a way that it is at-the-money (by combining just-in- and just-out-of-the-money options) and has a constant 28 calendar days to expiry (by combining the first nearby and second nearby options around the targeted 28 calendar days to maturity). Eight option prices are used, including four calls and four puts, to reduce any pricing bias and measurement errors caused by staleness in the recorded index level. Since options written on S&P100 are American-style, a cash-dividend adjusted binomial model was used to capture the effect of early exercise. The mid bid–ask option price is used instead of traded price because transaction prices are subject to bid–ask bounce. (See Whaley (1993) and Fleming, Ostdiek and Whaley (1995) for further details.) Owing to the calendar day adjustment, VIX is about 1.2 times (i.e. $\sqrt{365/252}$) greater than historical volatility computed using trading-day data.

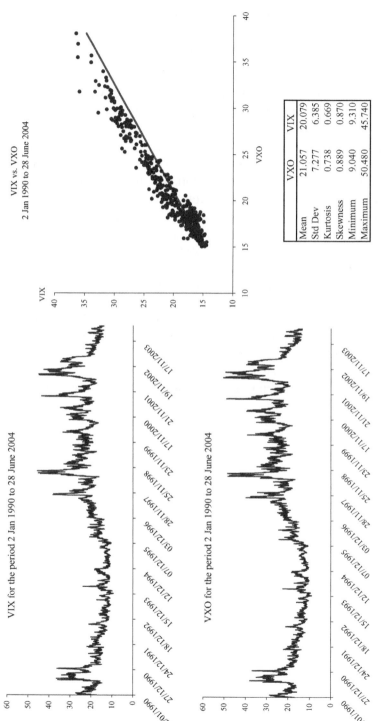

Figure 13.1 Chicago Board of Options Exchange volatility indices

13.3   REASON FOR THE CHANGE

There are many reasons for the change; if nothing else the new volatility index is hedgeable and the old one is not. The new VIX can be replicated with a static portfolio of S&P500 options or S&P500 futures. Hence, it allows hedging and, more importantly, the corrective arbitrage options of VIX derivatives if prices are not correct. The CBOE argues that the new VIX reflect information in a broader range of options rather than just the few at-the-money options. More importantly, the new VIX is aiming to capture the information in the volatility skew. It is linked to the broader-based S&P500 index instead of the S&P100 index. The S&P500 is the primary index for most portfolio benchmarking so derivative products that are more closely linked to S&P500 will facilitate risk management.

Although the two volatility indices are compiled very differently, their statistical properties are very similar. Figures 13.1(a) and 13.1(b) show the time series plots of VIX and VXO over the period 2 January 1990 to 28 June 2004, and Figure 13.1(c) provides a scatterplot showing the relationship between the two. The new VIX has a smaller mean and is more stable than the old VXO. There is no doubt that researchers are already investigating the new index and all the issues that it has brought about, such as the pricing and hedging of derivatives written on the new VIX.

14

Where Next?

The volatility forecasting literature is still very active. Many more new results are expected in the near future. There are several areas where future research could seek to make improvements. First is the issue about forecast evaluation and combining forecasts of different models. It would be useful if statistical tests were conducted to test whether the forecast errors from Model A are significantly smaller, in some sense, than those from Model B, and so on for all pairs. Even if Model A is found to be better than all the other models, the conclusion is NOT that one should henceforth forecast volatility with Model A and ignore the other models as it is very likely that a linear combination of all the forecasts might be superior. To find the weights one can either run a regression of empirical volatility (the quantity being forecast) on the individual forecasts, or as an approximation just use equal weights. Testing the effectiveness of a composite forecast is just as important as testing the superiority of the individual models, but this has not been done very often or across different data sets.

A mere plot of any measure of volatility against time will show the familiar 'volatility clustering' which indicates some degree of forecast-ability. The biggest challenge lies in predicting changes in volatility. If implied volatility is agreed to be the best performing forecast, on average, this is in agreement with the general forecast theory, which emphasizes the use of a wider information set than just the past of the process being forecast. Implied volatility uses option prices and so potentially the information set is richer. What needs further consideration is if all of its information is now being extracted and if it could still be widened to further improve forecast accuracy especially that of long horizon forecasts. To achieve this we need to understand better the cause of volatility (both historical and implied). Such an understanding will help to improve time series methods, which are the only viable methods when options, or market-based forecast, are not available.

Closely related to the above is the need to understand the source of volatility persistence and the volume-volatility research appears to be promising in providing a framework in which volatility persistence may be closely scrutinized. The mixture of distribution hypothesis (MDH) proposed by Clark (1973), the link between volume-volatility and market trading mechanism in Tauchen and Pitts (1983), and the empirical findings of the volume-volatility relationship surveyed in Karpoff (1987) are useful starting points. Given that Lamoureux and Lastrapes (1990) find volume to be strongly significant when it is inserted into the ARCH variance process, while returns shocks become insignificant, and that Gallant, Rossi and Tauchen (1993) find conditioning on lagged volume substantially attenuates the 'leverage' effect, the volume-volatility research may lead to a new and better way for modelling returns distributions. To this end, Andersen (1996) puts forward a generalized framework for the MDH where the joint dynamics of returns and volume are estimated, and reports a significant reduction in the estimated volatility persistence. Such a model may be useful for analysing the economic factors behind the observed volatility clustering in returns, but such a line of research has not yet been pursued vigorously.

There are many old issues that have been around for a long time. These include consistent forecasts of interest rate volatilities that satisfies the no-arbitrage relationship across all interest rate instruments, more tests on the use of absolute returns models in comparison with squared returns models in forecasting volatility, a multivariate approach to volatility forecasting where cross-correlation and volatility spillover may be accommodated, etc.

There are many new adventures that are currently under way as well.[1] These include the realized volatility approach, noticeably driven by Andersen, Bollerslev, Diebold and various co-authors, the estimation and forecast of volatility risk premium, the use of spot and option price data simultaneously (e.g. Chernov and Ghysels, 2000), and the use of Bayesian and other methods to estimate stochastic volatility models (e.g. Jones, 2001), etc.

It is difficult to envisage in which direction volatility forecasting research will flourish in the next five years. If, within the next five years, we can cut the forecast error by half and remove the option pricing bias in *ex ante* forecast, this will be a very good achievement indeed. Producing by then forecasts of large events will mark an important milestone.

---

[1] We thank a referee for these suggestions.

Appendix

No.	Author(s)	Asset(s)	Data period	Data frequency	Forecasting methods and rank	Forecasting horizon	Evaluation and R-squared	Comments
1.	Akigray (1989)	CRSP VW & EW indices	Jan63–Dec86 (pre-crash) split into 4 subperiods of 6 years each	D	GARCH(1,1) ARCH(2) EWMA HIS (ranked)	20 days ahead estimated from rolling 4 years data. Daily returns used to construct 'actual vol.'; adjusted for serial correlation	ME, RMSE, MAE, MAPE	GARCH is least biased and produced best forecast especially in periods of high volatility and when changes in volatility persist. Heteroscedasticity is less strong in low-frequency data and monthly returns are approximately Normal
2.	Alford and Boatman (1995)	6879 stocks listed in NYSE/ ASE & NASDAQ	12/66–6/87	W, M	'Shrinkage' forecast (HIS adjusted towards comparable firms) HIS Median HIS vol. of 'comparable' firm (ranked)	5 years starting from 6 months after firm's fiscal year	MedE, MedAE	To predict 5-year monthly volatility one should use 5 year's worth of weekly or monthly data. Adjusting historical forecast using industry and size produced best forecast

Continued

	Author(s)	Asset(s)	Data period	Data frequency	Forecasting methods and rank	Forecasting horizon	Evaluation and R-squared	Comments
3.	Amin and Ng (1997)	3M Eurodollar futures & futures options	1/1/88–1/11/92	D	Implied[American All Call+Put] (WLS, 5 variants of the HJM model) HIS (ranked)	20 days ahead (1 day ahead forecast produced from in-sample with lag implied in GARCH/GJR not discussed here)	R^2 is 21% for implied and 24% for combined. H_0: $\alpha_{\text{implied}} = 0$, $\beta_{\text{implied}} = 1$ cannot be rejected with robust SE	Interest rate models that incorporate volatility term structure (e.g. Vasicek) perform best. Interaction term capturing rate level and volatility contribute additional forecasting power
4.	Andersen and Bollerslev (1998)	DM/\$, ¥/\$	In: 1/10/87–30/9/92 Out: 1/10/92–30/9/93	D (5 min)	GARCH(1, 1)	1 day ahead, use 5-min returns to construct 'actual vol.'	R^2 is 5 to 10% for daily squared returns, 50% for 5-min square returns	R^2 increases monotonically with sample frequency
5.	Andersen, Bollerslev, Diebold and Labys (2001)	¥/US\$, DM/US\$ Reuters FXFX quotes	In: 1/12/86–30/6/99 In: 1/12/86–1/12/96, 10 years Out: 2/12/96–30/6/99, 2.5 years	Tick (30 min)	VAR-RV, AR-RV, FIEGARCH-RV GARCH-D, RM-D, FIEGARCH-D VAR-ABS (ranked)	1 and 10 days ahead. 'Actual vol.' derived from 30-min returns	1-day-ahead R^2 ranges between 27 and 40% (1-day-ahead) and 20 and 33% (10-days-ahead).	RV is realized volatility, D is daily return, and ABS is daily absolute return. VAR allows all series to share the same fractional integrated order and cross-series linkages. Forecast improvement is largely due to the use of high-frequency data (and realised volatility) instead of the model(s)

No.	Study	Data	Frequency	Models	Forecast horizon / 'actual vol.'	Error measure	Findings
6.	Andersen, Bollerslev and Lange (1999)	DM/US$ Reuters quotes	1/12/86–30/11/96 In: 1/10/87–30/9/92	5 min	GARCH(1, 1) at 5-min, 10-min, 1-hr, 8-hr, 1-day, 5-day, 20-day interval	1, 5 and 20 days ahead, use 5-min returns to construct 'actual vol.'	RMSE, MAE, HRMSE, HMAE, LL	HRMSE and HMAE are heteroscedasticity-adjusted error statistics; LL is the logarithmic loss function. High-frequency returns and high-frequency GARCH(1, 1) models improve forecast accuracy. But, for sampling frequencies shorter than 1 hour, the theoretical results and forecast improvement break down
7.	Bali (2000)	3-, 6-, 12-month T-Bill rates	8/1/54–25/12/98	W	NGARCH GJR, TGARCH AGARCH, QGARCH TSGARCH GARCH VGARCH Constant vol. (CKLS) (ranked, forecast both level and volatility)	1 week ahead. Use weekly interest rate absolute change to proxy 'actual vol.'	R^2 increases from 2% to 60% by allowing for asymmetries, level effect and changing volatility	CKLS: Chan, Karolyi, Longstaff and Sanders (1992)

Continued

	Author(s)	Asset(s)	Data period	Data frequency	Forecasting methods and rank	Forecasting horizon	Evaluation and R-squared	Comments
8.	Beckers (1981)	62 to 116 stocks options	28/4/75– 21/10/77	D	FBSD Implied$_{\text{ATM call, 5 days ave}}$ Implied$_{\text{vega call, 5 days ave}}$ RW$_{\text{last quarter}}$ (ranked, both implieds are 5-day average because of large variations in daily stock implied)	Over option's maturity (3 months), 10 non-overlapping cycles. Use sample SD of daily returns over option maturity to proxy 'actual vol.'	MPE, MAPE. Cross sectional R^2 ranges between 34 and 70% across models and expiry cycles. FBSD appears to be least biased with $\alpha = 0$, $\beta = 1$. $\alpha > 0$, $\beta < 1$ for the other two implieds	FBSD: Fisher Black's option pricing service takes into account stock vol. tend to move together, mean revert, leverage effect and implied can predict future. ATM, based on vega WLS, outperforms vega weighted implied, and is not sensitive to ad hoc dividend adjustment. Incremental information from all measures suggests option market inefficiency. Most forecasts are upwardly biased as actual vol. was on a decreasing trend
		50 stock options	4 dates: 18/10/76, 24/1/77, 18/4/77, 18/7/77	D (from Tick)	TISD$_{\text{vega}}$ Implied$_{\text{ATM call, 1 days ave}}$ (ranked)	ditto	Cross-sectional R^2 ranges between 27 and 72% across models and expiry cycles	TISD: Single intraday transaction data that has the highest vega. The superiority of TISD over implied of closing option prices suggest significant non-simultaneity and bid–ask spread problems

No.	Author	Data	Period	D/W/M	Models	Method	Error measure	Comments
9.	Bera and Higgins (1997)	Daily SP500, Weekly $/£, Monthly US Ind. Prod.	SP 1/1/88–28/5/93 $/£ 12/12/85–28/2/91 Ind. Prod. 1/60–3/93	D W M	GARCH Bilinear model (ranked)	One step ahead. Reserve 90% of data for estimation	Cox MLE RMSE (LE: logarithmic error)	Consider if heteroscedasticity is due to bilinear in level. Forecasting results show strong preference for GARCH
10.	Blair, Poon and Taylor (2001)	S&P100 (VXO)	2/1/87–31/12/99 Out: 4/1/93–31/2/99	Tick	Implied$_{VXO}$ GJR HIS$_{100}$ (ranked)	1, 5, 10 and 20 days ahead estimated using a rolling sample of 1000 days. Daily actual volatility is calculated from 5-min returns	1-day-ahead R^2 is 45% for VXO, and 50% for combined. VXO is downward biased in out-of-sample period	Using squared returns reduces R^2 to 36% for both VXO and combined. Implied volatility has its own persistence structure. GJR has no incremental information though integrated HIS vol. can almost match IV forecasting power
11.	Bluhm and Yu (2000)	German DAX stock index and VDAX the DAX volatility index	In: 1/1/88–28/6/96 Out: 1/7/66–30/6/99	D	Implied$_{VDAX}$ GARCH(-M), SV EWMA, EGARCH, GJR, HIS (approx. ranked)	45 calendar days, 1, 10 and 180 trading days. 'Actual' is the sum of daily squared returns	MAPE, LINEX	Ranking varies a lot depend on forecast horizons and performance measures

Continued

	Author(s)	Asset(s)	Data period	Data frequency	Forecasting methods and rank	Forecasting horizon	Evaluation and R-squared	Comments
12.	Boudoukh, Richard-son and Whitelaw (1997)	3-month US T-Bill	1983–1992	D	EWMA, MDE GARCH(1, 1), HIS (ranked)	1 day ahead based on 150-day rolling period estimation. Realized volatility is the daily squared changes averaged across $t + 1$ to $t + 5$	MSE and regression. MDE has the highest R^2 while EWMA has the smallest MSE	MDE is multivariate density estimation where volatility weights depend on interest rate level and term spread. EWMA and MDE have comparable performance and are better than HIS and GARCH
13.	Brace and Hodgson (1991)	Futures option on Australian Stock Index (marking to market is needed for this option)	1986–87	D	HIS$_{5, 20, 65 \text{ days}}$ Implied$_{\text{NTM call, 20–75 days}}$ (ranked)	20 days ahead. Use daily returns to calculate standard deviations	Adj R^2 are 20% (HIS), 17% (HIS + implied). All $\alpha > 0$ and sig. some uni regr coeff are sig negative (for both HIS and implied)	Large fluctuations of R^2 from month to month. Results could be due to the difficulty in valuing futures style options
14.	Brailsford and Faff (1996)	Australian Statex-Actuaries Accumulation Index for top 56	1/1/74–30/6/93 In: Jan74–Dec85 Out: Jan86–Dec93 (include 87's crash period)	D	GJR, Regr, HIS, GARCH, MA, EWMA, RW, ES (rank sensitive to error statistics)	1 month ahead. Models estimated from a rolling 12-year window	ME, MAE, RMSE, MAPE, and a collection of asymmetric loss functions	Though the ranks are sensitive, some models dominate others; MA12 > MA5 and Regr. > MA > EWMA > ES. GJR came out quite well but is the only model that always underpredicts

No.	Author	Asset	Period	Freq.	Models	Forecast/Estimation	Evaluation	Findings
15.	Brooks (1998)	DJ Composite	17/11/78–30/12/88 Out: 17/10/86–30/12/88	D	RW, HIS, MA, ES, EWMA, AR, GARCH, EGARCH, GJR, Neural network (all about the same)	1 day ahead squared returns using rolling 2000 observations for estimation	MSE, MAE of variance, % overpredict. R^2 is around 4% increases to 24% for pre-crash data	Similar performance across models especially when 87's crash is excluded. Sophisticated models such as GARCH and neural net did not dominate. Volume did not help in forecasting volatility
16.	Canina and Figlewski (1993)	S&P100 (OEX)	15/3/83–28/3/87 (pre-crash)	D	HIS$_{60 \text{ calendar days}}$ Implied$_{\text{Binomial Call}}$ (ranked) Implied in 4 maturity gp, each subdivided into 8 intrinsic gp	7 to 127 calendar days matching option maturity, overlapping forecasts with Hansen std error. Use sample SD of daily returns to proxy 'actual vol.'	Combined R^2 is 17% with little contribution from implied. All $\alpha_{\text{implied}} > 0$, $\beta_{\text{implied}} < 1$ with robust SE	Implied has no correlation with future volatility and does not incorporate info. contained in recently observed volatility. Results appear to be peculiar for pre-crash period. Time horizon of 'actual vol.' changes day to day. Different level of implied aggregation produces similar results
17.	Cao and Tsay (1992)	Excess returns for S&P, VW EW indices	1928–1989	M	TAR EGARCH(1, 0) ARMA(1, 1) GARCH(1, 1) (ranked)	1 to 30 months. Estimation period ranges from 684 to 743 months Daily returns used to construct 'actual vol.'	MSE, MAE	TAR provides best forecasts for large stocks. EGARCH gives best long-horizon forecasts for small stocks (may be due to leverage effect). Difference in MAE can be as large as 38%

	Author(s)	Asset(s)	Data period	Data frequency	Forecasting methods and rank	Forecasting horizon	Evaluation and R-squared	Comments
18.	Chiras and Manaster (1978)	All stock options from CBOE	23 months from Jun73 to Apr75	M	Implied (weighted by price elasticity) $HIS_{20 months}$ (ranked)	20 months ahead. Use SD of 20 monthly returns to proxy 'actual vol.'	Cross-sectional R^2 of implied ranges 13–50% across 23 months. HIS adds 0–15% to R^2	Implied outperformed HIS especially in the last 14 months. Find implied increases and better behave after dividend adjustments and evidence of mispricing possibly due to the use European pricing model on American style options
19.	Christensen and Prabhala (1998)	S&P100 (OEX) Monthly expiry cycle	Nov83–May95	M	$Implied_{BS\ ATM\ 1\text{-month Call}}$ $HIS_{18\ days}$ (ranked)	Non-overlapping 24 calendar (or 18 trading) days. Use SD of daily returns to proxy 'actual vol.'	R^2 of log var are 39% (implied), 32% (HIS) and 41% (combined). $\alpha < 0$ (because of log), $\beta < 1$ with robust SE. Implied is more biased before the crash	Not adj. for dividend and early exercise. Implied dominates HIS. HIS has no additional information in subperiod analysis. Proved that results in Canina and Figlewski (1993) is due to pre-crash characteristics and high degree of data overlap relative to time series length. Implied is unbiased after controlling for measurement errors using $implied_{t-1}$ and HIS_{t-1}

No.	Author	Asset	Period	Freq	Model	Horizon	Statistics	Findings
20.	Christoffersen and Diebold (2000)	4 stk indices 4 ex rates US 10-year T-Bond	1/1/73–1/5/97	D	No model. (no rank; evaluate volatility forecastability (or persistence) by checking interval forecasts)	1 to 20 days	Run tests and Markov transition matrix eigenvalues (which is basically 1st-order serial coefficient of the hit sequence in the run test)	Equity and FX: forecastability decrease rapidly from 1 to 10 days. Bond: may extend as long as 15 to 20 days. Estimate bond returns from bond yields by assuming coupon equal to yield
21.	Cumby, Figlewski and Hasbrouck (1993)	¥/$, stocks (¥, $), bonds (¥, $)	7/77 to 9/90	W	EGARCH HIS (ranked)	1 week ahead, estimation period ranges from 299 to 689 weeks	R^2 varies from 0.3% to 10.6%.	EGARCH is better than naive in forecasting volatility though R-squared is low. Forecasting correlation is less successful
22.	Day and Lewis (1992)	S&P100 OEX option Reconstructed S&P100	Out: 11/11/83–31/12/89 In: 2/1/76–11/11/83	W	Implied$_{BS\,Call}$ (shortest but > 7 days, volume WLS) HIS$_{1\,week}$ GARCH EGARCH (ranked)	1 week ahead estimated from a rolling sample of 410 observations. Use sample variance of daily returns to proxy weekly 'actual vol.'	R^2 of variance regr. are 2.6% (implied) and 3.8% (encomp.). All forecasts add marginal info. H_0: $\alpha_{implied} = 0, \beta_{implied} = 1$ cannot be rejected with robust SE	Omit early exercise. Effect of 87's crash is unclear. When weekly squared returns were used to proxy 'actual vol,' R^2 increase and was max for HIS contrary to expectation (9% compared with 3.7% for implied)

Continued

Author(s)	Asset(s)	Data period	Data frequency	Forecasting methods and rank	Forecasting horizon	Evaluation and R-squared	Comments
23. Day and Lewis (1993)	Crude oil futures options Crude oil futures	14/11/86–18/3/91 8/4/83–18/3/91 coincide with Kuwait invasion by Iraq in second half of sample	D	Implied$_{\text{Binomial ATM Call}}$ HIS$_{\text{forecast horizon}}$ GARCH-M EGARCH-AR(1) (ranked)	Option maturity of 4 nearby contracts, (average 13.9, 32.5, 50.4 and 68 trading days to maturity). Estimated from rolling 500 observations	ME, RMSE, MAE. R^2 of variance regr. are 72% (short mat.) and 49% (long maturity). With robust SE $\alpha > 0$ for short and $\alpha = 0$ for long, $\beta = 1$ for all maturity	Implied performed extremely well. Performance of HIS and GARCH are similar. EGARCH much inferior. Bias adjusted and combined forecasts do not perform as well as unadjusted implied. GARCH has no incremental information. Result likely to be driven by Kuwait invasion by Iraq
24. Dimson and Marsh (1990)	UK FT All Share	1955–89	Q	ES, Regression RW, HA, MA (ranked)	Next quarter. Use daily returns to construct 'actual vol.'	MSE, RMSE, MAE, RMAE	Recommend exponential smoothing and regression model using fixed weights. Find ex ante time-varying optimization of weights does not work well ex post

| 25. Doidge and Wei (1998) | Toronto 35 stock index & European options | In: 2/8/88–31/12/91 Out: 1/92–7/95 | D | Combine3 Combine2 GARCH EGARCH HIS$_{100\,days}$ Combine1 Implied$_{BS\,Call+Put}$ (All maturities > 7 days, volume WLS) (ranked) | 1 month ahead from rolling sample estimation. No mention on how 'actual vol' was derived | MAE, MAPE, RMSE | Combine1 equal weight for GARCH and implied forecasts. Combine2 weighs GARCH and implied based on their recent forecast accuracy. Combine3 puts implied in GARCH conditional variance. Combine3 was estimated using full sample due to convergence problem; so not really out-of-sample forecast |
| 26. Dunis, Laws and Chauvin (2000) | DM/¥, £/DM, £/$, $/CHF, $/DM, $/¥ | In: 2/1/91–27/2/98 Out: 2/3/98–31/12/98 | D | GARCH(1, 1) AR(10)-Sq returns AR(10)-Abs returns SV(1) in log form HIS$_{21\ or\ 63\ trading\ days}$ Implied$_{ATM\ quotes}$ 1- & 3-M forward Combine Combine (except SV) (rank changes across currencies and forecast horizons) | 1 and 3 months (21 and 63 trading days) with rolling estimation. Actual volatility is calculated as the average absolute return over the forecast horizon | RMSE, MAE, MAPE, Theil-U, CDC (Correct Directional Change index) | No single model dominates though SV is consistently worst, and implied always improves forecast accuracy. Recommend equal weight combined forecast excluding SV |

Continued

Author(s)	Asset(s)	Data period	Data frequency	Forecasting methods and rank	Forecasting horizon	Evaluation and R-squared	Comments
27. Ederington and Guan (1999) 'Frown'	S&P500 futures options	1Jan88–30Apr98	D	Implied$_{BK\ 16\,Calls\ 16\,Puts}$ HIS$_{40\ days}$ (ranked)	Overlapping 10 to 35 days matching maturity of nearest to expiry option. Use SD of daily returns to proxy 'actual vol.'	Panel R^2 19% and individual R^2 ranges 6–17% (calls) and 15–36% (puts). Implied is biased and inefficient, $\alpha_{implied} > 0$ and $\beta_{implied} < 1$ with robust SE	Information content of implied across strikes exhibit a frown shape with options that are NTM and have moderately high strikes possess largest information content. HIS typically adds 2–3% to the R^2 and nonlinear implied terms add another 2–3%. Implied is unbiased and efficient when measurement error is controlled using Implied$_{t-1}$ and HIS$_{t-1}$.

| 28. Ederington and Guan (2000a) 'Forecasting volatility' | 5 DJ Stocks S&P500 3m Euro$ rate 10yr T-Bond yield DM/$ | 2/7/62–30/12/94 2/7/62–29/12/95 1/1/73–20/6/97 2/1/62–13/6/97 1/1/71–30/6/97 | D | GW_{MAD} GW_{STD}, GARCH, EGARCH AGARCH $HIS_{MAD, n}$, $HIS_{STD, n}$ (ranked, error statistics are close; GW_{MAD} leads consistently though with only small margin) | $n = 10, 20, 40,$ 80 and 120 days ahead estimated from a 1260-day rolling window; parameters re-estimated every 40 days. Use daily squared deviation to proxy 'actual vol.' | RMSE, MAE | GW: geometric weight, MAD: mean absolute deviation, STD: standard deviation. Volatility aggregated over a longer period produces a better forecast. Absolute returns models generally perform better than square returns models (except GARCH > AGARCH). As horizon lengthens, no procedure dominates. GARCH and EGARCH estimations were unstable at times |

Continued

Author(s)	Asset(s)	Data period	Data frequency	Forecasting methods and rank	Forecasting horizon	Evaluation and R-squared	Comments
29. Ederington and Guan (2000b) 'Averaging'	S&P500 futures options	In: 4/1/88–31/12/91 Out: 2/1/92–31/12/92	D	Implied:* 99%, VXO HIS$_{40\ \text{trading days}}$ Implied: VXO > Eq4 Implied: WLS > vega > Eq32 > elasticity (ranked)	Overlapping 10 to 35 days matching maturity of nearest to expiry option. Use SD of daily returns to proxy 'actual vol.'	RMSE, MAE, MAPE '*' indicates individual implieds were corrected for biasedness first before averaging using in-sample regr. on realized	VXO: 2calls+2puts, NTM weighted to get ATM. Eq4/32: calls+puts equally weighted. WLS, vega and elasticity are other weighting scheme. 99% means 1% of regr. error used in weighting all implieds. Once the biasedness has been corrected using regr., little is to be gained by any averaging in such a highly liquid S&P500 futures market

| 30. Ederington and Guan (2002) 'Efficient predictor' | S&P500 futures options | 1/1/83–14/9/95 | D | Implied$_{\text{Black 4 NTM}}$ GARCH, HIS$_{40\,\text{days}}$ (ranked) | Overlapping option maturity 7–90, 91–180, 181–365 and 7–365 days ahead. Use sample SD over forecast horizon to proxy 'actual vol.' | R^2 ranges 22–12% from short to long horizon. Post 87's crash R^2 nearly doubled. Implied is efficient biased; $\alpha_{\text{implied}} > 0$ and $\beta_{\text{implied}} < 1$ with robust SE | GARCH parameters were estimated using whole sample. GARCH and HIS add little to 7–90 day R^2. When 87's crash was excluded HIS add sig. explanatory power to 181–365 day forecast. When measurement errors were controlled using implied$_{t-5}$ and implied$_{t+5}$ as instrument variables implied becomes unbiased for the whole period but remains biased when crash period was excluded |

Continued

Author(s)	Asset(s)	Data period	Data frequency	Forecasting methods and rank	Forecasting horizon	Evaluation and R-squared	Comments
31. Edey and Elliot (1992)	Futures options on A\$ 90d-Bill, 10yr bond, Stock index	Futures options: inception to 12/88	W	Implied$_{BK \, NTM,call}$ Implied$_{BK \, NTM, put}$ (No rank, 1 call and 1 put, selected based on highest trading volume)	Option maturity up to 3M. Use sum of (return square plus Implied$_{t+1}$) as 'actual vol.'	Regression (see comment). In most cases $\alpha_{implied} > 0$ and $\beta_{implied} < 1$ with robust SE. For stock index option $\beta_{implied} = 1$ cannot be rejected using robust SE	R^2 cannot be compared with other studies because of the way 'actual' is derived and lagged squares returns were added to the RHS
	A\$/US\$ options	A\$/US\$ option: 12/84–12/87	W		Constant 1M. Use sum of weekly squared returns to proxy 'actual vol.'		
32. Engle, Ng and Rothschild (1990)	1 to 12 months T-Bill returns, VW index of NYSE & AMSE stocks	Aug64–Nov85	M	1-factor ARCH Univariate ARCH-M (ranked)	1 month ahead volatility and risk premium of 2 to 12 months T-Bills	Model fit	Equally weighted bill portfolio is effective in predicting (i.e. in an expectation model) volatility and risk premia of individual maturities

No.	Author	Asset	Period	Data	Models	Forecast horizon / proxy	Error statistics	Comments
33.	Feinstein (1989b)	S&P500 futures options (CME)	Jun83–Dec88	Option expiry cycle	Implied: Atlanta > average > vega > elasticity Just-OTM$_{Call}$ > P+C > Put HIS$_{20 days}$ (ranked, note pre-crash rank is very different and erratic)	23 non-overlapping forecasts of 57, 38 and 19 days ahead. Use sample SD of daily returns over the option maturity to proxy 'actual vol.'	MSE, MAE, ME. T-test indicates all ME > 0 (except HIS) in the post-crash period which means implied was upwardly biased	Atlanta: 5-day average of Just-OTM call implied using exponential weights. In general Just-OTM Implied$_{call}$ is the best
34.	Ferreira (1999)	French & German interbank 1M mid-rate	In: Jan81–Dec89 Out: Jan90–Dec97 (ERM crises: Sep92–Sep93)	W	ES, HIS$_{26, 52, all}$ GARCH(-L) (E)GJR(-L) (rank varies between French and German rates, sampling method and error statistics)	1 week ahead. Use daily squared rate changes to proxy weekly volatility	Regression, MPE, MAPE, RMSPE. R^2 is 41% for France and 3% for Germany	L: interest rate level, E: exponential. French rate was very volatile during ERM crises. German rate was extremely stable in contrast. Although there are lots of differences between the two rates, best models are nonparametric; ES (French) and simple level effect (German). Suggest a different approach is needed for forecasting interest rate volatility

Continued

	Author(s)	Asset(s)	Data period	Data frequency	Forecasting methods and rank	Forecasting horizon	Evaluation and R-squared	Comments
35.	Figlewski (1997)	S&P500 3m US T-Bill 20yr T-Bond DM/$	1/47–12/95 1/47–12/95 1/50–7/93 1/71–11/95	M	HIS$_{6, 12, 24, 36, 48, 60m}$ GARCH(1, 1) for S&P and bond yield. (ranked)	6, 12, 24, 36, 48, 60 months. Use daily returns to compute 'actual vol.'	RMSE	Forecast of volatility of the longest of the longest horizon is the most accurate. HIS uses the longest estimation period is the best except for short rate
		S&P500 3m US T-Bill 20yr T-Bond DM/$	2/7/62– 29/12/95 2/1/62– 29/12/95 2/1/62– 29/12/95 4/1/71– 30/11/95	D	GARCH(1, 1) HIS$_{1, 3, 6, 12, 24, 60\,months}$ (S&P's rank, reverse for the others)	1, 3, 6, 12, 24 months	RMSE	GARCH is best for S&P but gave worst performance in all the other markets. In general, as out-of-sample horizon increases, the in-sample length should also increase

| 36. | Figlewski and Green (1999) | S&P500 US LIBOR 10yr T-Bond yield DM/\$ | D | HiS$_{3, 12, 60\,months}$ ES (rank varies) | 1, 3, 12 months for daily data | RMSE | ES works best for S&P (1–3 month) and short rate (all three horizons), HIS works best for bond yield, exchange rate and long horizon S&P forecast. The longer the forecast horizon, the longer the estimation period |
| | | | M | HiS$_{26, 60, \,all\,months}$ ES (ranked) | 24 and 60 months for monthly data | | For S&P, bond yield and DM/\$, it is best to use all available 'monthly' data. 5 year's worth of data works best for short rate |

Continued

	Author(s)	Asset(s)	Data period	Data frequency	Forecasting methods and rank	Forecasting horizon	Evaluation and R-squared	Comments
37.	Fleming (1998)	S&P100 (OEX)	10/85–4/92 (all observations that overlap with 87's crash were removed)	D	Implied$_{Fw\ ATM\ calls}$ Implied$_{Fw\ ATM\ puts}$ (both implieds are WLS using all ATM options in the last 10 minutes before market close) ARCH/GARCH HIS$_{H-L\ 28\ days}$ (ranked)	Option maturity (shortest but > 15 days, average 30 calendar days), 1 and 28 days ahead. Use daily square return deviations to proxy 'actual vol.'	R^2 is 29% for monthly forecast and 6% for daily forecast. All $\alpha_{implied} = 0$, $\beta_{implied} < 1$ with robust SE for the last two fixed horizon forecasts	Implied dominates. All other variables related to volatility such as stock returns, interest rate and parameters of GARCH do not possess information incremental to that contained in implied
38.	Fleming, Kirby and Ostdiek (2000)	S&P500, T-Bond and gold futures	3/1/83–31/12/97	D	Exponentially weighted var-cov matrix	Daily rebalanced portfolio	Sharpe ratio (portfolio return over risk)	Efficient frontier of volatility timing strategy plotted above that of fixed weight portfolio

No.	Author	Sample period	Freq.	Model	Forecasting horizon / proxy	Evaluation / results	Findings
39.	Fleming, Ostdiek and Whaley (1995)	S&P100 (VXO) Jan86–Dec92	D, W	Implied $_{VXO}$ $HIS_{20\,days}$ (ranked)	28 calendar (or 20 trading) day. Use sample SD of daily returns to proxy 'actual vol.'	R^2 increased from 15% to 45% when crash is excluded. $\alpha_{VXO} = 0$, $\beta_{VXO} < 1$ with robust SE	VXO dominates HIS, but is biased upward up to 580 basis points. Orthogonality test rejects HIS when VXO is included. Adjust VXO forecasts with average forecast errors of the last 253 days helps to correct for biasedness while retaining implied's explanatory power
40.	Franses and Ghijsels (1999)	Dutch, German, Spanish and Italian stock market returns, 1983–94	W	AO-GARCH (GARCH adjusted for additive outliers using the 'less-one' method) GARCH GARCH-t (ranked)	1 week ahead estimated from previous 4 years. Use weekly squared deviations to proxy 'actual vol.'	MSE and MedSE	Forecasting performance significantly improved when parameter estimates are not influenced by 'outliers'. Performance of GARCH-t is consistently much worse. Same results for all four stock markets

Continued

Author(s)	Asset(s)	Data period	Data frequency	Forecasting methods and rank	Forecasting horizon	Evaluation and R-squared	Comments
41. Franses and Van Dijk (1996)	Stock indices (Germany, Netherlands, Spain, Italy, Sweden)	1986–94	W	QGARCH RW GARCH GJR (ranked)	1 week ahead estimated from rolling 4 years. Use weekly squared deviations to proxy 'actual vol.'	MedSE	QGARCH is best if data has no extremes. RW is best when 87's crash is included. GJR cannot be recommended. Results are likely to be influenced by MedSE that penalize nonsymmetry. Brailsford and Faff (1996) support GJR as best model although it underpredicts over 70% of the time

| 42. | Frennberg and Hansson (1996) | VW Swedish stock market returns
Index option (European style) | M | In:
1919–1976
Out: 1977–82, 1983–90
Jan87–Dec90 | $AR_{12}(ABS)$-S RW, Implied$_{BS\ ATM\ Call}$ (option maturity closest to 1 month) GARCH-S, ARCH-S (ranked)
Models that are not adj. for seasonality did not perform as well | 1 month ahead estimated from recursively re-estimated expanding sample. Use daily ret. to compile monthly vol., adjusted for autocorrelation | MAPE, R^2 is 2–7% in first period and 11–24% in second, more volatile period. H_0: $\alpha_{implied} = 0$ and $\beta_{implied} = 1$ cannot be rejected with robust SE | S: seasonality adjusted. RW model seems to perform remarkably well in such a small stock market where returns exhibit strong seasonality. Option was introduced in 86 and covered 87's crash; outperformed by RW. ARCH/ GARCH did not perform as well in the more volatile second period |
| 43. | Fung, Lie and Moreno (1990) | £/$, C$/$, FFr$, DM/$, ¥/$ & SrFr/$ options on PHLX | D | 1/84–2/87 (pre-crash) | Implied$_{OTM>ATM}$ Implied$_{vega,\ elasticity}$ Implied$_{equal\ weight}$ HIS$_{40\ days}$, Implied$_{TTM}$ (ranked, all implied are from calls) | Option maturity; overlapping periods. Use sample SD of daily returns over option maturity to proxy 'actual vol.' | RMSE, MAE of overlapping forecasts | Each day, 5 options were studied; 1 ATM, 2 just in and 2 just out. Define ATM as S = X, OTM marginally outperformed ATM. Mixed together implied of different contract months |

Continued

Author(s)	Asset(s)	Data period	Data frequency	Forecasting methods and rank	Forecasting horizon	Evaluation and R-squared	Comments
44. Fung and Hsieh (1991)	S&P500, DM$ US T-bond Futures and futures options	3/83–7/89 (DM/$ futures from 26 Feb 85)	D (15 min)	RV-AR(n) Implied$_{BAW\,NTM\,Call/Put}$ RV, RW (C-t-C) HL (ranked, some of the differences are small)	1 day ahead. Use 15-min data to construct 'actual vol.'	RMSE and MAE of $\log \sigma$	RV: Realized vol. from 15-min returns. AR(n): autoregressive lags of order n. RW (C-t-C): random walk forecast based on close to close returns. HL: Parkinson's daily high-low method. Impact of 1987 crash does not appear to be drastic possibly due to taking log. In general, high-frequency data improves forecasting power greatly

| 45. | Gemmill (1986) | 13 UK stocks LTOM options. Stock price | May78–Jul83 M
Jan 78–Nov83 D | Implied$_{ITM}$
Implied$_{ATM, vega\ WLS}$
Implied$_{equal, OTM, elasticity}$
HIS$_{20\ Weeks}$
(ranked, all implied are from calls) | 13–21 non-overlapping option maturity (each average 19 weeks). Use sample SD of weekly returns over option maturity to proxy 'actual vol.' | ME, RMSE, MAE aggregated across stocks and time. R^2 are 6–12% (pooled) and 40% (panel with firm specific intercepts). All $\alpha > 0, \beta < 1$ | Adding HIS increases R^2 from 12% to 15%. But *ex ante* combined forecast from HIS and Implied$_{ITM}$ turned out to be worse than individual forecasts. Suffered small sample and nonsynchroneity problems and omitted dividends |

Continued

Author(s)	Asset(s)	Data period	Data frequency	Forecasting methods and rank	Forecasting horizon	Evaluation and R-squared	Comments
46. Gray (1996)	US 1m T-Bill	1/70–4/94	W	RSGARCH with time varying probability GARCH Constant variance (ranked)	1 week ahead (model not re-estimated). Use weekly squared deviation to proxy volatility	R^2 calculated without constant term, is 4 to 8% for RSGARCH, negative for some CV and GARCH. Comparable RMSE and MAE between GARCH and RSGARCH	Volatility follows GARCH and CIR square root process. Interest rate rise increases probability of switching into high-volatility regime Low-volatility persistence and strong rate level mean reversion at high-volatility state. At low-volatility state, rate appears random walk and volatility is highly persistent

| 47. | Guo (1996a) | PHLX US$/¥ options | Jan91–Mar93 | D | $\text{Implied}_{\text{Heston}}$ $\text{Implied}_{\text{HW}}$ $\text{Implied}_{\text{BS}}$ GARCH HIS_{60} (ranked) | Information not available | Regression with robust SE. No information on R^2 and forecast biasedness | Use mid of bid-ask option price to limit 'bounce' effect. Eliminate 'nonsynchroneity' by using simultaneous exchange rate and option price. HIS and GARCH contain no incremental information. $\text{Implied}_{\text{Heston}}$ and $\text{Implied}_{\text{HW}}$ are comparable and are marginally better than $\text{Implied}_{\text{BS}}$. *Only have access to abstract* |

Author(s)	Asset(s)	Data period	Data frequency	Forecasting methods and rank	Forecasting horizon	Evaluation and R-squared	Comments
48. Guo (1996b)	PHLX US$/¥, US$/DM options Spot rate	Jan86–Feb93	Tick D	Implied$_{HW}$ (WLS, 0.8 < S/X < 1.2, 20 < T < 60 days) GARCH (1, 1) HIS$_{60 \text{ days}}$ (ranked)	60 days ahead. Use sample variance of daily returns to proxy actual volatility	US$/DM R^2 is 4, 3, 1% for the three methods. (9, 4, 1% for US$/¥) All forecasts are biased $\alpha > 0$, $\beta < 1$ with robust SE	Conclusion same as Guo (1996a). Use Barone-Adesi/Whaley approximation for American options. No risk premium for volatility variance risk. GARCH has no incremental information. Visual inspection of figures suggests implied forecasts lagged actual
49. Hamid (1998)	S&P500 futures options	3/83–6/93	D	13 schemes (including HIS, implied cross-strike average and intertemporal averages) (ranked, see comment)	Non-overlapping 15, 35 and 55 days ahead	RMSE, MAE	Implied is better than historical and cross-strike averaging is better than intertemporal averaging (except during very turbulent periods)

No.	Study	Series	Freq.	Period	Model	Horizon	Evaluation	Findings
50.	Hamilton and Lin (1996)	Excess stock returns (S&P500 minus T-Bill) & Ind. Production	M	1/65–6/93	Bivariate RSARCH Univariate RSARCH GARCH+L ARCH+L AR(1) (ranked)	1 month ahead. Use squared monthly residual returns to proxy volatility	MAE	Found economic recessions drive fluctuations in stock returns volatility. 'L' denotes leverage effect. RS model outperformed ARCH/GARCH+L
51.	Hamilton and Susmel (1994)	NYSE VW stock index	W	3/7/62– 29/12/87	RSARCH+L GARCH+L ARCH+L (ranked)	1, 4 and 8 weeks ahead. Use squared weekly residual returns to proxy volatility	MSE, MAE, MSLE, MALE. Errors calculated from variance and log variance	Allowing up to 4 regimes with t distribution. RSARCH with leverage (L) provides best forecast. Student-t is preferred to GED and Gaussian
52.	Harvey and Whaley (1992)	S&P100 (OEX)	D	Oct85–Jul89	Implied$_{\text{ATM calls+puts}}$ (American binomial, shortest maturity > 15 days) (predict changes in implied)	1 day ahead implied for use in pricing next day option	R^2 is 15% for calls and 4% for puts (excluding 1987 crash)	Implied volatility changes are statistically predictable, but market was efficient, as simulated transactions (NTM call and put and delta hedged using futures) did not produce profit

Continued

	Author(s)	Asset(s)	Data period	Data frequency	Forecasting methods and rank	Forecasting horizon	Evaluation and R-squared	Comments
53.	Heynen and Kat (1994)	7 stock indices and 5 exchange rates	1/1/80–31/12/92 In: 80–87 Out: 88–92 (87's crash included in in-sample)	D	SV(?) EGARCH GARCH RW (ranked, see also comment)	Non-overlapping 5, 10, 15, 20, 25, 50, 75, 100 days horizon with constant update of parameters estimates. Use standard sample standard deviations of daily returns to proxy 'actual vol.'	MedSE	SV appears to dominate in index but produces errors that are 10 times larger than (E)GARCH in exchange rate. The impact of 87's crash is unclear. Conclude that volatility model forecasting performance depends on the asset class
54.	Hol and Koopman (2002)	S&P100 (VXO)	2/1/86–29/6/2001 Out: Jan97–Jun01	D	SIV SVX⁺ SV (ranked)	1, 2, 5, 10, 15 and 20 days ahead. Use 10-min returns to construct 'actual vol.'	R^2 ranges between 17 and 33%, MSE, MedSE, MAE. α and β not reported. All forecasts underestimate actuals	SVX is SV with impliedvxo as an exogenous variable while SVX⁺ is SVX with persistence adjustment. SIV is stochastic implied with persistence parameter set equal to zero

No.	Author	Market	Freq	Model	Sample	Forecast horizon / method	Error measure	Findings
55.	Hwang and Satchell (1998)	LIFFE stock options	D	Log-ARFIMA-RV Scaled truncated Detrended Unscaled truncated $MA_{opt\ n=20}$-IV Adj $MA_{opt\ n=20}$-RV GARCH-RV (ranked, forecast implied)	23/3/92–7/10/96. 240 daily out-of-sample forecasts.	1, 5, 10, 20,..., 90, 100, 120 days ahead IV estimated from a rolling sample of 778 daily observations. Different estimation intervals were tested for robustness	MAE, MFE	Forecast implied$_{ATM\,BS}$ of shortest maturity option (with at 15 trading days to maturity). Build MA in IV and ARIMA on log (IV). Error statistics for all forecasts are close except those for GARCH forecasts. The scaling in Log-ARFIMA-RV is to adjust for Jensen inequality
56.	Jorion (1995)	DM/$, ¥/$, SrFr/$ futures options on CME	D	Implied$_{ATM\,BS\ call+put}$ GARCH (1, 1), MA_{20} (ranked)	1/85–2/92, 7/86–2/92, 3/85–2/92	1 day ahead and option maturity. Use squared returns and aggregate of square returns to proxy actual volatility	R^2 is 5% (1-day) or 10–15% (option maturity). With robust SE, $\alpha_{implied} > 0$ and $\beta_{implied} < 1$ for long horizon and is unbiased for 1-day forecasts	Implied is superior to the historical methods and least biased. MA and GARCH provide only marginal incremental information

Continued

Author(s)	Asset(s)	Data period	Data frequency	Forecasting methods and rank	Forecasting horizon	Evaluation and R-squared	Comments
57. Jorion (1996)	DM/\$ futures options on CME	Jan85–Feb92	D	Implied$_{\text{Black, ATM}}$ GARCH(1, 1) (ranked)	1 day ahead, use daily squared to proxy actual volatility	R^2 about 5%. H_0: $\alpha_{\text{implied}} = 0$, $\beta_{\text{implied}} = 1$ cannot be rejected with robust SE	R^2 increases from 5% to 19% when unexpected trading volume is included. Implied volatility subsumed information in GARCH forecast, expected futures trading volume and bid–ask spread
58. Karolyi (1993)	74 stock options	13/1/84–11/12/85	M	Bayesian implied$_{\text{Call}}$ Implied$_{\text{Call}}$ HIS$_{20,60}$ (Predict option price not 'actual vol.')	20 days ahead volatility	MSE	Bayesian adjustment to implied to incorporate cross-sectional information such as firm size, leverage and trading volume useful in predicting next period option price

59.	Klaassen (1998)	US\$/£, US\$/DM and US\$/¥	D	3/1/78–23/7/97 Out: 20/10/87–23/7/97	RSGARCH RSARCH GARCH(1, 1) (ranked)	1 and 10 days ahead. Use mean adjusted 1- and 10-day return squares to proxy actual volatility	MSE of variance, regression though R^2 is not reported	GARCH(1, 1) forecasts are more variable than RS models. RS provides statistically significant improvement in forecasting volatility for US\$/DM but not the other exchange rates
60.	Kroner, Kneafsey and Claessens (1995)	Futures options on cocoa, cotton, corn, gold, silver, sugar, wheat Futures prices	D	Jan87–Dec90 (kept last 40 observations for out-of-sample forecast) Jan87–Jul91	GR > COMB Implied$_{BAW}$ Call (WLS > AVG > ATM) HIS$_{7\ weeks}$ > GARCH (ranked)	225 calendar days (160 working days) ahead, which is longer than average	MSE, ME	GR: Granger and Ramanathan (1984)'s regression weighted combined forecast, COMB: lag implied in GARCH conditional variance equation. Combined method is best suggests option market inefficiency

Continued

Author(s)	Asset(s)	Data period	Data frequency	Forecasting methods and rank	Forecasting horizon	Evaluation and R-squared	Comments
61. Lamoureux and Lastrapes (1993)	Stock options for 10 non-dividend-paying stocks (CBOE)	19/4/82–31/3/84	D	Implied$_{Hull-White}$ NTM Call (intermediate term to maturity, WLS) HIS$_{updated\ expanding\ estimate}$ GARCH (ranked, based on regression result)	90 to 180 days matching option maturity estimated using rolling 300 observations and expanding sample. Use sample variance of daily returns to proxy 'actual vol.'	ME, MAE, RMSE. Average implied is lower than actual for all stocks. R^2 on variance varies between 3 and 84% across stocks and models	Implied volatility is best but biased. HIS provides incremental info. to implied and has the lowest RMSE. When all three forecasts are included; $\alpha > 0$, $1 > \beta_{implied} > 0$, $\beta_{GARCH} = 0$, $\beta_{HIS} < 0$ with robust SE. Plausible explanations include option traders overreact to recent volatility shocks, and volatility risk premium is nonzero and time-varying

62. Latane and Rendleman (1976)	24 stock options from CBOE	5/10/73– 28/6/74	W	Implied $_{vega\ weighted}$ HIS$_{4\ years}$ (ranked)	In-sample forecast and forecast that extend partially into the future. Use weekly and monthly returns to calculate actual volatility of various horizons	Cross-section correlation between volatility estimates for 38 weeks and a 2-year period	Used European model on American options and omitted dividends. 'Actual' is more correlated (0.686) with 'Implied' than HIS volatility (0.463) Highest correlation is that between implied and actual standard deviations which were calculated partially into the future
63. Lee (1991)	$/DM, $/£, $/¥, $/FFr, $/C$ (Fed. Res. Bulletin)	7/3/73– 4/10/89, Out: 21 Oct81 –11 Oct89.	W (Wed, 12pm)	Kernel (Gaussian, truncated) Index (combining ARMA and GARCH) EGARCH (1, 1) GARCH (1, 1) IGARCH with trend (rank changes see comment for general assessment)	1 week ahead (451 observations in sample and 414 observations out-of-sample)	RMSE, MAE. It is not clear how actual volatility was estimated	Nonlinear models are, in general, better than linear GARCH. Kernel method is best with MAE. But most of the RMSE and MAE are very close. Over 30 kernel models were fitted, but only those with smallest RMSE and MAE were reported. It is not clear how the nonlinear equivalence was constructed. Multi-step forecast results were mentioned but not shown

Author(s)	Asset(s)	Data period	Data frequency	Forecasting methods and rank	Forecasting horizon	Evaluation and R-squared	Comments
64. Li (2002)	$/DM, $/£, $/¥ OTC ATM options $/£, $/¥ $/DM	3/12/86– 30/12/99 In: 12/8/86– 11/5/95 19/6/94– 13/6/99 19/6/94– 30/12/98	Tick (5 min) D D	Implied GK OTC ATM ARFIMA realised (implied better at shorter horizon and ARFIMA better at long horizon)	1, 2, 3 and 6 months ahead. Parameters not re-estimated. Use 5-min returns to construct 'actual vol.'	MAE. R^2 ranges 0.3–51% (implied), 7.3–47% (LM), 16–53% (encompass). For both models, H$_0$: $\alpha = 0, \beta = 1$ are rejected and typically $\beta < 1$ with robust SE	Both forecasts have incremental information especially at long horizon. Forcing: $\alpha = 0, \beta = 1$ produce low/negative R^2 (especially for long horizon). Model realized standard deviation as ARFIMA without log transformation and with no constant, which is awkward as a theoretical model for volatility

Study	Data	Period		Models	Forecast	Evaluation	Comments
65. Lopez (2001)	C$/US$, DM/US$, ¥/US$, US$/£	1980–1995 In: 1980–1993 Out: 1994–1995	D	SV-AR(1)-normal GARCH-gev EWMA-normal GARCH-normal, -t EWMA-t AR(10)-Sq, -Abs Constant (approx. rank, see comments)	1 day ahead and probability forecasts for four 'economic events', viz. cdf of specific regions. Use daily squared residuals to proxy volatility. Use empirical distribution to derive cdf	MSE, MAE, LL, HMSE, GMLE and QPS (quadratic probability scores)	LL is the logarithmic loss function from Pagan and Schwert (1990), HMSE is the heteroscedasticity-adj. MSE from Bollerslev and Ghysels (1996) and GMLE is the Gaussian quasi-ML function from Bollerslev, Engle and Nelson (1994). Forecasts from all models are indistinguishable. QPS favours SV-n, GARCH-g and EWMA-n
66. Loudon, Watt and Yadav (2000)	FT All Share	Jan71–Oct97 Sub-periods: Jan71–Dec80 Jan81–Dec90 Jan91–Oct97	D	EGARCH, GJR, TS-GARCH, TGARCH NGARCH, VGARCH, GARCH, MGARCH (no clear rank, forecast GARCH vol.)	Parameters estimated in period 1 (or 2) used to produce conditional variances in period 2 (or 3). Use GARCH squared residuals as 'actual' volatility	RMSE, regression on log volatility and a list of diagnostics. R^2 is about 4% in period 2 and 5% in period 3	TS-GARCH is an absolute return version of GARCH. All GARCH specifications have comparable performance though nonlinear, asymmetric versions seem to fare better. Multiplicative GARCH appears worst, followed by NGARCH and VGARCH (Engle and Ng 1993)

Continued

Author(s)	Data Asset(s)	Data period	Forecasting frequency	Forecasting methods and rank	Evaluation horizon	and R-squared	Comments
67. Martens and Zein (2004)	S&P500 futures, ¥/US$ futures, Crude oil futures	Jan94–Dec2000 Jan96–Dec2000 Jun93–Dec2000	Tick	Implied$_{BAW}$ VXO$_{style}$ Log-ARFIMA GARCH (ranked, see comment also)	Non-overlapping 1, 5, 10, 20, 30 and 40 days ahead. 500 daily observations in in-sample which expands on each iteration	Heteroscedasticity adjusted RMSE. R^2 ranges 25–52% (implied), 15–48% (LM) across assets and horizons. Both models provide incremental info. to encompassing regr.	Scaled down one large oil price. Log-ARFIMA truncated at lag 100. Based on R^2, Implied outperforms GARCH in every case, and beats Log-ARFIMA in ¥/US$ and crude oil. Implied has larger HRMSE than Log-ARFIMA in most cases. *Difficult to comment on implied's biasedness from information presented*
68. McKenzie (1999)	21 A$ bilateral exchange rates	Various length from 1/1/86 or 4/11/92 to 31/10/95	D	Square vs. power transformation (ARCH models with various lags. See comment for rank)	1 day ahead absolute returns	RMS, ME, MAE. Regressions suggest all ARCH forecasts are biased. No R^2 was reported	The optimal power is closer to 1 suggesting squared return is not the best specification in ARCH type model for forecasting purpose

| 69. McMillan, Speight and Gwilym (2000) | FTSE100
FT All Share

Jan84–Jul96
Jan69–Jul96

Out:
1996–1996 for both series. | D, W, M | RW, MA, ES, EWMA
GARCH,
TGARCH,
EGARCH,
CGARCH
HIS, regression,
(ranked) | j = 1 day, 1 week and 1 month ahead based on the three data frequencies. Use j period squared returns to proxy actual volatility | ME, MAE, RMSE for symmetry loss function. MME(U) and MME(O), mean mixed error that penalize under/over predictions | CGARCH is the component GARCH model. Actual volatility is proxied by mean adjusted squared returns, which is likely to be extremely noisy. Evaluation conducted on variance, hence forecast error statistics are very close for most models. RW, MA, ES dominate at low frequency and when crash is included. Performances of GARCH models are similar though not as good |

Continued

Author(s)	Data Asset(s)	Data period	Forecasting frequency	Forecasting methods and rank	Evaluation horizon	and R-squared	Comments
70. Noh, Engle and Kane (1994)	S&P500 index options	Oct85–Feb92	D	GARCH adj. for weekend and hols Implied$_{BS}$ weighted by trading volume (ranked, predict option price not 'actual vol.')	Option maturity. Based on 1000 days rolling period estimation	Equate forecastability with profitability under the assumption of an inefficient option market	Regression with call+put implieds, daily dummies and previous day returns to predict next day implied and option prices. Straddle strategy is not vega neutral even though it might be delta neutral assuming market is complete. It is possible that profit is due to now well-documented post 87's crash higher option premium
71. Pagan and Schwert (1990)	US stock market	1834–1937 Out: 1900–1925 (low volatility), 1926–1937 (high volatility)	M	EGARCH(1, 2) GARCH(1, 2) 2-step conditional variance RS-AR(m) Kernel (1 lag) Fourier (1 or 2 lags) (ranked)	1 month ahead. Use squared residual monthly returns to proxy actual volatility	R^2 is 7–11% for 1900–25 and 8% for 1926–37. Compared with R^2 for variance, R^2 for log variance is smaller in 1900–25 and larger in 1926–37	The nonparametric models fared worse than the parametric models. EGARCH came out best because of the ability to capture volatility asymmetry. Some prediction bias was documented

Study	Asset	Data	Period	Models	Horizon	Evaluation	Findings
72. Pong, Shackleton, Taylor and Xu (2004)	US$/£	5-, 30-min futures Tick	In: Jul87–Dec93 Out: Jan94–Dec98	Implied$_{ATM}$, OTC quote (bias adj. using rolling regr. on last 5 years monthly data) Log-ARMA(2, 1) Log-ARFIMA (1, d, 1) GARCH(1, 1) (ranked)	1 month and 3 months ahead at 1-month interval	ME, MSE, R^2 regression. R^2 ranges between 22 and 39% (1-month) and 6 and 21% (3-month)	Implied, ARMA and ARFIMA have similar performance. GARCH(1, 1) clearly inferior. Best combination is Implied + ARMA (2, 1). Log-AR(FI)MA forecasts adjusted for Jensen inequality. *Difficult to comment on implied's biasedness from information presented*
73. Poteshman (2000)	S&P500 (SPX) & futures S&P500	D futures Tick M	1Jun88–29Aug97 Heston estimation: 1Jun93–29Aug97 7Jun62–May93	Implied$_{Heston}$ Implied$_{BS}$ (both implieds are from WLS of all options <7 months but >6 calendar days) HIS$_{1, 2, 3, 6 \text{ months}}$ (ranked)	Option maturity (about 3.5 to 4 weeks, non-overlapping). Use 5-min futures inferred index return to proxy 'actual vol.'	BS R^2 is over 50%. Heston implied produced similar R^2 but very close to being unbiased	F test for H$_0$: $\alpha_{BS} = 0$, $\beta_{BS} = 1$ are rejected though t-test supports H$_0$ on individual coefficients. Show biasedness is not caused by bid-ask spread. Using in σ, high-frequency realized vol., and Heston model, all help to reduce implied biasedness

Continued

Author(s)	Asset(s)	Data period	Data frequency	Forecasting methods and rank	Forecasting horizon	Evaluation and R-squared	Comments
74. Randolph and Najand (1991)	S&P500 futures options ATM calls only	2/1/1986–31/12/88 (crash included) In: First 80 observations	Daily opening Tick	MRM$_{ATM}$ HIS MRM$_{ATM}$ implied GARCH(1, 1) HIS$_{20\ day}$ Implied$_{Black}$ (ranked though the error statistics are close)	Non-overlapping 20 days ahead, re-estimated using expanding sample.	ME, RMSE, MAE, MAPE	Mean reversion model (MRM) sets drift rate of volatility to follow a mean reverting process taking implied$_{ATM}$ (or HIS) as the previous day vol. Argue that GARCH did not work as well because it tends to provide a persistent forecast, which is valid only in period when changes in vol. are small
75. Schmalensee and Trippi (1978)	6 CBOE stock options	29/4/74–23/5/75 W 56 weekly observations		Implied$_{BS}$ call (simple average of all strikes and all maturities) (Forecast implied not actual volatility)	1 week ahead. 'Actual' proxied by weekly range and average price deviation	Statistical tests reject the hypothesis that IV responds positively to current volatility	Find implied rises when stock price falls, negative serial correlation in changes of IV and a tendency for IV of different stocks to move together. Argue that IV might correspond better with *future* volatility

76. Scott and Tucker (1989)	DM/$, £/$, C$/S, ¥/$ & SrFr/$ American options on PHLX	14/3/83/– 13/3/87 (pre-crash)	Daily closing tick	Implied$_{GK}$ (vega, Inferred ATM, NTM) Implied$_{CEV}$ (similar rank)	Non-overlapping option maturity: 3, 6 and 9 months. Use sample SD of daily returns to proxy 'actual vol.'	MSE, R^2 ranges from 42 to 49%. In all cases, $\alpha > 0$, $\beta < 1$. HIS has no incremental info. content	Simple B-S forecasts just as well as sophisticated CEV model. Claimed omission of early exercise is not important. Weighting scheme does not matter. Forecasts for different currencies were mixed together
77. Sill (1993)	S&P500	1959–1992	M	HIS with exo variables HIS (see comment)	1 month ahead	R^2 increase from 1% to 10% when additional variables were added	Volatility is higher in recessions than in expansions, and the spread between commercial-paper and T-Bill rates predict stock market volatility
78. Szakmary, Ors, Kim and Davidson (2002)	Futures options on S&P500, 9 interest rates, 5 currency, 4 energy, 3 metals, 10 agriculture, 3 livestock	Various dates between Jan 83 and May 2001	D	Implied$_{BK}$, NTM 2Calls + 2Puts eq al weight HIS$_{30}$, GARCH (ranked)	Overlapping option maturity, shortest but >10 days. Use sample SD of daily returns over forecast horizon to proxy 'actual vol.'	R^2 smaller for financial (23–28%), higher for metal and agricult. (30–37%), highest for livestock and energy (47–58%)	HIS$_{30}$ and GARCH have little or no incremental information content. $\alpha_{implied} > 0$ for 24 cases (or 69%), all 35 cases $\beta_{implied} < 1$ with robust SE

Continued

Author(s)	Asset(s)	Data period	Data frequency	Forecasting methods and rank	Forecasting horizon	Evaluation and R-squared	Comments
79. Taylor JW (2004)	DAX, S&P500, Hang Seng, FTSE 100, Amsterdam EOE, Nikkei, Singapore All Share	6/1/88–30/8/95 (equally split between in- and out-)	W	STES (E, AE, EAE) GJR (+Smoothed variations) GARCH MA$_{20\text{ weeks}}$, Riskmetrics (ranked)	1 week ahead using a moving window of 200 weekly returns. Use daily squared residual returns to construct weekly 'actual' volatility	ME, MAE, RMSE, R^2 (about 30% for HK and Japan and 6% for US)	Models estimated based on minimizing in-sample forecast errors instead of ML. STES-EAE (smooth transition exponential smoothing with return and absolute return as transition variables) produced consistently better performance for 1-step-ahead forecasts
80. Taylor SJ (1986)	15 US stocks FT30 6 metal £/$ 5 agricultural futures 4 interest rate futures	Jan66–Dec76 Jul75–Aug82 Various length Nov74–Sep82 Various length Various length	D	EWMA Log-AR(1) ARMACH-Abs ARMACH-Sq HIS (ranked) ARMACH-Sq is similar to GARCH	1 and 10 days ahead absolute returns. 2/3 of sample used in estimation. Use daily absolute returns deviation as 'actual vol.'	Relative MSE	Represent one of the earliest studies in ARCH class forecasts. The issue of volatility stationarity is not important when forecast over short horizon. Nonstationary series (e.g. EWMA) has the advantage of having fewer parameter estimates and forecasts respond to variance change fairly quickly

	Asset	Data period	Freq	Models	Forecast horizon	Evaluation	Comment
81. Taylor SJ (1987)	DM/$ futures	1977–83	D	High, low and closing prices (see comment)	1, 5, 10 and 20 days ahead. Estimation period, 5 years	RMSE	Best model is a weighted average of present and past high, low and closing prices with adjustments for weekend and holiday effects
82. Taylor SJ and Xu (1997)	DM/$ DM/$ options on PHLX	1/10/92–30/9/93 In: 9 months Out: 3 months	Quote D	Implied + ARCH combined Implied, ARCH HIS$_{9\ months}$ HIS$_{last\ hour\ realised\ vol}$ (ranked) See comment for details on implied and ARCH	1 hour ahead estimated from 9 months in-sample period. Use 5-min returns to proxy 'actual vol.'	MAE and MSE on std deviation and variance	5-min return has information incremental to daily implied when forecasting hourly volatility Friday macro news seasonal factors have no impact on forecast accuracy ARCH model includes with hourly and 5-min returns in the last hour plus 120 hour/day/week seasonal factors. Implied derived from NTM shortest maturity (>9 calendar days) Call+Put using BAW

Continued

Author(s)	Asset(s)	Data period	Data frequency	Forecasting methods and rank	Forecasting horizon	Evaluation and R-squared	Comments
83. Tse (1991)	Topix Nikkei Stock Average	In: 1986–1987 Out: 88–89	D	EWMA HIS ARCH, GARCH (ranked)	25 days ahead estimated from rolling 300 observations	ME, RMSE, MAE, MAPE of variance of 21 non-overlapping 25-day periods	Use dummies in mean equation to control for 1987 crash. Nonnormality provides a better fit but a poorer forecast. ARCH/GARCH models are slow to react to abrupt change in volatility. EWMA adjust to changes very quickly
84. Tse and Tung (1992)	Singapore, 5 VW market & industry indices	19/3/75 to 25/10/88	D	EWMA HIS GARCH (ranked)	25 days ahead estimated from rolling 425 observations	RMSE, MAE	EWMA is superior, GARCH worst. Absolute returns > 7% are truncated. Sign of nonstationarity. Some GARCH nonconvergence

85. Vasilellis and Meade (1996)	Stock options 12 UK stocks (LIFFE)	In: 28/3/86–27/6/86 In2 (for combined forecast): 28/6/86–25/3/88 Out: 6/7/88–21/9/91	W	Combine (Implied + GARCH) Implied (various, see comment) GARCH EWMA HIS$_{3 months}$ (ranked, results not sensitive to basis use to combine)	3 months ahead. Use sample SD of daily returns to proxy 'actual vol.'	RMSE	Implied: 5-day average dominates 1-day implied vol. Weighting scheme: max vega > vega weighted > elasticity weighted > max elasticity with '>', indicates better forecasting performance. Adjustment for div. and early exercise: Rubinstein > Roll > constant yield. Crash period might have disadvantaged time series methods
86. Vilasuso (2002)	C\$/\$, FFr/\$, DM/\$, ¥/\$, £/\$	In: 13/3/79–31/12/97 Out: 1/1/98–31/12/99	D	FIGARCH GARCH, IGARCH (ranked, GARCH marginally better than IGARCH)	1, 5 and 10 days ahead. Used daily squared returns to proxy actual volatility	MSE, MAE, and Diebold-Mariano's test for sig. difference	Significantly better forecasting performance from FIGARCH. Built FIARMA (with a constant term) on conditional variance without taking log. Truncated at lag 250

Continued

Author(s)	Asset(s)	Data period	Data frequency	Forecasting methods and rank	Forecasting horizon	Evaluation and R-squared	Comments
87. Walsh and Tsou (1998)	Australian indices: VW20, VW50 & VW300	1 Jan 93– 31 Dec95 In: 1 year Out: 2 years	5-min to form H, D and W returns	EWMA GARCH (not for weekly returns) HIS, IEV (improved extreme-value method) (ranked)	1 hour, 1 day and 1 week ahead estimated from a 1-year rolling sample. Use square of price changes (non-cumulative) as 'actual vol.'	MSE, RMSE, MAE, MAPE	Index with larger number of stock is easier to forecast due to diversification, but gets harder as sampling interval becomes shorter due to problem of nonsynchronous trading. None of the GARCH estimations converged for the weekly series, probably too few observations
88. Wei and Frankel (1991)	SrFr/\$, DM/\$, ¥/\$, £/\$ options (PHLX) Spot rates	2/83–1/90	M D	Implied GK ATM call (shortest maturity)	Non-overlapping 1 month ahead. Use sample SD of daily exchange rate return to proxy 'actual vol.'	R^2 30%(£), 17% (DM), 3%(SrFr), 0%(¥). $\alpha > 0$, $\beta < 1$ (except that for £/\$, $\alpha > 0$, $\beta = 1$) with heterosced. consistent SE	Use European formula for American style option. Also suffers from nonsynchronicity problem. Other tests reveal that implied tends to overpredict high vol. and underpredict low vol. Forecast/implied could be made more accurate by placing more weight on long-run average

Study	Asset/Market	Period	Model	Forecast	Evaluation	Findings
89. West and Cho (1995)	C$/$, FFr/$, DM/$, ¥$/$, £/$	14/3/73–20/9/89 In: 14/3/73–17/6/81 Out: 24/6/81–12/4/89	W GARCH(1,1) IGARCH (1,1) AR(12) in absolute AR(12) in squares Homoscedastic Gaussian kernel (no clear rank)	$j = 1, 12, 24$ weeks estimated from rolling 432 weeks. Use j period squared returns to proxy actual volatility	RMSE and regression test on variance, R^2 varies from 0.1% to 4.5%	Some GARCH forecasts mean revert to unconditional variance in 12 to 24 weeks. It is difficult to choose between models. Nonparametric method came out worst though statistical tests for do not reject null of no significance difference in most cases
90. Wiggins (1992)	S&P500 futures	4/82–12/89	D ARMA model with 2 types of estimators: 1. Parkinson/Garmen-Klass extreme value estimators 2. Close-to-close estimator (ranked)	1 week ahead and 1 month ahead. Compute actual volatility from daily observations	Bias test, efficiency test, regression	Modified Parkinson approach is least biased. C-t-C estimator is three times less efficient than EV estimators. Parkinson estimator is also better than C-t-C at forecasting. 87's crash period excluded from analysis

Continued

Author(s)	Asset(s)	Data period	Data frequency	Forecasting methods and rank	Forecasting horizon	Evaluation and R-squared	Comments
91. Xu and Taylor (1995)	£/$, DM/$, ¥/$ & SrFr/$ PHLX options Corresponding futures rates	In: Jan 85–Oct89 Out: 18Oct89–4Feb92	D	Implied_{BAW NTM TS or short} GARCH_{Normal or GED} HIS_{4 weeks} (ranked)	Non-overlapping 4 weeks ahead, estimated from a rolling sample of 250 weeks daily data. Use cumulative daily squared returns to proxy 'actual vol.'	ME, MAE, RMSE, When $\alpha_{implied}$ is set equal to 0, $\beta_{implied} = 1$ cannot be rejected	Implied works best and is unbiased. Other forecasts have no incremental information. GARCH forecast performance not sensitive to distributional assumption about returns. The choice of implied predictor (term structure, TS, or short maturity) does not affect results
92. Yu (2002)	NZSE40	Jan80–Dec98 In: 1980–1993 Out: 1994–1998	D	SV (of log variance) GARCH (3, 2), GARCH (1, 1) HIS, MA_{5 yr or 10 yr} ES and EWMA (monthly revision) Regression_{lag-1} ARCH(9), RW, (ranked)	1 month ahead estimated from previous 180 to 228 months of daily data. Use aggregate of daily squared returns to construct actual monthly volatility	RMSE, MAE, Theil-U and LINEX on variance	Range of the evaluation measures for most models is very narrow. Within this narrow range, SV ranked first, performance of GARCH was sensitive to evaluation measure; regression and EWMA methods did not perform well. Worst performance from ARCH(9) and RW. Volatile periods (Oct 87 and Oct 97) included in in- and out-of-samples

93. Zumbach (2002)	USD/CHF, USD/JPY	1/1/89– 1/7/2000	H LM-ARCH F-GARCH GARCH And their integrated counterparts (ranked)	1 day ahead estimated from previous 5.5 years	RMSE. Realized volatility measured using hourly returns	LM-ARCH, aggregates high-frequency squared returns with a set of power law weights, is the best though difference is small. All integrated versions are more stable across time

Ranked: models appear in the order of forecasting performance; best performing model at the top. If two weighting schemes or two forecasting models appear at both sides of ' > ', it means the l.h.s. is better than the r.h.s. in terms of forecasting performance. **SE:** Standard error. **ATM:** At the money. **NTM:** Near the money. **OTM:** Out of the money. **WLS:** an implied volatility weighting scheme used in Whaley (1982) designed to minimize the pricing errors of a collection of options. In some cases the pricing errors are multiplied by trading volume or vega to give ATM implied a greater weight. **HIS:** Historical volatility constructed based on past variance/standard deviation. **VXO:** Chicago Board of Option Exchange's volatility index derived from S&P100 options. VXO was renamed VXO in September 2003. The current VXO is compiled using a model-free implied volatility estimate. All the research papers reviewed have used VXO (i.e. the old VIX.) **RS:** Regime switching. **BS:** Black–Scholes. **BK:** Black model for pricing futures option. **BAW:** Barone-Adesi and Whaley American option pricing formula. **HW:** Hull and White option pricing model with stochastic volatility. **FW:** Fleming and Whaley (1994) modified binomial method that takes into account wildcard option. **GK:** Garman and Kohlhagan model for pricing European currency option. **HJM:** Heath, Jarrow and Morton (1992) forward rate model for interest rates.

References

Aggarwal, R., C. Inclan and R. Leal (1999) Volatility in emerging stock markets, *Journal of Financial and Quantitative Analysis*, **34**, 1, 33–55.

Ait-Sahalia, Y., P. A. Mykland and L. Zhang (2003) How often to sample a continuous-time process in the presence of market microstructure noise, Working paper, University of Princeton.

Akgiray, V. (1989) Conditional heteroskedasticity in time series of stock returns: evidence and forecasts, *Journal of Business*, **62**, 55–80.

Alexander, C. (2001), *Market Models: A Guide to Financial Data Analysis*, John Wiley & Sons Ltd, Chichester.

Alford, A.W., and J.R. Boatsman (1995) Predicting long-term stock return volatility: Implications for accounting and valuation of equity derivatives, *Accounting Review*, **70**, 4, 599–618.

Alizadeh, S., M.W. Brandt and F.X. Diebold (2002) Range-based estimation of stochastic volatility models, *Journal of Finance*, **57**, 3, 1047–1092.

Amin, K., and V. Ng (1997) Inferring future volatility from the information in implied volatility in Eurodollar options: A new approach, *Review of Financial Studies*, **10**, 333–367.

Andersen, T.G. (1996) Return volatility and trading volume: An information flow interpretation of stochastic volatility, *Journal of Finance*, **51**, 1, 169–204.

Andersen, T.G., L. Benzoni and J. Lund (2002) An empirical investigation of continuous time equity return models, *Journal of Finance*, **57**, 1239–1284.

Andersen, T., and T. Bollerslev (1998) Answering the skeptics: Yes, standard volatility models do provide accurate forecasts, *International Economic Review*, **39**, 4, 885–905.

Andersen, T.G., T. Bollerslev, F.X. Diebold and H. Ebens (2001) The distribution of realized stock return volatility, *Journal of Financial Economics*, **61**, 1, 43–76.

Andersen, T.G., T. Bollerslev, F.X. Diebold and P. Labys (2001) The distribution of realized exchange rate volatility, *Journal of American Statistical Association*, **96**, 453, 42–57.

Andersen, T.G., T. Bollerslev and S. Lange (1999) Forecasting financial market volatility: Sample frequency vis-à-vis forecast horizon, *Journal of Empirical Finance*, **6**, 5, 457–477.

Andersen, T.G., T. Bollerslev, F.X. Diebold and P. Labys, 2003, Modeling and forecasting realized volatility, *Econometrica*, **71**, 2, 529–626.

Andersen, T.G., and B.E. Sorensen (1997) GMM and QML asymptotic standard deviations in stochastic volatility models, *Journal of Econometrics*, **76**, 397–403.

Artzner, P., F. Delbaen, J. Eber and D. Heath (1997) Thinking coherently, *RISK Magazine*, **10**, 11, 68–71.

Artzner, P., F. Delbaen, J. Eber and D. Heath (1999) Coherent measures of risk, *Mathematical Finance*, **9**, 3, 203–228.

Baillie, R.T., and T. Bollerslev (1989) The message in daily exchange rates: a conditonal-variance tale, *Journal of Business and Economic Statistics*, **7**, 3, 297–305.

Baillie, R.T., T. Bollerslev and H.O. Mikkelsen (1996) Fractionally integrated generalized autoregressive conditional heteroskedasticity, *Journal of Econometrics*, **74**, 1, 3–30.

Baillie, R.T., T. Bollerslev and M.R. Redfearn (1993) Bear squeezes, volatility spillovers and speculative attacks in the hyperinflation 1920s foreign exchange, *Journal of International Money and Finance*, **12**, 5, 511–521.

Bakshi, G., C. Cao and Z. Chen (1997) Empirical performance of alternative option pricing models, *Journal of Finance*, **52**, 5, 2003–2049.

Bakshi, G., and N. Kapadia (2003) Delta-hedged gains and the negative market volatility risk premium, *Review of Financial Studies*, **16**, 2, 527–566.

Bali, T.G. (2000) Testing the empirical performance of stochastic volatility models of the short-term interest rate, *Journal of Financial and Quantitative Analysis*, **35**, 2, 191–215.

Ball, C.A., and W.N. Torous (1984) The maximum likelihood estimation of security price volatility: Theory, evidence and application to option pricing, *Journal of Business*, **57**, 1, 97–113.

Bandi, F.M., and J.R. Russell (2004) Separating microstructure noise from volatility, Working paper, University of Chicago.

Banks, E. (2004) Alternative risk transfer: Integrated risk management through insurance, reinsurance and the capital markets, John Wiley & Sons Ltd, Chichester.

Barndorff-Nielsen, O.E., and N. Shephard (2003) Power and bipower variation with stochastic volatility and jumps, Working paper, Oxford University.

Barone-Adesi, G., and R.E. Whaley (1987) Efficient analytic approximation of American option values, *Journal of Finance*, **42**, 2, 301–320.

Bates, D.S. (1996) Testing option pricing models, in: Maddala, G.S., and C.R. Rao (eds), *Handbook of Statistics*, vol. 14: *Statistical Methods in Finance*, Elsevier, North Holland, Amsterdam, pp. 567–611.

Bates, D.S. (2000) Post-87 crash fears in S&P 500 futures options, *Journal of Econometrics*, **94**, 181–238.

Beckers, S. (1981) Standard deviations implied in option prices as predictors of future stock price variability, *Journal of Banking and Finance*, **5**, 363–382.

Beckers, S, (1993) Variances of security price returns based on high, low and closing prices, *Journal of Business*, **56**, 97–112.

Benzoni, L. (2001) Pricing options under stochastic volatility: An empirical investigation, Working paper, Carlson School of Management, Minneapolis, MN.

Bera, A.K., and M.L. Higgins (1993) ARCH models: properties, estimation and testing, *Journal of Economic Surveys*, **7**, 4, 305–365.

Bera, A., and M. Higgins (1997) ARCH and bilinearity as competing models for nonlinear dependence, *Journal of Business and Economic Statistics*, **15**, 1, 43–50.

Beran, J. (1994) *Statistics for Long Memory Process*, John Ryland, Chapman & Hall.

Black, F. (1975) Fact and fantasy in the use of options, *Financial Analysts Journal*, **31**, 36–41.

Black, F, (1976) Studies of stock price volatility of changes, *American Statistical Association Journal*, 177–181.

Blair, B., S.-H. Poon and S.J. Taylor (2001) Forecasting S&P 100 volatility: The incremental information content of implied volatilities and high frequency index returns, *Journal of Econometrics*, **105**, 5–26.

Bluhm, H.H.W., and J. Yu (2000) Forecasting volatility: Evidence from the German stock market, Working paper, University of Auckland.

Bollen, B., and B., Inder (2002) Estimating daily volatility in financial markets utilizing intraday data, *Journal of Empirical Finance*, **9**, 551–562.

Bollerslev, T. (1986) Generalized autoregressive conditional heteroskedasticity, *Journal of Econometrics*, **31**, 307–328.

Bollerslev, T. (1987) A conditionally heteroskedastic time series model for speculative prices and rates of return, *Review of Economics and Statistics*, **69**, 3, 542–547.

Bollerslev, T. (1990) Modelling the coherence in short-run nominal exchange rates: A multivariate generalized ARCH model, *Review of Economics and Statistics*, **72**, 498–505.

Bollerslev, T., R.Y. Chou and K.P. Kroner (1992) ARCH modeling in finance: A Review of the theory and empirical evidence, *Journal of Econometrics*, **52**, 5–59.

Bollerslev, T., R.F. Engle and D.B. Nelson (1994) ARCH models, in: Engle, R.F., and D.L. McFadden (eds), *Handbook of Econemetrics*, Vol. IV, North Holland, Amsterdam, pp. 2959–3038.

Bollerslev, T., R.F. Engle and J.M. Wooldridge (1988) A capital asset pricing model with time-varying covariances, *Journal of Political Economy*, **96**, 1, 116–131.

Bollerslev, T., and E. Ghysels (1996) Periodic autoregressive conditional heteroskedasticity, *Journal of Business and Economic Statistics*, **14**, 2, 139–151.

Bollerslev, T., and H.O. Mikkelsen (1996) Modeling and pricing long memory in stock market volatility, *Journal of Econometrics*, **73**, 1, 151–184.

Bollerslev, T., and H. O. Mikkelsen (1999) Long-term equity anticipation securities and stock market volatility dynamics, *Journal of Econometrics*, **92**, 75–99.

Boudoukh, J., M. Richardson and R.F. Whitelaw (1997) Investigation of a class of volatility estimators, *Journal of Derivatives*, **4**, 3, 63–71.

Brace, A., and A. Hodgson (1991) Index futures options in Australia – An empirical focus on volatility, *Accounting and Finance*, **31**, 2, 13–31.

Brailsford, T.J., and R.W. Faff (1996) An evaluation of volatility forecasting techniques, *Journal of Banking and Finance*, **20**, 3, 419–438.

Brooks, C. (1998) Predicting stock market volatility: Can market volume help? *Journal of Forecasting*, **17**, 1, 59–80.

Buraschi, A., and J. C. Jackwerth (2001) The price of a smile: Hedging and spanning in option markets, *Review of Financial Studies*, **14**, 2, 495–527.

Canina, L., and S. Figlewski (1993) The informational content of implied volatility, *Review of Financial Studies*, **6**, 3, 659–681.

Cao, C.Q., and R.S. Tsay (1992) Nonlinear time-series analysis of stock volatilities, *Journal of Applied Econometrics*, December, Supplement, **1**, S165–S185.

Chan, K.C., G.A. Karolyi, F.A. Longstaff and A.B. Sanders (1992) An empirical comparision of alternative models of the short-term interest rate, *Journal of Finance*, **47**, 3, 1209–1227.

Chernov, M. (2001) Implied volatilities as forecasts of future volatility, the market risk premia, and returns variability, Working paper, Columbia Business School.

Chernov, M., and E. Ghysels (2000) A study towards a unified approach to the joint estimation of objective and risk neutral measures for the purposes of options valuation, *Journal of Financial Economics*, **56**, 3, 407–458.

Chiras, D., and S. Manaster (1978) The information content of option prices and a test of market efficiency, *Journal of Financial Economics*, **6**, 213–234.

Chong, Y.Y., and D.F. Hendry, (1986) Econometric evaluation of linear macro-economic models, *Review of Economics Studies*, **53**, 671–690.

Christensen, B.J., and N.R. Prabhala (1998) The relation between implied and realized volatility, *Journal of Financial Economics*, **50**, 2, 125–150.

Christie, A.A. (1982) The stochastic behaviour of common stock variances: Value, leverage, and interest rate effect, *Journal of Financial Economics*, **10**, 407–432.

Christodoulakis, G.A., and S.E. Satchell (1998) Hashing GARCH: A re-assessment of volatility forecast and perfomance, Chapter 6, pp. 168–192, in: Knight, J., and S. Satchell (eds), *Forecasting Volatility in the Financial Markets*, Butterworth.

Christoffersen, P.F., and F.X. Diebold (2000) How relevant is volatility forecasting for risk management? *Review of Economics and Statistics,* **82**, 1, 12–22.

Clark, P. (1973) A subordinated stochastic process model with finite variance for speculative prices, *Econometrica*, **41**, 135–156.

Corradi, V. (2000) Reconsidering the continuous time limit of the GARCH(1,1) process, *Journal of Econometrics*, **96**, 145–153.

Cox, J.C., S.A. Ross and M. Rubinstein (1979) Option pricing: A simplified approach, *Journal of Financial Economics*, **7**, 229–263.

Cumby, R., S. Figlewski and J. Hasbrouck (1993) Forecasting volatilities and correlations with EGARCH models, *Journal of Derivatives*, **1**, 51–63.

Danielsson, J. (1994) Stochastic volatility in asset prices: Estimation with simulated maximum likelihood, *Journal of Econometrics*, **64**, 375–400.

Danielsson, J., and C.G. de Vries (1997) Tail index and quantile estimation with very high frequency data, *Journal of Empirical Finance*, **4**, 241–257.

Das, S.R., and R.K. Sundaram (1999) Of smiles and smirks: A term structure perpective, *Journal of Financial and Quantitative Analysis*, **34**, 2.

Davidian, M., and R.J. Carroll (1987) Variance function estimation, *Journal of American Statistical Association*, **82**, 1079–1091.

Day, T.E., and C.M. Lewis (1992) Stock market volatility and the information content of stock index options, *Journal of Econometrics*, **52**, 267–287.

Day, T.E., and C.M. Lewis (1993) Forecasting futures market volatility, *Journal of Derivatives*, **1**, 33–50.

Diebold, F.X. (1988) *Empirical Modeling of Exchange Rate Dynamics*, Springer Verlag, New York.

Diebold, F.X., A. Hickman, A. Inoue and T. Schuermann (1998) Scale models, *RISK Magazine*, **11**, 104–107.

Diebold, F.X., and A. Inoue (2001) Long memory and regime switching, *Journal of Econometrics*, **105**, 1, 131–159.

Diebold, F.X., and J.A. Lopez (1995) Modelling volatility dynamics, in: Hoover, K. (ed.), *Macroeconomics: Developments, Tensions and Prospects, Kluwer, Dordtecht,* pp. 427–466.

Diebold, F.X., and R.S. Mariano (1995) Comparing predictive accuracy, *Journal of Business and Economic Statistics*, **13**, 253–263.

Dimson, E., and P. Marsh (1990) Volatility forecasting without data-snooping, *Journal of Banking and Finance*, **14**, 2–3, 399–421.

Ding, Z., C.W.J. Granger and R.F. Engle (1993) A long memory property of stock market returns and a new model, *Journal of Empirical Finance*, **1**, 83–106.

Doidge, C., and J.Z. Wei (1998) Volatility forecasting and the efficiency of the Toronto 35 index options market, *Canadian Journal of Administrative Science*, **15**, 1, 28–38.

Drost, F.C., and T.E. Nijman (1993) Temporal aggregation of GARCH process, *Econometrica*, **61**, 4, 909–927.

Duan, J. (1997) Augmented GARCH(p,q) process and its diffusion limit, *Journal of Econometrics*, **79**, 97–127.

Duffie, D., and K.J. Singleton (1993) Simulated moments estimation of Markov models of asset prices, *Econometrica*, **61**, 929–952.

Dunis, C.L., J. Laws and S. Chauvin (2000) The use of market data and model combination to improve forecast accuracy, Working paper, Liverpool Business School.

Durbin, J., and S.J. Koopman (2000) Time series analysis of non-Gaussian observations based on state space models from both classical and Bayesian perpectives, *Journal of Royal Statistical Society Series*, **62**, 1, 3–56.

Ederington, L.H., and W. Guan (1999) The information frown in option prices, Working paper, University of Oklahoma.

Ederington, L.H., and W. Guan (2000a) Forecasting volatility, Working paper, University of Oklahoma.

Ederington, L.H., and W. Guan (2000b) Measuring implied volatility: Is an average better? Working paper, University of Oklahoma.

Ederington, L.H., and W. Guan (2002) Is implied volatility an informationally efficient and effective predictor of future volatility? *Journal of Risk*, **4**, 3.

Ederington, L.H., and J.H. Lee (2001) Intraday volatility in interest rate and foreign exchange markets: ARCH, announcement, and seasonality effects, *Journal of Futures Markets*, **21**, 6, 517–552.

Edey, M., and G. Elliot (1992) Some evidence on option prices as predictors of volatility, *Oxford Bulletin of Economics & Statistics*, **54**, 4, 567–578.

Engle, R.F. (1982) Autoregressive conditional heteroscedasticity with estimates of the variance of United Kingdom inflation, *Econometrica*, **50**, 4, 987–1007.

Engle, R.F. (1993) Statistical models for financial volatility, *Financial Analysts Journal*, **49**, 1, 72–78.

Engle, R.F., and T. Bollerslev (1986) Modelling the persistence of conditional variances, *Econometric Reviews*, **5**, 1–50.

Engle, R., and K.F. Kroner (1995) Multivariate simultaneous generalized ARCH, *Econometric Theory*, **11**, 122–150.

Engle, R.F., and G.J. Lee (1999) A long-run and short-run component model of stock return volatility, in: Engle, R.F., and H. White (ed.), *Cointegration, Causality and Forecasting*, Oxford University Press, Oxford, Chapter 10, pp. 475–497.

Engle, R.F., and V.K. Ng (1993) Measuring and testing the impact of news on volatility, *Journal of Finance*, **48**, 1749–1778.

Engle, R. F., V. Ng and M. Rothschild (1990) Asset pricing with a factor-ARCH covariance structure: Empirical estimates for Treasury Bills, *Journal of Econometrics*, **45**, 213–239.

Fair, R.C., and R.J. Shiller (1989) The informational content of ex ante forecasts, *Review of Economics and Statistics,* **71**, 2, 325–332.

Fair, R.C., and R.J. Shiller (1990) Comparing information in forecasts from econometric models, *American Economic Review,* **80**, 3, 375–380.

Feinstein, S.P. (1989a) The Black–Scholes formula is nearly linear in sigma for at-the-money options; therefore implied volatilities from at-the-money options are virtually unbiased, Working paper, Federal Reserve Bank of Atlanta.

Feinstein, S.P. (1989b) Forecasting stock market volatility using options on index futures, *Economic Review* (Federal Reserve Bank of Atlanta), **74**, 3, 12–30.

Ferreira, M.A. (1999) Forecasting interest rate volatility from the information in historical data, Working paper, Department of Finance, University of Wisconsin-Madison.

Figlewski, S. (1997) Forecasting volatility, *Financial Markets, Institutions and Instruments* (New York University Salomon Center), **6**, 1, 1–88.

Figlewski, S., and T.C. Green (1999) Market risk and model risk for a financial institution writing options, *Journal of Finance*, **54**, 4, 1465–1999.

Fiorentini, G., A. Leon and G. Rubio (2002) Estimation and empirical performance of Heston's stochastic volatility model: The case of a thinly traded market, *Journal of Empirical Finance*, **9**, 225–255.

Fleming, J. (1998) The quality of market voltility forecasts implied by S&P 100 index option prices, *Journal of Empirical Finance*, **5**, 4, 317–345.

Fleming, J., and C. Kirby (2003) A closer look at the relation between GARCH and stochastic autoregressive volatility, *Journal of Financial Econometrics*, **1**, 365–419.

Fleming, J., and R.E. Whaley (1994) The value of wildcard options, *Journal of Finance*, **49**, 1, 215–236, March.

Fleming, J., C. Kirby and B. Ostdiek (2000) The economic value of volatility timing *Journal of Finance*, **56**, 1.

Fleming, J., C. Kirby and B. Ostdiek (2002) The economic value of volatility timing using realized volatility, *Journal of Financial Economics*, **67**, 473–509.

Fleming, J., B. Ostdiek and R.E. Whaley (1995) Predicting stock market volatility: A new measure, *Journal of Futures Market*, **15**, 3, 265–302.

Forbes, K.J., and R. Rigobon (2002) No contagion, only interdependence: measuring stock market co-movements, *Journal of Finance*, **57**, 5, 2223–2262.

Fouque, J.-P., G. Papanicolaou and K.R. Sircar (2000) *Derivatives in Financial Markets with Stochastic Volatility*, Cambridge University Press, Cambridge.

Franke, G., R.C. Stapleton and M.G. Subrahmanyam (1998) Who buys and who sells options: The role of options in an economy with background risk, *Journal of Economic Theory*, **82**, 1, 89–109.

Franses, P.H., and H. Ghijsels (1999) Additive outliers, GARCH and forecasting volatility, *International Journal of Forecasting*, **15**, 1–9.

Franses, P.H., and D. Van Dijk (1996) Forecasting stock market volatility using (nonlinear) Garch models, *Journal of Forecasting*, **15**, 3, 229–235.

Franses, P.H. and D. van Dijk (2000) *Non-Linear Time Series Models in Empirical Finance*, Cambridge University Press, Cambridge.

French, K.R., G.W. Schwert and R.F. Stambaugh (1987) Expected stock returns and volatility, *Journal of Financial Economics*, **19**, 1, 3–30.

Frennberg, P., and B. Hansson (1996) An evaluation of alternative models for predicting stock volatility, *Journal of International Financial Markets, Institutions and Money*, **5**, 117–134.

Fridman, M., and L. Harris (1998) A maximum likelihood approach for non-Gaussian stochastic volatility models, *Journal of Business and Economic Statistics*, **16**, 284–291.

Friedman, B.M., and D.I. Laibson (1989) Economic implications of extraordinary movements in stock prices, *Brooking Papers on Economic Activity*, **2**, 137–189.

Fung, H.-G., C.-J. Lie and A. Moreno (1990) The forecasting performance of the implied standard deviation in currency options, *Managerial Finance*, **16**, 3, 24–29.

Fung, W.K.H., and D.A. Hsieh (1991) Empirical analysis of implied volatility: Stocks, bonds and currencies, Working paper, Department of Finance, Fuqua School of Business.

Gallant, A.R., P.E. Rossi and G. Tauchen (1993) Nonlinear dynamic structures, *Econometrica*, **61**, 4, 871–907.

Garman, M.B., and M.J. Klass (1980) On the estimation of security price volatilities from historical data, *Journal of Business*, **53**, 1, 67–78.

Gemmill, G. (1986) The forecasting performance of stock options on the London Traded Options Markets, *Journal of Business Finance and Accounting*, **13**, 4, 535–546.

Geske, R. (1979) The valuation of compound options, *Journal of Financial Economics*, **7**, 63–81.

Ghysels, E., A. Harvey and E. Renault (1996) Stochastic volatility, pp. 119–191, in: Maddala, G.S., and C.R. Rao (eds), *Handbook of Statistics: Statistical Methods in Finance*, Vol. 14, Elsevier Science, Amsterdam.

Glosten, L.R., R. Jagannathan and D.E. Runkle (1993) On the relation between the expected value and the volatility of the nominal excess return on stocks, *Journal of Finance*, **48**, 1779–1801.

Gourieroux, C. (1997) *ARCH Models and Financial Applications*, Springer, New York.

Granger, C.W.R. (1999) *Empirical Modeling in Economics. Specification and Evaluation*. Cambridge University Press, Cambridge.

Granger, C.W.J. (2001) Long memory processes – an economist's viewpoint, Working paper, University of California, San Diego.

Granger, C.W.J., and Z. Ding (1995) Some properties of absolute return: An alternative measure of risk, *Annales dEconomie et de Statistique*, **40**, 67–91.

Granger, C.W.J., Z. Ding and S. Spear (2000) Stylized facts on the temporal and distributional properties of absolute returns: An update, Working paper, University of California, San Diego.

Granger, C.W.J., and N. Hyung (2004) Occasional structural breaks and long memory with an application to the S&P500 absolute stock returns, *Journal of Empirical Finance*, **11**, 3, 399–421.

Granger, C.W.J., and R. Joyeux (1980) An introduction to long memory time series and fractional differencing, *Journal of Time Series Analysis*, **1**, 15–39.

Gray, S.F. (1996) Modeling the conditional distribution of interest rates as a regime-switching process, *Journal of Financial Economics*, **42**, 1, 27–62.

Guo, D. (1996a) The predictive power of implied stochastic variance from currency options, *Journal of Futures Markets*, **16**, 8, 915–942.

Guo, D. (1996b) The information content of implied stochastic volatility from currency options, *Canadian Journal of Economics*, **29**, S, 559–561.

Hamao, Y., R.W. Masulis and V. Ng (1989) Correlations in price changes and volatility across international stock markets, *Review of Financial Studies*, **3**, 281–307.

Hamid, S. (1998) Efficient consolidation of implied volatilities and a test of intertemporal averaging, *Derivatives Quarterly*, **4**, 3, 35–49.

Hamilton, J.D. (1989) A new approach to the economic analysis of nonstationary time series and the business cycle, *Econometrica*, **57**, 357–384.

Hamilton, J.D., and G. Lin (1996) Stock market volatility and the business cycle, *Journal of Applied Econometrics*, **11**, 5, 573–593.

Hamilton, J.D., and R. Susmel (1994) Autoregressive conditional heteroskedasticity and changes in regime, *Journal of Econometrics*, **64**, 1–2, 307–333.

Hansen, L.P., and R.J. Hodrick (1980) Forward exchange rates as optimal predictors of future spot rates: An econometric analysis, *Journal of Political Economy*, **88**, 829–853.

Hansen, P.R., and A. Lunde (2004a) A forecast comparison of volatility models: Does anything beat a GARCH(1,1), *Journal of Applied Econometrics*, Forthcoming.

Hansen, P.R., and A. Lunde (2004b) Consistent ranking of volatility models, *Journal of Econometrics*, Forthcoming.

Harvey, A.C. (1998) Long memory in stochastic volatility, Chapter 12, pp. 307–320, in: Knight, J., and S. Satchell (eds), *Forecasting Volatility in the Financial Markets*, Butterworth, Oxford.

Harvey, A.C., E. Ruiz and N. Shephard (1994) Multivariate stochastic variance models, *Review of Economic Studies*, **61**, 247–264.

Harvey, C.R., and R.E. Whaley (1992) Market volatility prediction and the efficiency of the S&P100 Index option market, *Journal of Financial Economics*, **31**, 1, 43–74.

Heath, D., R. Jarrow, and A. Morton (1992) Bond pricing and the term structure of interest rates: A new methodology for contingent claim valuation, *Econometrica*, **60**, 77–105.

Hentschel, L. (2001) Errors in implied volatility estimation, working paper, University of Rochester.

Heston, S.L (1993) A closed solution for options with stochastic volatility, with application to bond and currency options, *Review of Financial Studies*, **6**, 2, 327–343.

Heynen, R.C. (1995) *Essays on Derivatives Pricing Theory*, Thesis Publishers, Amsterdam.

Heynen, R.C., and H.M. Kat (1994) Volatility prediction: A comparison of stochastic volatility, GARCH(1,1) and EGARCH(1,1) models, *Journal of Derivatives*, **2**, 50–65.

Hol, E., and S.J. Koopman (2002) Forecasting the variability of stock index returns with stochastic volatility models and implied volatility, Working paper, Free University, Amsterdam.

Hong, Y. (2001) A test for volatility spillover with application to exchange rates, *Journal of Econometrics*, **103**, 183–224.

Hosking, J.R.M. (1981) Fractional differencing, *Biometrika*, **68**, 165–176.

Hsieh, D.A. (1989) Modeling heteroscedasticity in daily foreign exchange rates, *Journal of Business and Economic Statistics*, **7**, 3, 307–317.

Huber, P.J. (1981) *Robust Statistics*, John Wiley and Sons Canada Ltd, Ontario.

Hull, J. (2002) *Options, Futures and Other Derivative Securities*, 5th edn, Prentice Hall, Englewood Cliffs, NJ.

Hull, J., and A. White (1987) The pricing of options on assets with stochastic volatilities, *Journal of Finance*, **42**, 2, 281–300.

Hull, J., and A. White (1988) An analysis of the bias in option pricing caused by a stochastic volatility, *Advances in Futures and Options Research*, **3**, 27–61.

Hwang, S., and S. Satchell (1998) Implied volatility forecasting: A comparison of different procedures including fractionally integrated models with applications to UK equity options, Chapter 7, pp. 193–225, in: Knight, J., and S. Satchell (eds), *Forecasting Volatility in the Financial Markets*, Butterworth, Oxford.

Jacquier, E., N.G. Polson and P.E. Rossi (1994) Bayesian analysis of stochastic volatility models: reply, *Journal of Business and Economic Statistics*, **12**, 4, 413–417.

Jarrow, R. (ed) (1998) *Volatility: New Estimation Techniques for Pricing Derivatives*, Risk Books, London.

Johnson, H., and D. Shanno (1987) Option pricing when the variance is changing, *Journal of Financial and Quantitative Analysis*, **22**, 143–151.

Jones, C.S. (2001) The dynamics of stochastic volatility: Evidence from underlying and options markets, Working paper, Simon School of Business, University of Rochester.

Jones, C., O. Lamont and R. Lumsdaine (1998) Macroeconomic news and bond market volatility, *Journal of Financial Economics*, **47**, 315–337.

Jorion, P. (1995) Predicting volatility in the foreign exchange market, *Journal of Finance*, **50**, 2, 507–528.

Jorion, P. (1996) Risk and turnover in the foreign exchange market, in: Frankel, J.A., G. Galli and A. Giovannini (eds), *The Microstructure of Foreign Exchange Markets*, The University of Chicago Press, Chicago.

Jorion, P. (2001) *Value at Risk: The New Benchmark for Managing Financial Risk*, 2nd edn, McGraw-Hill, New York.

Karatzas, I., and S.E. Shreve (1988) *Brownian Motion and Stochastic Calculus*, Springer Verlag, New York.

Karolyi, G.A. (1993) A Bayesian approach to modeling stock return volatility and option valuation, *Journal of Financial and Quantitative Analysis*, **28**, 4, 579–595.

Karolyi, G.A. (1995) A multivariate GARCH model of international transimissions of stock returns and volatility: The case of the United States and Canada, *Journal of Business and Economic Statistics*, **13**, 1, 11–25.

Karpoff, J.M. (1987) The relation between price changes and trading volume: A survey, *Journal of Financial and Quantitative Analysis*, **22**, 1, 109–126.

Kearns, P., and A.R. Pagan (1993) Australian stock market volatility, 1875–1987, *Economic Record*, **69**, 163–178.

Kim, S., N. Shephard and S. Chib (1998) Stochastic volatility: likelihood inference and comparison with ARCH models, *Review of Economic Studies*, **65**, 361–393.

King, M.A., and S. Wadhwani (1990) Transmission of volatility between stock markets, *Review of Financial Studies*, **3**, 1, 5–33.

Klaassen, F. (1998) Improving GARCH volatility forecasts, *Empirical Economics*, **27**, 363–394.

Knight, J., and S. Satchell (ed) (2002) *Forecasting Volatility in the Financial Markets*, 2nd edn, Butterworth, Oxford.

Koutmos, G., and G.G. Booth (1995) Asymmetric volatility transmission in international stock markets, *Journal of International Money and Finance*, **14**, 6, 747–762.

Kroner, K., Kneafsey K. and S. Claessens (1995) Forecasting volatility in commodity markets, *Journal of Forecasting*, **14**, 77–95.

Kroner, K.F., and V.K. Ng (1998) Modeling asymmetric co-movements of asset returns, *Review of Financial Studies*, **11**, 4, 817–844.

Lamoureux, C.G., and W.D. Lastrapes (1990) Persistence in variance, structural change and the GARCH model, *Journal of Business and Economic Statistics*, **8**, 2, 225–234.

Lamoureux, C., and W. Lastrapes (1993) Forecasting stock-return variance: toward an understanding of stochastic implied volatilities, *Review of Financial Studies*, **6**, 2, 293–326.

Latane, H., and R.J. Rendleman (1976) Standard deviations of stock price ratios implied in option prices, *Journal of Finance*, **31**, 2, 369–381.

Lee, K.Y. (1991) Are the GARCH models best in out-of-sample performance? *Economics Letters*, **37**, 3, 305–308.

Li, K. (2002) Long-memory versus option-implied volatility prediction, *Journal of Derivatives*, **9**, 3, 9–25.

Liesenfeld, R., and J.-F. Richard (2003) Univariate and multivariate stochastic volatility models: estimation and diagnostics, *Journal of Empirical Finance*, **10**, 4, 505–531.

Lin, Y., N. Strong and X. Xu (2001) Pricing FTSE-100 index options under stochastic volatility, *Journal of Futures Markets*, **21**, 3, 197–211.

Lopez, J.A. (1998) Methods for evaluating value-at-risk estimates, *Economic Policy Review* (Federal Reserve Bank of New York), **4**, 3, 119–129.

Lopez, J.A. (2001) Evaluating the predictive accuracy of volatility models, *Journal of Forecasting*, **20**, 2, 87–109.

Loudon, G.F., W.H. Watt and P.K. Yadav (2000) An empirical analysis of alternative parametric ARCH models, *Journal of Applied Econometrics*, **15**, 117–136.

Martens, M., and S.-H. Poon (2001) Returns synchronization and daily correlation dynamics between international stock markets, *Journal of Banking and Finance*, **25**, 10, 1805–1827.

Martens, M., and J. Zein (2004) Predicting financial volatility: High-frequency time-series forecasts vis-à-vis implied volatility, *Journal of Futures Markets*, **24**, 11, 1005–1028.

Mayhew, S. (1995) Implied volatility, *Financial Analyst Journal*, **51**, 8–20.

McCurdy, T.H., and I. Morgan (1987) Tests of the martingale hypothesis for foreign currency futures with time varying volatility, *International Journal of Forecasting*, **3**, 131–148.

McKenzie M.D. (1999) Power transformation and forecasting the magnitude of exchange rate changes, *International Journal of Forecasting*, **15**, 49–55.

McMillan, D.G., A.H. Speight and O.A.P. Gwilym (2000) Forecasting UK stock market volatility, *Journal of Applied Economics*, **10**, 435–448.

McNeil, A.J., and R. Frey (2000) Estimation of tailed-related risk measures for heteroscedastic financial time series: An extreme value approach, *Journal of Empirical Finance*, **7**, 271–300.

Merton, R.C. (1980) On estimating expected return on the market: An exploratory investigation, *Journal of Financial Economics*, **8**, 323–361.

Milhoj, A. (1987) A conditional variance model for daily observations of an exchange rate, *Journal of Business and Economic Statistics*, **5**, 99–103.

Nandi, S. (1998) How important is the correlation between returns and volatility in a stochastic volatility model? Empirical evidence from pricing and hedging S&P500 index option market, *Journal of Banking and Finance*, **22**, 5, 589–610.

Nelson, D.B. (1991) Conditional heteroskedasticity in asset returns: A new approach, *Econometrica*, **59**, 2, 347–370.

Nelson, D.B. (1992) Filtering and forecasting with misspecified ARCH models I: Getting the right variance with the wrong model, *Journal of Econometrics*, **52**, 61–90.

Nelson, D.B., and C.Q. Cao (1992) Inequality constraints in the univariate GARCH model, *Journal of Business and Economic Statistics*, **10**, 2, 229–235.

Nelson, D.B., and D.P. Foster (1995) Filtering and forecasting with misspecified ARCH models II: Making the right forecast with the wrong model, *Journal of Econometrics*, **67**, 2, 303–335.

Noh, J. R.F., Engle and A. Kane (1994) Forecasting volatility and option prices of the S&P 500 index, *Journal of Derivatives*, **2**, 17–30.

Ohanissian, A., J.R. Russell and R.S. Tsay (2003) True or spurious long memory in volatility: Does it matter for pricing options? Working Paper, University of Chicago.

Pagan, A.R., and G.W. Schwert (1990) Alternative models for conditional models for conditional stock volatility, *Journal of Econometrics*, **45**, 1–2, 267–290.

Parkinson, M. (1980) The extreme value method for estimating the variance of the rate of return, *Journal of Business*, **53**, 61–65.

Pitt, M.J., and N. Shephard (1997) Likelihood analysis of non-Gaussian measurement time series, *Biometrika*, **84**, 653–667.

Peria, M.S.M. (2001) A regime-switching approach to the study of speculative attacks: A focus on EMS crises. Working paper, World Bank.

Pong, S., M.B. Shackleton, S.J. Taylor and X. Xu (2004) Forecasting Sterling/Dollar volatility: A comparison of implied volatilities and AR(FI)MA models, *Journal of Banking and Finance*, **28**, 2541–2563.

Poon, S.-H., and C.W.J. Granger (2003) Forecasting financial market volatility: A review, *Journal of Economic Literature*, **41**, 2, 478–539.

Poon, S.-H., and C.W.J. Granger (2005) Practical issues in forecasting volatility, *Financial Analyst Journal*, **61**, 1, 45–65.

Poon, S.-H., M. Rockinger and J. Tawn (2003) Extreme value dependence in international stock markets and financial applications, *Statistica Sinica*, **13**, 929–953.

Poon, S.-H., M. Rockinger and J. Tawn (2004) Extreme-value dependence in financial markets: Diagnostics, models and financial implications, *Review of Financial Studies*, **17**, 2, 581–610.

Poon, S., and S.J. Taylor (1992) Stock returns and stock market volatilities, *Journal of Banking and Finance*, **16**, 37–59.

Poteshman, A.M. (2000) Forecasting future volatility from option prices, Working paper, University of Illinois at Urbana-Champaign.

Randolph, W.L., and M. Najand (1991) A test of two models in forecasting stock index futures price volatility, *Journal of Futures Markets*, **11**, 2, 179–190.

Robinson, P.M. (ed.) (2003) *Time Series with Long Memory*. Oxford University Press, Oxford.

Rogers, L.C.G., and S.E. Satchell (1991) Estimating variance from high, low and closing prices, *Annals of Applied Probability*, **1**, 504–512.

Rogers, L.C.G., S.E. Satchell and Y. Yoon (1994) Estimating the volatility of stock prices: A comparison of methods that use high and low prices, *Applied Financial Economics*, **4**, 3, 241–248.

Roll, R. (1977) An analytic valuation formula for unprotected American call options on stocks with known dividends, *Journal of Financial Economics*, **5**, 251–258.

Rossi, P. (ed.) (1996) *Modelling Stock Market Volatility: Bridging the Gap to Continuous Time*, Academic Press, London.

Schmalensee, R., and R.R. Trippi (1978) Common stock volatility expectations implied by option premia, *Journal of Finance*, **33**, 1, 129–147.

Scott, E., and A.L. Tucker (1989) Predicting currency return volatility, *Journal of Banking and Finance*, **13**, 6, 839–851.

Scott, L.O. (1987) Option pricing when the variance changes randomly: Theory, estimation and an application, *Journal of Financial and Quantitative Analysis*, **22**, 419–438.

Sentana, E. (1998) The relation between conditionally heteroskedastic factor models and factor GARCH models, *Econometrics Journal*, **1**, 1–9.

Sentana, E., and G. Fiorentini (2001) Identification, estimation and testing of conditionally heteroskedastic factor models, *Journal of Econometrics*, **102**, 143–164.

Shephard, N. (2003) *Stochastic Volatility*, Oxford University Press, Oxford.

Sill, D.K. (1993) Predicting stock-market volatility, *Business Review* (Federal Reserve Bank of Philadelphia), Jan./Feb., 15–27.

Singleton, K. (2001) Estimation of affine asset pricing models using the empirical characteristic function, *Journal of Econometrics*, **102**, 111–141.

Stein, E., and C.J. Stein (1991) Stock priced distributions with stochastic volatility: An analytical approach, *Review of Financial Studies*, **4**, 4, 727–752.

Szakmary, A., E. Ors, J.K. Kim and W.D. Davidson III (2002) The predictive power of implied volatility: Evidence from 35 futures markets, Working paper, Southern Illinois University.

Tauchen, G., and M. Pitts (1983) The price variability–volume relationship on speculative markets, *Econometrica*, **51**, 485–505.

Taylor, J.W. (2004) Volatility forecasting with smooth transition exponential smoothing, *International Journal of Forecasting*, **20**, 273–286.

Taylor, S.J. (1986) *Modelling Financial Time Series*, John Wiley & Sons Ltd, Chichester.

Taylor, S.J. (1987) Forecasting of the volatility of currency exchange rates, *International Journal of Forecasting*, **3**, 159–170.

Taylor, S.J. (1994) Modeling stochastic volatility: A review and comparative study, *Mathematical Finance*, **4**, 2, 183–204.

Taylor, S.J. (2000) Consequences for option pricing of a long memory in volatility, Working paper, University of Lancaster.

Taylor, S. (2005) *Asset Price Dynamics and Prediction*, Princeton University Press.

Taylor, S.J., and G.X. Xu (1997) The incremental volatility information in one million foreign exchange quotations, *Journal of Empirical Finance*, **4**, 4, 317–340.

Theil, H. (1966) *Applied Economic Forecasting*, North-Holland, Amsterdam.

Tsay, R.S. (2002) *Analysis of Financial Time Series: Financial Econometrics*, John Wiley & Sons Ltd, Chichester.

Tse, Y.K. (1991) Stock return volatility in the Tokyo Stock Exchange, *Japan and the World Economy*, **3**, 285–298.

Tse, Y., and G.G. Booth (1996) Common volatility and volatility spillovers between U.S. and Eurodollar interest rates: Evidence from the futures market, *Journal of Economics and Business*, **48**, 3, 299–313.

Tse, T.Y.K., and S.H. Tung (1992) Forecasting volatility in the Singapore stock market, *Asia Pacific Journal of Management*, **9**, 1, 1–13.

Vasilellis, G.A., and N. Meade (1996) Forecasting volatility for portfolio selection, *Journal of Business Finance and Accounting*, **23**, 1, 125–143.

Vilasuso, J. (2002) Forecasting exchange rate volatility, *Economics Letters*, **76**, 59–64.

Walsh, D.M., and G.Y.-G. Tsou (1998) Forecasting index volatility: Sampling integral and non-trading effects, *Applied Financial Economics*, **8**, 5, 477–485.

Wei, S.J., and J.A. Frankel (1991) Are option-implied forecasts of exchange rate volatility excessively variable? NBER working paper No. 3910.

West, K.D., (1996) Asymptotic inference about predictive ability, *Econometrica*, **64**, 1067–1084.

West, K.D., and D. Cho (1995) The predictive ability of several models of exchange rate volatility, *Journal of Econometrics*, **69**, 2, 367–391.

West, K.D., H.J. Edison and D. Cho (1993) A utility based comparison of some methods of exchange rate volatility, *Journal of International Economics*, **35**, 1–2, 23–45.

West, K.D., and M. McCracken (1998) Regression based tests of predictive ability, *International Economic Review*, **39**, 817–840.

Whaley, R.E. (1981) On the valuation of American call options on stocks with known dividends, *Journal of Financial Economics*, **9**, 207–211.

Whaley, R.E. (1982) Valuation of American call options on dividend-paying stocks, *Journal of Financial Economics*, **10**, 29–58.

Whaley, R.E. (1993) Derivatives on market volatility: Hedging tools long overdue, *Journal of Derivatives*, Fall, 71–84.

Wiggins, J.B. (1987) Option values under stochastic volatility: Theory and empirical estimates, *Journal of Financial Economics*, **19**, 351–372.

Wiggins, J.B. (1992) Estimating the volatility of S&P 500 futures prices using the Extreme-Value Method, *Journal of Futures Markets*, **12**, 3, 256–273.

Xu, X., and S.J. Taylor (1995) Conditional volatility and the informational efficiency of the PHLX currency options market, *Journal of Banking and Finance*, **19**, 5, 803–821.

Yu, J., (2002) Forecasting volatility in the New Zealand Stock Market, *Applied Financial Economics*, **12**, 193–202.

Zakoïan, J.-M. (1994) Threshold heteroskedastic models, *Journal of Economic Dynamics and Control*, **18**, 5, 931–955.

Zumbach, G. (2002) Volatility processes and volatility forecast with long memory, Working paper, Olsen Associates.

Index

Index compiled by Annette Musker

Printed and bound by CPI Group (UK) Ltd, Croydon, CR0 4YY

23/04/2025

14660956-0001